# GLOBAL RESTRUCTURING AND TERRITORIAL DEVELOPMENT

# Global Restructuring and Territorial Development

*Edited by*
Jeffrey Henderson and Manuel Castells

(S) SAGE Publications
London ● Newbury Park ● Beverly Hills ● New Delhi

3 38.9
G 562

SAGE Publications Ltd
28 Banner Street
London EC1Y 8QE

SAGE Publications Inc
2111 West Hillcrest Street
Newbury Park, California 91320

SAGE Publications Inc
275 South Beverly Drive
Beverly Hills, California 90212

SAGE Publications India Pvt
Ltd C-236 Defence Colony
New Delhi 110 024

**British Library Cataloguing in Publication Data**
Global restructuring and territorial development.
  1. Economic development — Social aspects
  I. Henderson, Jeff    II. Castells, Manuel
  306′.3        HD75

ISBN 0-8039-8059-0
ISBN 0-8039-8060-4 Pbk

**Library of Congress catalog card number 87-062030**

Printed in Great Britain by J.W. Arrowsmith Ltd, Bristol

# Contents

# Preface and Acknowledgements

This book grew out of a conference on the 'Urban and Regional Impact of the New International Division of Labour' which was organized by the International Sociological Association's Research Committee on Regional and Urban Development in association with the Centre of Urban Studies and Urban Planning and the Department of Sociology of the University of Hong Kong. With the exception of chapters 1, 3 and 8, the book brings together a small selection of versions of the papers originally presented at that conference.

We are indebted to a number of people and organizations who helped to make the conference possible and this book a reality. The University of Hong Kong's Urban Studies and Urban Planning Trust Fund provided a grant to cover organizational costs, while the ISA's Research Committee provided funds to support the participation of a number of scholars from developing countries. The Research Committee's then President, Enzo Mingione, provided considerable support and encouragement, as did the staff and graduate students of the Centre of Urban Studies and Urban Planning and the Department of Sociology. In addition, we obviously owe a great debt to all the participants at the conference for presenting their work and stimulating debate.

A number of individuals in Hong Kong were particularly helpful. The efficient organization and running of the conference would have been inconceivable without the assistance of Teresa Fong, Diana Martin, Yan Yuk Fung, and especially Priscilla Chiu. Similarly, Diana Martin and Tam Suk Tak made our editorial tasks much easier, while Angela Chung drew the figures and maps, and Belinda Man and Samantha Chan transmitted the manuscript to a word processor with their usual speed and efficiency. We are most grateful to them all for their assistance.

Finally, we wish to thank our editor at Sage, David Hill, for his interest, advice and commitment to the project. We trust that the final product proves to be a fitting culmination to the collective efforts of all those who participated in the enterprise.

JH and MC
*Hong Kong and Berkeley*

# The Contributors

**Manuel Castells** is Professor of Planning at the University of California, Berkeley. Formerly he taught sociology at the University of Paris where he directed the urban sociology seminar at the Ecole des Hautes Etudes en Sciences Sociales. In addition, he has held Visiting Professorships at the Universities of Montreal, Chile, Wisconsin (Madison), Copenhagen, Boston, Mexico, Hong Kong, Southern California and Madrid. His most recent books are *The City and the Grassroots* (Edward Arnold and University of California Press, 1983) which won the 1983 C. Wright Mills Award, and *High Technology, Space and Society* (Sage, 1985). He is currently working on the relationship between new technologies and economic restructuring in a comparative perspective.

**Robin Cohen** is Director of the Centre for Research in Ethnic Relations and Professor of Sociology at the University of Warwick. He was previously Professor of Sociology at the University of the West Indies, Trinidad, and Senior Lecturer in Sociology at the University of Birmingham. He has held visiting appointments at the Universities of California (Berkeley) and Toronto. His publications include *Labour and Politics in Nigeria* (Heinemann, 1974 and 1982), *Endgame in South Africa*? (James Currey and UNESCO Press, 1986) and *The New Helots: Migrants in the International Division of Labour* (Gower, 1987).

**Dieter Ernst** is currently a Senior Research Fellow at the OECD Development Centre in Paris. Formerly Director of the IDPAD Project on Microelectronics at the Institute of Social Studies, The Hague, he has worked extensively as a consultant for various UN agencies, governments, trade unions, and for non-governmental organizations such as the Pugwash Conference on Science and World Affairs, and the North-South Roundtable. His recent publications include *The Global Race in Microelectronics* (Campus Verlag, 1983), as well as numerous articles on the electronics industry, automation and development in the Third World.

**Jeffrey Henderson** is Lecturer in Sociology and Urban Studies at the University of Hong Kong. Previously a Research Fellow at the Centre for Urban and Regional Studies, University of Birmingham, he has held visiting appointments at the Universities of California (Berkeley),

Glasgow, Lodz, Melbourne and Warwick. He is the co-author of *Race, Class and State Housing* (Gower, 1987) and co-editor of *Urban Political Economy and Social Theory* (Gower, 1982). He is a member of the Board of the International Sociological Association's Research Committee on Urban and Regional Development and a Corresponding Editor of the *International Journal of Urban and Regional Research*. His current research is concerned with the social and spatial dynamics of the changing international division of labour, with particular regard to semiconductor production.

**Richard Child Hill** is Professor of Sociology and Urban Affairs at Michigan State University, and has held visiting appointments at the University of California (Santa Cruz), the Royal Danish Academy of Fine Arts, and the Centre of Urban Studies and Urban Planning, University of Hong Kong. He is the co-author of *Restructuring the City* (Longman, 1983) and of *Detroit: Race and Uneven Development* (Kenikat, 1986). In addition, he has published articles on urban theory, urban fiscal crises, race relations, and transnational corporations and industrial policy. He has been a member of the Editorial Advisory Board of the *International Journal of Urban and Regional Research* and his current research interests include studies of regional deindustrialization and industrial policy; and the social ramifications of the crisis and reorganization of the world automobile industry.

**Vivian Kwang-Wen Lin** was born in Taiwan, and raised in the United States. She studied biology and political science at Yale University and public health at the University of California, Berkeley. The research discussed in this volume is drawn from her doctoral dissertation. Vivian has worked in academia as well as government, and has been an activist around occupational health issues. She currently works for the New South Wales Department of Health in Sydney.

**Manuel Perlo Cohen** is Associate Professor in the Faculty of Political and Social Sciences and a Tenured Researcher at the Institute of Social Research, Universidad Nacional Autonoma de Mexico, and a Visiting Professor in the Urban Studies Program, Stanford University. He has written numerous articles on housing, urban social movements, national urban policy and urban politics. He is also the author of *Estado, Vivienda y Estructura Urbana en el Cardenismo* (Universidad Nacional Autonoma de Mexico).

**Kamal Salih** is Director of the Malaysian Institute of Economic Research, Kuala Lumpur. Formerly Deputy Vice-Chancellor and Professor of Development Studies at the Universiti Sains Malaysia, he has also been a Visiting Professor at the Australian National University. He is the co-author (with Fu-Chen Lo) of *Growth Pole*

*Strategy and Regional Development Policy: Asian Problems and Alternatives* (Pergamon, 1978) and author or co-author of numerous articles on regional development, regional economics and urbanization and industrialization in Malaysia. He is a member of the editorial advisory boards of *Geoforum*, the *Canadian Journal of Development Studies* and *Society and Space*. He has been a consultant for UNCRD, APDC and the East-West Population Institute as well as a member of a number of Malaysian government advisory bodies. His current research is concerned with labour force formation and the household economy in Malaysia.

**Saskia Sassen-Koob** is Associate Professor of Urban Planning at Columbia University. She is completing a three-year research project on 'Hispanic Women in the Electronics and Garments Industries of New York and California' sponsored by the Revson Foundation. Also underway is a project on the informal sector in New York City. She is the author of *The Mobility of Labour and Capital* (Cambridge University Press, 1987), as well as numerous articles on migrant labour and the informal economy.

**Michael Peter Smith** is Professor of Community Studies and Development and Chairperson of the Department of Applied Behavioral Sciences, University of California, Davis. Previously a Professor of Political Science at Tulane University, he is the author of *The City and Social Theory* (St. Martin's Press, 1979; Blackwell, 1980) and of the forthcoming book, *The Political Economy of Urban Problems*. His co-authored books include *Restructuring the City* (Longman, 1983). He has written numerous articles on urban theory, bureaucracy, and state policy and is the editor of *Cities in Transformation: Class, Capital, and the State* (Sage, 1984) and co-editor of *The Capitalist City: Global Restructuring and Community Politics* (Blackwell, 1987). His current research is concerned with the interplay between global capital and labour flows and community politics.

**Nigel Thrift** is Co-Director of the Centre for the Study of Britain and the World Economy and a lecturer in Geography at the University of Bristol. He has taught and carried out research at the Universities of Cambridge and Leeds, and at the Australian National University. His books include (with D. Parkes) *Times, Spaces and Places* (Wiley, 1980) and (with D. Forbes) *The Price of War: Urbanization in Vietnam 1954-1985* (Allen & Unwin, 1986). He is also the co-editor of *Environment and Planning A* and a member of the Editorial Board of *Society and Space*.

**Mei Ling Young** is a Lecturer in Development Studies at the Universiti Sains Malaysia. She is the author or co-author of numerous articles on labour migration, labour force formation, urbanization, industrialization and family demography in Malaysia. She has been a programme co-ordinator and resource person at the East-West Center, Hawaii, and for a number of United Nations conferences. Her current research is concerned with industrialization and the household economy in rural Malaysia.

# I
# INTRODUCTION

## 1

# Techno-economic Restructuring, Socio-political Processes and Spatial Transformation: a Global Perspective

### *Manuel Castells and Jeffrey Henderson*

The world economy is undergoing a process of global restructuring that redefines capital–labour relationships, and the role of the state, while furthering the asymmetrical interdependency of economic functions across national boundaries. This process manifests itself differently in different contexts, thus triggering diverse social and political conflicts upon which its outcome will ultimately depend. Yet, it has some common features that allow us to consider it as a global process, albeit with specific developments and different social effects in each territorial unit (country, region, city). In all instances, this restructuring process results from the effort to supersede the economic crisis that has affected the capitalist world system at least since the early 1970s.

Efforts to treat the crisis have relied, in part, on forms of restructuring similar to those that have been used in previous economic crises. So, for instance, social relations of production have been altered by means of a reorganization of labour processes thus allowing for increases in the pace of work and in supervisory control. This, together with reductions in excess productive capacity, have resulted in growing and longer term unemployment in many core economies. These developments, combined with an increased belligerence of some governments towards organized labour, have led to a weakened trade union capacity to improve wages and working conditions. As in earlier crises, new technologies also have been utilized as part of the restructuring process. Furthermore, a process of capital concentration has taken place associated with the elimination (or incorporation) of weaker competitors.

In previous crises restructuring was usually confined to the given territorial unit. What is new about the contemporary period, however, is that restructuring 'internal' to the territorial unit has been combined with spatial (intra- and inter-national) shifts in investment (of prac- ically all forms of capital) and a massive expansion of the radii of organizational control. It is precisely these latter dimensions that have given the current restructuring process its global character and dynamic.

This 'global option' has been able to take advantage of the revolution associated with information technologies. So potent has this combination become that a particular model of development, and hence a new form of expansion of the capitalist system, has emerged. This model has a logic of its own that transcends specific countries, along the lines we describe below.

Under the impact of the restructuring process, and of the socio-political conflicts surrounding its implementation (or the political alternatives to it), profound social and spatial transformations are under way. However, it would be absurd to pretend that a specific spatial form will derive automatically from the characteristics of the model of capitalist development implicit in the restructuring process. Specific spatial forms and processes will result from the interaction between the historically concrete restructuring policies and the attributes of each society, including its territorial basis. This volume explores, on the basis of theoretically informed empirical research, the range of urban and regional processes associated with the current restructuring in different societies. The assumption, however, is *not* that these processes can be treated as direct representations of the overall tendency. Rather, what we sustain is the methodological prescription that we must start with the analysis of the process of global restructuring, in its different, specific manifestations, in order to understand much of the current social and spatial change in capitalist countries. Thus we need to introduce the subject by summarizing the fundamental features of the restructuring process, and by emphasizing some spatial tendencies that appear to develop as general trends. The consideration of the specificity of the relationship between society and space in each territorial and historical context will be addressed by the studies presented in this volume. It is this combination of a global theoretical approach, with concrete, empirical analyses, that characterizes the intellectual style we consider most fruitful for the study of current developments in the urban and regional arena.

**A New Model of Development**
The basic hypothesis that underlies our perspective is that a new model of capitalist development is being put forward in the core countries of the world economic system, and is being imposed upon the rest of the system by means of transnational organizations (industrial, financial, service capital, aid/development agencies, etc.). After several years of

implementation of anti-inflationary policies in a variety of countries, we think that the model of economic growth that has emerged represents a similar sort of departure from Keynesianism and welfare-state capitalism that that model itself represented vis-à-vis liberal capitalism before the 1930s Depression. For the sake of the analysis we undertake in this volume, it is necessary to outline, very schematically, the characteristics of this new model of economic development.

This development model is not necessarily linked to a particular political party, administration, or even to a country, even if the Reagan and Thatcher governments seem to be the closest examples of the fulfilment of its policies. Very similar policies have emerged, for instance, in most Western European countries; in those governed by Christian Democrats and Liberals, as well as in those governed by Socialists, and even in Communist-led regions (Italy) or governments with Communist participation (France, for a certain period). At the same time, in most Third World countries, austerity policies, inspired or dictated by the International Monetary Fund and other world financial institutions, have also developed along the same lines. These have established (though riddled with contradictions and conflicts), a new economic logic, that is not only capitalist, but a very specific kind of capitalism. Obviously, the generalization of such a model of economic policy (which is not historically irreversible) does not imply that all governments are alike or that politics does not matter. The issue is that when a system reaches an historical limit, and the socio-political process is unable to transform it any further, the only possibility for society to avoid disintegration is for it to consolidate, reinforce, and make more dynamic, the already institutionalized structural logic. Because the economy (under capitalism) structures society, and because economies are now highly interdependent at the international level, national governments find themselves faced with the dilemma of either adjusting to the dominant logic in the most advantageous manner, or undertaking an uphill battle that is unlikely to succeed as an isolated enterprise. Not surprisingly, then, most countries are embarking along the lines of a new model of economic development that is organized around a major series of measures which originate, at one and the same time, from governments and private business alike. These measures take the following forms.

1. Inflation is controlled through fiscal austerity, monetary restriction and policies aimed at the partial dismemberment of the welfare state.

2. Labour costs are reduced by means of forcing down wages while at the same time reducing expenditure on working conditions and social

benefits. Consequently, other conditions being equal, profit ratios increase proportionately.

3. Productivity and profitability of companies are increased by means of redundancies, reductions of working time, technological innovation, and speed-ups of work.

4. Industrial sectors are restructured. This results in massive disinvestments in those sectors, regions and companies that have become less profitable, and investment in new products and activities, generally in high-technology manufacturing, corporate services, miscellaneous consumer services, and real estate. A major development within industrial restructuring (particularly in Europe and Latin America) is the shrinkage of the public sector and the associated 'privatization' of state assets.

5. There is tremendous growth of the 'informal economy', that is, of all kinds of economic activities unregulated and uncontrolled by the state, regardless of their legality. This includes, certainly, the astronomic cash-flows associated with criminal activities (particularly in the production and distribution of drugs), but it mainly refers to undeclared waged work, unpaid taxes, absence of compliance with health and safety regulations, labour legislation, etc. In countries like the United States, massive immigration from undocumented workers fuels the process of the increasing penetration of the centre by the periphery. The informal economy represents today a key element of all economies, not only for the survival of the poor, but for the dynamism of small businesses, accounting for much of the growth and new employment (but also, usually, the 'super-exploitation' of the workforce) and for the transfer of value from the informal sector to large corporations via subcontracting arrangements and networks, and decentralized production.

6. There is an increasing internationalization of the economy, taking advantage of the most favourable locations for production, management and control of the markets, while maintaining an interconnected worldwide system. This is a common strategy for both companies and governments, and paradoxically, it simultaneously tends to trigger protectionist reactions in the core economies as soon as industrial sectors, regions, or countries, start to lose out in the cut-throat competition which ensues.

7. Finally, there are attempts by core economies to control world prices of raw materials and energy thus ensuring the stability of the price system and exchange flows.

This sketchy presentation of the emergent economic model inevitably emphasizes its coherence and internal logic, without considering its contradictions, and the potentially destructive deviations from its own rationality. For instance, in the case of the United States the call for fiscal austerity and a balanced budget is translated into a greater deficit, with a shift within the budget from social to military expenditures (what, following Herbert Marcuse, we call the transition from the Welfare State to the Warfare State) financed, without inflation, thanks to the influx of capital from all over the world. As a result, sources of investment elsewhere tended to dry up and the dollar, for a time, was pushed upward, thus wrecking the US balance of trade, and sending a series of connected negative effects reverberating throughout the world system.

**Global Restructuring as a Techno-economic Process**
Another element in our analysis concerns the definition of the current restructuring as a *techno-economic process*. This is because we believe that the revolution in information technologies strongly affects the possibilities for the implementation of the new development model. This is not to say that new technologies result from capitalist austerity policies, but rather that their current use and applications are basically shaped by such policies. As a result, technological progress is being captured within an historically limited economic logic. The chances of this economic logic being imposed are dramatically enhanced, however, by the power of the new technological means at its disposal.

New technologies are at the core of the current process of economic restructuring in the following ways. They contribute to a qualitative increase in productivity, across the board, in manufacturing, agriculture (down the line, through biotechnology), and services. In fact, productivity growth is particularly crucial in the service sector of the economy. Because new technologies are primarily aimed at processing information, and this is precisely the substance of most service industries, the deepest economic impact of new technologies probably will occur in these areas.

For the moment, however, the most immediate impact on productivity has been in manufacturing, and particularly in the automobile industry. During the 1980s the automobile industry has experienced a major transformation in its labour processes and in the overall logic of its operation. This has resulted from the fact that it has become the main user of industrial robots, and of CAD/CAM systems of flexible manufacturing. If we add to this developments in new materials, it seems that in a few years' time the automobile industry will have shifted from an electro-mechanical to an electronics-plastics industry with dramatic increases in productivity and reductions in production employment. Similar trends can be observed in key industries such as electronics and telecommunications.

While the employment effects of new technologies are still unclear, and thus in some countries they could have negative implications, their impact is a more complex issue than this. Other considerations, therefore, must be taken into account. Amongst these, the fact that new technologies tend to help reduce costs, increase productivity and improve the quality of products, is of some importance. In addition they contribute a good deal to the stimulation of investment and the possibilities of resolving the economic crisis. However, in the absence of mechanisms designed to redistribute the wealth generated, the application of new technologies is likely to contribute to the growing inequality and social polarization associated with current economic policies.

Secondly, new technologies help place management in an advantageous position with regard to workers and trade unions. They enhance managerial control over work routines, and help obtain concessions on improvements in wages and working conditions in exchange for the maintenance of employment, or, more usually, a slow-down in the phasing-out of jobs. Thus, although technology per se is not an instrument of capital, it is imbued with capitalist relations of production, and hence can be (and is being) used as a bargaining factor in the redefinition of power relations between management and labour. This, in itself, is a key component of overall economic restructuring.

Thirdly, new technologies, and particularly telecommunications, are a material condition necessary for the internationalization of the economy, and this is probably *the* key feature of the new model of development. Only through an integrated system of telecommunications and computers is it possible at one and the same time both to integrate and to decentralize production, distribution, and management, in a worldwide, flexible, interconnected system. The new telecommunications technologies are the electronic highways of the informational age, equivalent to the role played by railway systems in the process of industrialization.

Finally, worldwide production and distribution is only possible because of the perfect standardization of parts (that can be assembled into final products even if separately produced in very distant locations), and flexible customized production (that can adapt a basic product to specific characteristics targeted on a particular final market). Both processes are dependent upon automated production, and flexible re-programmable electronic tools. The global assembly line and the planetary bazaar require both the electronic factory and on-line management.

Thus, new technologies are a key component in the process of economic restructuring that determines a new international division of labour whose characteristics are decisive for the making of our future world, including its emergent spatial profile.

**Contours of Spatial Transformation**

A number of key urban–regional *processes* appear to be associated, in general, with the process of restructuring we have described. We must emphasize, however, that we pinpoint processes whose specific spatial forms might vary according to historical circumstances in each region or city.

The first of such major developments is the tendency for a *space of flows* to supersede the *space of places*. By such a cumbersome expression we mean that the actual dynamics of a given territory rely mainly on the connection of the population and activities of that territory to activities and decisions that go far beyond the boundaries of each locality. The development of the international economy, the dramatic growth of new information and communications technologies, the formation of powerful transnational organizations linked by subordinated, decentralized networks, are crucial factors in the process that provides the structural meaning for each territory in terms of the functions that territory performs in the broader framework of interdependent operations. We certainly still have spatial forms, since societies and economies develop on a given territory and unevenly across the globe. Yet the logic and dynamics of territorial development are increasingly placeless from the point of view of the dominant organizations and social interests.

At the same time, a second territorial process grows in importance. While dominant interests may be losing their sense of place with regard to the development process, 'community' social relations and socio-political mobilizations continue to operate, for the most part, according to a local, place-oriented logic. In fact, the more the dominant logic is based upon flows, the more the defence of specific interests or of autonomous identities takes the form of irreducible *local* experience. Community organizations, regional and urban movements, ethnic, racial, gender, class and age-based social networks all over the world tend to oppose their local, specific experience to the abstract, flow-oriented logic of worldwide organizations and interests. The new territorial dynamics, then, tend to be organized around the contradiction between placeless power and powerless places,[1] the former relying upon communication flows, the latter generating their own communication codes on the basis of an historically specific territory.

The socio-spatial functions so created are likely to be intensified by the acceleration of the process of uneven development, linked to economic restructuring. Yet, the spatial consequences of the current form of uneven development are very peculiar, in the sense that they tend not to be cumulative vis-a-vis pre-existing developed regions and cities. New areas of the world and new regions within countries are experiencing growth and increasing their relative weight in the spatial division of labour. In this sense, some secular trends towards increasing metropolitan dominance of these same areas are being moderated, with entire regions decaying, while new territorial units rise to prominence. In this way Schumpeter's 'creative destruction' of capitalist development is being given a new spatial form, and supplementing it, among other things, is the destructive creation of a new built environment. Very often the processes of growth and decline take place simultaneously within the same metropolitan area. As a result, they lead to increasingly contrasted urban forms and social structures.

Overall, the urban and regional problematic is increasingly diversified around the world. While Western Europe is witnessing the maturity of its metropolitan areas, with stagnant or even negative rates of growth, most of the Third World is experiencing an urban explosion, with the largest cities accounting for much of this unbalanced process of accelerated urbanization. In some countries, like the United States, some older industrial areas experience substantial urban decline, particularly in the Midwest, while new booming suburbs sprawl in the sunrise regions of 'post-industrial' America.

Such diversity of the current spatial experience requires an increasingly international perspective in order to generate a new territorial theory appropriate for understanding a new territorial world. This theory, to the development of which we would like to contribute with the present volume, has to bring together the structural commonalities of global processes and the specific forms the socio-spatial dynamics take. It has also to take into account the interaction between dominant economic–political interests and the resistance or alternative projects arising from communities and political actors which the furthering of these interests engender. Though the essays in this volume are informed by differing intellectual orientations, it is from within this broader theoretical perspective that we can better understand their combined contribution.

**Towards a New Theory of Territorial Development**

The essays collected here are indications of the type of work that is necessary, if we are to develop a theory adequate to the task of explaining socio-spatial change in the contemporary world. All of the essays take the global economy and its changing structures as their starting point. They then attempt, in their various ways, to specify some of the social and spatial consequences of global restructuring for particular economic sectors, regions, or cities.

The book begins with a number of essays which deal with the dynamics of capital and labour in the restructuring process (Part II). These essays, however, examine those dynamics with regard to particular industries and/or particular forms of labour. The subsequent essays (Part III) seek to examine some of the implications of incorporation into the world economy, both historically and contemporaneously, for two important areas of the developing world. The final essays (Part IV), on the other hand, explore some of the consequences of global capital restructuring for urban areas in predominantly core economies.

Underlying economic restructuring are structurally-induced crisis tendencies, which in the contemporary period originate at the level of the world economy. In periods of crisis the logic of capitalist development tends towards the reorganization of the bases for accumulation such that better and indeed new opportunities for accumulation can become possible in the future. The chapters by Hill and Ernst examine the relationship between crisis and restructuring in two important sectors of industrial capital.

Richard Child Hill emphasizes the relationship between economic crisis and the internationalization strategies of the American and Japanese automobile industries. His argument is cast in terms of a critical appraisal of one of the more important bodies of literature that has attempted to grasp the determinants and significance of global restructuring: new international division of labour (NIDL) theory. He suggests that, while the link between labour costs and internationalization emphasized by the most well-known version of the NIDL thesis may go some way towards explaining the global organization of the US automobile industry, it cannot explain the enormous success of the Japanese auto industry nor its (recent) mode of internationalization. The success of the Japanese industry has been built not on the basis of a 'global factory', nor indeed on cheap labour or sophisticated technology, but rather on a spatially-concentrated organization of both production and the lives of its workforce associated with the development of the 'company town'.

In his chapter, Hill shows why an adequate explanation of the determinants of productive forms of automobile manufacture and their socio-spatial impact, can be achieved only when the NIDL, or similar models, are historically and empirically specified in relation to particular national industries, and perhaps also, particular firms. Furthermore, he shows how the spatial reorganization of automobile manufacture has in very recent years been determined principally by the desire to protect major market segments (in the face of increasingly protectionist state policies) rather than by concerns with cost reduction. Finally, Hill points towards the convergence of global factory– company town stategies in the contemporary period, coupled with the development of strategic alliances, in both production and marketing, between US, Japanese and European manufacturers. Given the

the financial, technological and marketing power that will emerge from these alliances, the chances that Third World automobile companies could become significant world actors would appear very slim indeed.

Dieter Ernst also points to the significance of strategic alliances between American and Japanese companies as a response to economic crisis in the semiconductor industry. Like Hill, he argues that crisis is a structural feature which is propelling the global reorganization of semiconductor production. As with automobiles, American (rather than Japanese) semiconductor production has been internationalized in the last quarter-century in ways broadly consistent with those suggested by the NIDL thesis. In recent years, however, Ernst shows that the driving forces behind internationalization in the industry, the US 'merchant' firms, have been subject to very serious competition from their Japanese counterparts. The result has been that they have all but vacated standardized memory-chip production (the semiconductor most frequently used in computers and VCRs), leaving Japanese firms to dominate world markets. Furthermore, while Japanese firms have yet to be able to challenge the technological superiority of the Americans in regard to the most sophisticated types of semiconductors (microprocessors, etc.), their most important end-product markets (computers, etc.) have collapsed under the impact of the economic crisis. The result in the United States has been the growth of strategic alliances between merchant firms and major electronics systems corporations such as IBM. Ernst foresees the gradual elimination of US merchant manufacturers in favour of market domination by the systems houses, both American and Japanese.

In spatial terms, Ernst sees these developments as likely to result in a 'multi-polarization of production', with the control centres (and, by implication, technological cores) of the industry becoming ever more entrenched in the United States and Japan. While acknowledging the attempts of certain 'newly industrializing countries' (NICs — South Korea and Taiwan in particular) to become semiconductor producers of global significance, Ernst's analysis in terms of economic crisis, restructuring on the basis of strategic alliances, and growing protectionist pressure in the major markets (US and EEC), points to pessimistic conclusions for the NICs. Although he is more hopeful for the possibilities of the development of European semiconductor production, he argues that it needs to emphasize the EEC, rather than export markets, and hence resist the '. . . whims of global competition'.

An integral part of the process of restructuring the bases for capital accumulation is the restructuring of the relationship of labour power to the production of value. Restructuring this relationship can take many forms. The attempt to organize the totality of working peoples' lives by means of the 'company town' phenomenon, as Hill shows in his chapter, can be one of them. But, as we indicated earlier, there are others which can be used alone, or more usually in various combinations. As well as tighter supervisory controls, work speed-ups, the expulsion of human labour by means of an application of new technologies, supression of trade unions by national states, etc., it is now clear that the export of capital in search of a non- (or semi-) proletarianized workforce and the importation of labour to the metropolitan heartland are two moments of the same process, and that this process is central to contemporary global restructuring. Furthermore it is also clear that much of the labour which comes to be employed, be it as a result of the migration of capital, or of human beings, is female.

The chapters which complete Part II of the volume concentrate on particular aspects of the global restructuring of labour and some of their consequences. Those by Sassen-Koob and Cohen deal with the dynamics, significance and contradictions of the use of migrant labour, while the chapter by Lin looks at some of the consequences for Malaysian and Singaporean women who are brought into wage labour as a result of foreign investment.

In her chapter, Saskia Sassen-Koob shows that the massive flows of migrant workers, both from periphery to core, as well as from one peripheral (or semi-peripheral) country to another, have in recent years been directly associated with global restructuring. She suggests that there are three ways in which this association has been forged. Firstly, rural to urban migration has fuelled industrialization in many NICs by providing a largely female workforce already culturally habituated to the acceptance of authority and low wages (a point also made by Lin in her chapter). Secondly, as a result of the surplus value generated from the employment of millions of migrant workers (from the Philippines, Pakistan, etc.) in OPEC countries, capital has been injected into the world economy in the form of finance capital in search of lucrative investment opportunities. It is this money that has resulted in construction booms in a variety of cities across the globe, and in Third World governments being pressured into accepting loans for development projects that they do not necessarily need. Finally, Sassen-Koob points to the use of migrant workers (many of them illegals) in low-paid, labour-intensive industrial and service jobs, many of which arise within the informal sector of the control centres of the international economy: the 'global cities'. She argues that the element which renders particularly the first and third migration patterns interdependent is class struggle. She sees migration as the use by capital of unorganized Third World workers in its struggle against workers in the core economies.

Furthermore, Sassen-Koob argues that the restructuring of the economies of global cities promotes the conditions for the informalization of a wide range of productive activities. Coupled with the use of migrant labour, 'developed' societies thus have become competitive with 'developing' societies in industrial sectors such as electronics and textiles. As a result, and in the context of technical and locational constraints (such as those raised by Ernst), increasing wages and emergent class struggles in developing societies, Sassen-Koob suggests that there is a growing tendency for industrial capital to become reconcentrated in the core economies. Global restructuring, then, is creating conditions which will allow, once again, the spatial reintegration of production with principal markets.

Robin Cohen continues our interest with migrant labour, though in his chapter the discussion is shifted to the role of national states in regulating labour supplies. He shows how states within their respective 'regional political economies' always have had to negotiate the contradiction between allowing cheap labour supplies to fuel their economies and the risk of negative political fall-out, legitimation problems and increased welfare expenditure that might result from allowing large numbers of ethnically (and often racially) distinct people to settle within the metropolitan homeland. So, whereas capital has always been able to benefit from the 'uneven distribution of the world's productive forces', workers have been unable to benefit in a similar fashion (in terms of jobs and improved living standards) because of restrictions on their movement across international boundaries.

Cohen examines state responses to migration control in the United States, Western Europe and South Africa. He shows that, while the Western European states (Britain, Germany, France, Switzerland) have had a reasonable record in matching migration to labour power needs, it is only South Africa that has come close to a total system of labour regulation. This has only been possible, however, by instituting a brutal system of repression at which other states, thus far, have baulked.

Of all of them, it is the United States that has had the greatest difficulty in restricting migrant flows. Focusing on Cuban and Haitian migrants, Cohen suggests that while geographic size and the large volume of passenger movements may have contributed to the 'poor record' of the US, pressure from big business for cheap labour power and an ideological commitment to 'freedom' vis-a-vis socialist societies, are more significant determinants. Like Sassen-Koob, he suggests that illegal immigrants in the US have been central to the profitability of agribusness, services, textiles and other manufacturing industries.

Vivian Lin shifts our concern from the political economy of migrant labour to questions of the social impact of industrialization. Her particular interest is in Malaysian and Singaporean women who experience industrial labour for the first time, largely as a result of foreign penetration of these Southeast Asian economies. Drawing on her own studies of semiconductor workers, Lin, in contradistinction to previous research, argues that female electronics workers are beginning to constitute a relatively permanent section of the working class. While there are differences between the racial groups (Malay, Chinese, Indian) and between Malaysia and Singapore, she finds that the women workers tend to be older, more of them married, and more with a continuous involvement with wage labour, than earlier. Furthermore, she shows that the women appreciate the increased status they achieve within their families, as well as the growing relative independence, which results from their role as factory workers.

Lin suggests that the family-centred orientations (and, we might add, obligations), typical of rural, pre-capitalist social formations, are beginning to wane. In their place are appearing the types of peer-group orientations and affiliations more typical of industrial society. Lin argues that in effect what is taking place in Malaysia and Singapore is that women factory workers are being constituted as a working class. While they are a long way from becoming a class 'for themselves', they are becoming culturally proletarianized and more liberated as women. By drawing parallels with nineteenth-century female proletarianization in Europe and America, Lin implies the possibility of class struggle on the industrializing periphery. As we have seen, Sassen-Koob links this phenomenon to capital reconcentration in the core.

In Part III we shift our focus to the relationship between global restructuring and regional development. In both the chapters which comprise this section, our interest is in societies in two important parts of the developing world: Latin America and Southeast Asia. In both cases, the authors are not content with accounts which abstract the present situation from their respective historical contexts. Rather they are concerned to show that contemporary economic, social and spatial arrangements in each region are products of the processes by which they have been incorporated historically in the world economy and the articulation of these processes with the developmental specificities internal to these regions and states themselves.

As with a number of other chapters in the volume, Manuel Perlo Cohen begins his discussion of regional development in Mexico by distancing himself from the NIDL account of global economic restructuring. He cautions against the use of any general model of internationalization, such as the NIDL thesis, which attempts to grasp economic development in the Third World as a whole. He suggests that such models usually fail to appreciate the significance of indigenous economic and social variation for the development of particular territorial units once they are incorporated into the world economy. He emphasizes that rather than operate with a monadic, undifferentiated concept of capital, it is far better to study the spatial effects of economic internationalization by means of attention to the circuits of capital (productive, commodity or money capital) which connect the territorial unit to the global economy. Furthermore, not only is the circuit of capital within which a firm operates important, but so too is its organizational form (transnational or national), whether it operates in a competitive or monopolistic sector, and whether it produces for export or for the internal market.

In order to explore the relation between capital circuit, organizational form, economic sector, market orientation and local variation, Perlo Cohen analyses, historically, spatial development in two regions of Mexico which have been firmly incorporated into the world (in this case, overwhelmingly US) economy. In the case of Sonora–Sinaloa, its development has been predicated on agricultural production for both the US and Mexican markets, and more recently on industrial production and tourism. In the case of the zone along the US border, however, development has focused on foreign-owned industrial production (predominantly automobiles) solely for the world market. Whereas the economic development of Sonora and Sinaloa has been multifaceted, with extensive links to both national and international markets, the border region has been subject to a more intense form of 'dependent development', associated, as it has been, with the productive circuit of capital, and indeed largely with one product. The economic linkages in the border zone are international and intraregional: it has almost no connection with the national economy. The significance of industrialization on the border for Mexican development as a whole has been merely the provision of employment opportunities. Even so, un- and under-employment remain significant problems in the region.

On the basis of his analysis of these Mexican regions, Perlo Cohen argues that regional economies with diverse and extensive links to both world and national economies (such as Sonora–Sinaloa) may well experience more dynamic and balanced socio-spatial development compared with those (such as the border region) which are linked to the world economy by means of a few transnational corporations concentrated in a few production branches.

The chapter by Kamal Salih and Mei Ling Young complements Perlo Cohen's contribution in the sense that it examines one part of Malaysia, Penang, which in recent years has become connected to the world economy precisely by means of 'a few transnational corporations concentrated in a few production branches'. Their discussion, however, is couched in terms of an historical account of Malaysia's incorporation in the world economy during British colonial domination and subsequent to independence in 1957.

Salih and Young show that the course of Malaysia's economic development in the last 30 years has been determined not only by its mode of incorporation in the world economy, but also, and crucially, by state policies which themselves have been a reflection of the balance of social forces (race and class) which has emerged within the society itself. The balance of social forces has certainly altered in the period since independence — in part as a result of changes in Malaysia's role in the world economy — but always it has affected economic and political policy via the ideological mediation of the state's commitment to the advancement of the interests of the Malay majority.

Having sketched the internal social and political dynamics, Salih and Young turn their attention to the region in Malaysia that has been most affected by the recent restructuring of the global economy, particularly that aspect of restructuring associated with the internationalization of manufacturing industry. The state of Penang has become throughly incorporated into the world economy since the early 1970s as a result of the development of export-processing zones there, and the subsequent attraction of subsidiaries of transnational textile/garment and electronics manufacturers. The economy of Penang has thus been transformed from one based on the entrepot trade and agriculture, to one linked to the world economy (and thus its vicissitudes) by a few industrial transnationals (though tourism is also of significance).

Focusing particularly on semiconductor production, Salih and Young show that while Malaysia has become the developing world's largest exporter of semiconductors, and while, by providing employment, the industry has helped raise the living standards of thousands of Malays (most of the industry's workers being Malay women from rural areas), it has been in a weak position (technologically and organizationally) in the global structure of the industry. As a result, the global crisis in the semiconductor industry (discussed in Ernst's chapter) has reverberated badly in Penang. Thousands of redundancies have resulted with their consequent damaging effects on the lives of the workers.

Although not addressing the question directly, Salih and Young's contribution raises the issue broached by Perlo Cohen: is export-oriented industrialization likely to provide a secure foundation for economic and social development in peripheral societies?

The final section of the book (Part IV) again alters the range of our spatial lens and turns our attention to some of the more specifically urban consequences of global restructuring.

While debates about global restructuring have focused heavily on industrial capital and to a far lesser extent on banking capital, there is very little work that directly addresses the role of commercial capital. Nigel Thrift's chapter serves to inform debates on this increasingly important sector of international capital development. He focuses on merchant capital (trading in commodities), money market organizations (merchant banks, etc.), securities firms (stockbrokers, etc.), and particularly on corporate services (accounting, insurance, real estate, etc.), and shows how their increasing internationalization has been related to the growth of international financial centres. While London, Paris and New York retain their pre-eminence as world finance centres, the period since the early 1970s has seen the growth of a number of secondary centres (Tokyo, Hong Kong, Singapore, Sydney, etc.). International commercial capital has been largely responsible for this development, which in turn has been facilitated by the rapid expansion and increased sophistication of information and communications technologies.

Having surveyed the global dynamics of commercial capital, Thrift turns to examine in more detail the internationalization of the City of London and especially its accounting and real estate firms. He shows how many such firms are now constituted as significant multinational corporations in their own right, with branches and/or participation arrangements in those cities across the globe where financial transactions of international moment are undertaken. The activities of international commercial capital have significant consequences for the cities in which its agents locate. They help polarize the urban social structure and push up housing prices and living costs generally. Thrift's chapter, then, helps to 'unpack' a crucial dimension of the 'world city' concept, and as such has an affinity with the more strictly sociological account of the impact of related phenomena developed in the latter parts of Sassen-Koob's chapter.

The volume is brought to a close by Michael Peter Smith's study of some of the political consequences of global restructuring for American cities. While it is well recognized that capital restructuring can help resolve economic crises, at least in the short and medium term, Smith argues that by sparking urban political conflict, restructuring may compound and hence prolong problems of accumulation.

Conceptualizing the contemporary crisis as taking three related forms — structural, sectoral and spatial — Smith suggests that structural crises at the global level have only been offset by activities that have provoked sectoral and spatial crises at the local level. He focuses on three responses to economic crisis that have had significance for US cities. Specifically he examines state and city government pressure to establish urban enterprise zones; the emergence of 'new' sweatshops and the growth of informal sector activities which 'employ' the increasing numbers of illegal immigrants; and finally he looks at the changing character of urban political mobilization.

Though a result of the desire of politicians to bring jobs to their localities, Smith argues that the development of enterprise zones can only result in the provision of low-skill, low-paid jobs and, if anything, is likely to encourage employers to informalize their activities and recruit vulnerable workers such as illegal immigrants. The growth in sweatshops producing garments and electronics and the increasing informalization of many productive activities have negative consequences, Smith suggests, for government revenues. In this sense the informalization of urban economies helps to deepen the fiscal crisis, and thus colludes in the supression of public — and hence formal — sector jobs. A vicious spiral is thus set in motion which could, in the long run, lead to intraclass, racial (and possibly gender) struggles.

Smith suggests, however, that for the moment, the situation is more optimistic. The urban impact of global restructuring is engendering new, interclass political movements which increasingly have a decentralized, pro-neighbourhood and anti-urban growth orientation. As a result, then, while informalization may in the short run have conservative economic and political implications, in the long run it could, both in itself and via its local political consequences, undermine what Smith regards as the 'twin pillars of social control under advanced capitalism': wage labour and the bureaucratic state.

The contributions to this book, in their various ways, show how the interaction of global economic restructuring, technological revolution, and the emergence of socio-political processes, are producing new spatial forms and new urban–regional policies that are becoming arenas of contention and contest. The collective endeavour of territorial researchers should be the development of a new theory that is flexible enough to be useful in very different contexts, yet rigorous enough to allow a cumulative process of knowledge-generation. This volume represents a tentative step towards such an intellectual horizon.

### Notes

1. We recognize, of course, that globally organized 'placeless power' will always continue to originate from within particular places. Our use of this phrase is meant to stress the fact that the power of core economies has been massively enhanced by the utilization and control over an historically new phenomenon: information-flow technologies. Similarly, the phrase 'powerless places' does not imply a zero-sum notion of power. Rather it connotes the fact that locally based socio-political movements are organized according to a logic of power which is distinct from, and at odds with, the global logic which increasingly penetrates and determines the lives of local populations.

# II
# CAPITAL, LABOUR AND THE DYNAMICS
# OF GLOBAL RESTRUCTURING

## 2
## Global Factory and Company Town: the Changing Division of Labour in the International Automobile Industry

*Richard Child Hill*

In the 1960s, the wealthier nations of the world began to confront severe problems of structural unemployment, underutilized plant capacity, stagnating domestic investment, capital flight abroad, and fiscal crises of the state. The poorer nations found themselves locked into a trajectory of worsening rural poverty and expanding urban slums as an ever higher proportion of their national economic activity was targeted to foreign markets, usually in the wealthier regions of the world.

In *The New International Division of Labour* Folker Frobel, Jurgen Heinrichs and Otto Kreye (1980) argue that these world events mirror a changing international division of labour. In the 1960s, a new international division of labour (NIDL) began to supersede the preceding one as multinational companies relocated industrial production from high-wage sites in wealthier nations to low-wage sites in poorer ones — all with 'far reaching consequences for the working and living conditions of people in all parts of the world' (Frobel et al., 1980: 1).

Theoretically bold, empirically grounded and ominous, the NIDL thesis captured the imagination of social scientists in many parts of the world. My aim in this paper is to evaluate how well the NIDL thesis, as set down by Frobel, Heinrichs and Kreye, fits the global transformation now underway in the automobile industry.

It would be hard to find a more significant test case for the NIDL thesis than the international auto industry. In sheer size, car production has dominated the industrial organization of advanced capitalist societies.[1] Auto production tips a nation's balance of payments and sustains or undermines world trade.[2] Car manufacture has been concentrated among a small number of companies, in a small number of regions, in a small number of wealthy nations: Piedmonte in Italy; Niedersachsen in West Germany; Ile de France in France; West Midlands in England; Tokyo, Nagoya and Hiroshima in Japan; and the Great Lakes states in the USA.[3] And because employment has been concentrated in a few large and well organized plants, the car industry has set standards of pay and work emulated by unions throughout the whole of manufacturing.

The auto industry has been experiencing a crisis since the early 1970s, and the car companies have responded by reorganizing their global operations. Employment changes have been abrupt, have occurred in large units, and have had a sharp regional impact; and the crisis has wreaked havoc in the national balance of payments and local fiscal accounts. Since the size and strength of many industries — steel, machine tools, electrical equipment, automotive components, rubber and electronics — depend heavily upon car production, a debilitated auto industry harbours severe implications for the future of all these industries, the communities which host them, and the industrial power of a nation. So the global reorganization of the auto industry raises fundamental questions of industrial policy, and managing the transition has become a priority item on the agenda of many national governments.

Can the NIDL theory make sense of the crisis and the international changes taking place in the world auto industry? Before we can address this question we have to dig more deeply into the NIDL argument itself.

## The New International Division of Labour

The world economy is not simply a sum total of national economies each of which functions essentially according to its own laws of motion with only marginal interconnections, such as those established by external trade. These national economies are, rather, organic elements of one all embracing system, namely a world economy which in fact is a single world-wide capitalist system ... the structural changes in individual nations are interrelated within this single world economy and mutually determine one another. (Frobel et al. 1980: 8)

For Frobel, Heinrichs and Kreye, the choice of the term *international* division of labour is hardly fortuitous. In their view, the economic direction taken by individual nations can only be explained by reference to the role each plays in a world capitalist system. What then, does the international *division of labour* mean from the vantage point of this world-embracing assumption? It means, the authors inform us, '... different forms of control over labour for different types of production in different regions of the capitalist world economy' (Frobel et al., 1980: 32).

Central to the NIDL thesis is an historical and an analytic contrast between a *classical* international division of labour and a *new* international division of labour. The classical international division of labour existed when

> a few industrial countries producing capital goods and consumer goods confronted the vast majority of underdeveloped countries which were integrated into the world economy as producers of raw materials (1980: 44). The new international division of labour comes about when the profitable production of manufactures for the world market ... finally become(s) possible to a significant and increasing extent, not only in the industrialized countries, but also ... in the developing countries ... [and when] ... commodity production... is increasingly subdivided into fragments which can be assigned to whichever part of the world can provide the most profitable combination of capital and labour. (1980: 13–14)

In sum, Frobel, Heinrichs and Kreye (1980: 45) use the term, the new international division of labour, to designate a tendency which:

1. undermines the traditional bisection of the world into a few industrialized countries on one hand, and a great majority of developing countries integrated into the world economy solely as raw material producers on the other, and
2. compels the increasing subdivision of manufacturing processes into a number of partial operations at different industrial sites throughout the world.

Let us call statement (1), the industrial diffusion hypothesis, and statement (2), the global factory hypothesis, and note in passing that (1) does not neccessarily imply (2); that is, the international diffusion of industry does not necessarily imply international industry organized like a global factory.

What is the source of this transformation? The moving force is the 'valorization and accumulation of capital' driven by capitalist competition. But rivalry among enterprises is a constant feature of capitalism. Why does the NIDL emerge in the 1960s and not earlier? In the past, the authors argue, capitalists survived competition through 'rationalization' — through the introduction of more efficient machinery and the reduction in size and skills of the labour force. But today,

> this device alone (along with other 'classical' devices) is no longer adequate. The development of the world economy has increasingly created conditions [forcing the development of the new international division of labour] in

which the survival of more and more companies can only be assured through the relocation of production to new industrial sites, where labour power is cheap to buy, abundant, and well disciplined; in short through the transnational reorganization of production. (Frobel et al., 1980: 15)

We shall have occasion to look more closely at this assertion in the light of recent developments in the international auto industry. But at this point it bears noting that Frobel, Heinrichs and Kreye have identified two corporate competitive strategies: *rationalization* (the introduction of more efficient machinery and production organization); and *relocation* (shifting production to new low-cost industrial sites). Several questions arise: what is the relationship between rationalization and relocation? Under what conditions is relocation an imperative? Are there yet other competitive strategies available to corporate enterprises?

According to the authors the preconditions forcing the development of the new international division of labour include: a world reserve army; advances in transportation and communication technologies; which together make possible 'world market oriented industrialization', that is, a global factory in which a detailed division of labour spans the globe. The division of labour, we learn, has three 'decisive advantages' for the valorization and accumulation of capital. The annexation of workers to a single operation increases productivity; the fragmentation of skills increases management's control over labour; and maximizing the replacement of skilled labour by simple labour reduces labour costs. But of the three, the authors give almost exclusive weight to competitive pressure to reduce wage costs (Frobel et al., 1980: 37–44).

Let us call these the productivity theorem, the labour control theorem, and the wage cost theorem, respectively. In honour of Harry Braverman whose work (1974) underpins this part of the NIDL thesis, let us call this the deskilling model of the international division of labour. But note that one can accept the argument that productivity, labour control and wage cost control are integral to the accumulation of capital *without* accepting the author's thesis that deskilling is the only means to those ends today, or that reducing wage costs is the critical imperative. Rather, these are generalizations that need to be weighed against the available evidence.

## Abstract and Concrete

The will toward concreteness, the fervor to do justice to the real, compels style and form into being. (Updike, 1985)

It is hard to carry an abstract discussion of the NIDL very far. If, for example, we want to ascertain the truth of the NIDL global factory claim that there is 'an increasing subdivision of manufacturing processes into a number of partial operations at different industrial sites throughout the world', then we soon have to discuss concrete cases of production chains, industries, and nations. When we try to do that some difficulties arise.

For one thing, when we cast a scrutinizing light on the NIDL concept, its meaning is not very clearly revealed. Analytic vagueness is hard to avoid because the internationalization idea assumes flesh only in the body of specific industrial companies located in specific countries. So, concreteness raises contingencies of its own, such as the following:

1.   The elements making up production chains and the way these elements are geographically arranged may vary among industries (contrast, for example, the textile and auto industries).
2.   Companies in the same industry but headquartered in different nations may organize their production chains differently (contrast, for example, the Japanese and US auto companies).
3.   Even companies in the same industry and headquartered in the same nation may organize their production chains differently (contrast, for example, Nissan and Toyota in Japan).

If these concrete contingencies are real, which I believe they are, then identification of general tendencies in the international division of labour becomes more difficult: the textile industry may fit the NIDL thesis better than the Japanese auto industry; and Nissan may approximate the theory better than Toyota. But before we start worrying about these kinds of issues we need to know more about the production chain in the world auto industry.

The complexity of the automobile industry is daunting. Elements that make up the production chain include *raw materials* of various kinds that go into the *production* of parts (some 15,000 in all!) which are *assembled* into finished motor vehicles for *distribution* to markets for sale. These products must be *designed, engineered*, and the whole process *financed* and *controlled* from beginning to end. So auto production is actually a joint effort among a handful of major assemblers, their many divisions, and thousands of suppliers, distributors and financing sources whose actions must be closely co-ordinated.

The auto industry tends to be identified with the major assemblers, but in fact auto suppliers account for as much as 55 percent of the purchase value of a car, and they provide 40 to 50 percent more jobs than do the assemblers.[4] In the USA alone, some 40,000 auto suppliers, ranging from steel and rubber to plastics and electronics producers, sold $40 billion worth of goods and services to the four domestic manufacturers in 1980.[5] This suggests that the relationships among the major assemblers and their suppliers play a critical role in auto production.

The chain in auto parts production can be broken down into four basic elements: *major mechanicals*, like the engine and drive train, which tend to be produced by the major assemblers themselves, or by joint ventures with big supply companies; *vehicle systems*, like lighting, braking, suspension, steering, and instrumentation, which are generally produced by transnational special system suppliers like Bendix (USA), Robert Bosch (West Germany), and Nippondenso (Japan); *finished parts*, for which fit and appearance are crucial, like seats, dashboards, and major stampings — these are mostly produced by the majors or in close collaboration with suppliers; and *minor parts*, like fasteners, trim, glass and tyres, which are usually purchased from outside suppliers (Altschuler et al., 1984: 189).

How then might we begin to describe the international division of labour in the auto industry? Hervey and Cole (1983: 1) provide a typical definition of internationalization: 'the diffusion of production, consumption, and capital investment of finished vehicles and auto components from established world centers to new centers'. But this kind of conception still does not take us very far, for at least two reasons. First, Hervey and Cole do not sufficiently distinguish among elements in the production chain (between the *production* of different *kinds* of components, for example, and their *assembly* into cars). Second, the authors compound the confusion by putting different temporal moments in the international expansion of industry into one historical category. For example, if the term 'consumption' refers to the marketing of finished vehicles, then the auto industry went global half a century ago. But if the reference point is control over finance capital, then auto companies are local and are likely to remain so.

So the following analytic points are worth bearing in mind. The international division of labour in an industry is a variable, a matter of *degree*. Structural elements in the production chain can be joined together in different international configurations, or *types*. Viewed historically, we should be able to speak of *phases* in the international division of labour defined by degree and type. The determinants, and indeed, even the meaning of internationalization may well vary among phases. Different phases in the international division of labour may suggest quite different corporate and labour strategies, patterns of urban and regional development, and government fiscal and industrial policies. In addition, the meaning of the international division of labour today is all the more complicated because the present phase is layered upon past ones with a result that looks less like a layer cake than like the batter, composed of folded-in elements, that gives the dessert substance.

How then do the NIDL industrial diffusion hypothesis, global factory hypothesis, and wage costs thesis hold up against recent developments in the world auto industry?

*Rationalization and Relocation*
National economies are, to be sure, organic parts of an embracing world system. But the structure of the whole emerges out of alliances and clashes among the parts. It is competition and collaboration among companies and governments in Japan and the United States that is shaping the international division of labour in the world auto industry today.

US-based transnational companies have been front-runners in the international car race during most of this century; until recently the world was their oyster. It is the US companies that have stretched the NIDL tendency the furthest. But the US oligarchs have recently more than met their match in competition from the Japanese. Yet Japan's auto companies are profitably organized along lines that do not fit the NIDL thesis at all.

Japanese and US companies now seem to be converging in the way they divide up and organize production, and that convergence foretells the international shape of things to come. Japanese companies are investing more abroad, as one would expect from the NIDL diffusion hypothesis, but they are doing so for reasons other than the wage costs theorem emphasized by Frobel, Heinrichs and Kreye. The US industry, on the other hand, is moving more in the direction of agglomeration that has proven so profitable for the Japanese in the past, and this tendency too fails to fit NIDL assumptions. The consequence is certainly a new international division of labour in the auto industry, but one more complicated, contradictory, and flexible than that allowed for by the NIDL theory.

**The New International Division of Labour in the Auto Industry**
To understand what is distinctive about the international division of labour in the auto industry today, one must know what preceded it. Juxtaposing present to past reveals three phases in the internationalization of the front-running US industry, timed roughly 25 to 30 years apart: the late 1920s, the late 1950s, and the early 1980s.[6] All three phases have certain features in common. Each occurred in a period of economic slump, stagnant domestic demand, excess capacity, and rising national protectionism. The first phase established the international presence of the industry on all five continents, primarily through assembly plants. The second phase sketched throughout Europe what the third phase is inscribing on other regions of the world today.

Excess capacity and slackening domestic demand first became critical in the latter half of the 1920s. Then as now the response was exports. Exports as a proportion of US domestic production rose from 4 percent in 1919 to 11.1 percent in 1927 (Mutlu, 1979: 189). The auto firms backed their export drive with foreign assembly plants. Foreign assembly allowed the companies to reduce transportation costs, overcome tariff barriers, protect their market shares against foreign competition, and utilize excess cash reserves for which there was no equally profitable investment to be found at home.

The US companies built 34 foreign plants between 1925 and 1929 — almost twice the number constructed during the preceding 20 years — and spread their tentacles to all five continents. US firms were the only ones engaged in foreign assembly and manufacturing, and by the close of the decade they held a virtual monopoly in Canada, Latin America and Australia. But with a handful of exceptions in Canada and Western Europe, the newly constructed facilities were all assembly plants (Mutlu, 1979: 195).

The second massive wave of US foreign investment came in the late 1950s and early 1960s. In 1958–59, 39 subsidiaries were established abroad, two more than all those created during the previous 13 years. In 1960–61 came 28 more; and in 1962, an additional 18 were established (Mutlu, 1979: 362). Factors responsible for this second phase of international expansion included: stagnant conditions of domestic demand and excess capacity at home; the formation of the European Economic Community (EEC) in 1957; and the import-substitution development policies mounted by Third World nations.

The investment exodus after 1955 indicates that the corporate giants were seeking outlets for excess capital and markets for excess products — resources which could not be disposed of at home but which could be incorporated into assembly operations and sales networks abroad (Mutlu, 1979: 9, Table VI). Behind this capital flight was a 'European strategy'.[7] With the formation of the EEC in 1957, Western Europe became one huge market as tariffs and restrictions were eliminated among member nations but maintained against outsiders. Goods and services were now more freely mobile among nations within the EEC and new opportunities were provided for economies of scale and corporate integration on a regional basis.

The EEC enabled US corporations to make a major leap forward in their transnational operations. Now the European subsidiaries of the US transnationals could penetrate all major European markets, and compete with rival indigenous firms, without having to have local assembly and manufacturing facilities in each separate nation. They could reach the economies of scale required to compete effectively within the EEC, and become significant bases for exports to world markets including the United States. So the EEC helped abate a crisis of overaccumulation in the world auto industry by absorbing excess funds seeking profitable employment, and by fostering a more 'rationalized' production structure among the firms within the European Economic Community (Mutlu, 1979: 309–331).

Finally, those Third World nations without an indigenous auto industry but desiring one, imposed a host of protective measures — tariffs, quotas, local content requirements, licensing and exchange controls — all meant to induce the transnational car companies to locate assembly, and sometimes manufacturing facilities, inside their borders. The US auto companies did not begin investing heavily in the Third World until the late 1950s. So long as demand and profits were buoyant at home and demand in Third World markets was not high, auto companies had no inclination to invest in the periphery. But when the market stagnated at home, investment opportunities south of the border looked much better, so capital moved. Moreover, Third World import substitution policies in the latter half of the 1950s (Brazil in 1956, Argentina in 1958, Mexico in 1962) happened to coincide with a period of stagnant demand in the USA.

We are now in the midst of the third phase of internationalization in the auto industry. The current wave of foreign investment shares features in common with the preceding two, for it has occurred in the midst of economic slump, stagnating demand, excess capacity, and rising national protectionism. Yet the nature of the third phase differs so considerably from the two that came before it, that one cannot help describing it as an epoch making transition in the history of the world auto industry. It is a transition that conforms in the following particulars to the trajectory forecast by the NIDL theory.

*Global competition.* By the 1970s, European and Japanese firms had reached the economies of scale required to challenge the monopoly held by US companies in world markets.

*A global market.* The oil shocks of 1973 and 1979, and government regulations to promote higher fuel efficiency and safety, led to a big expansion of the market for small, fuel-efficient cars in the USA and Canada and an unprecedented convergence in product characteristics between North America and the rest of the globe.

*Global integration.* The global convergence in car-buying habits has afforded car manufacturers unprecedented opportunities to pursue a global strategy, one where firms produce different parts and assemble finished vehicles in different countries depending upon the advantages offered in each, and where they integrate their operations on a transnational plane.

One expression of the global integration strategy is the *world car* — designing cars for production in all major markets to gain economies of scale in product development, component design and production. Ford recognized the cost advantages of this kind of integration in Europe as early as 1967. This strategy, Ford concluded, would eliminate duplication of research and design staff in its German and British subsidiaries, spread design and some retooling costs over a larger volume, make possible bulk buying and longer production runs with standardized components, and give added flexibility in responding to strikes and production breakdowns (Hainer and Koslofsky, 1979). In the 1970s, Ford gave birth to the Fiesta — a car designed in Europe, with engines produced in Valencia, Spain, and transaxles made in Bordeaux, France. The Fiesta was assembled in Valencia, in Dagenham, England, and in Saarlouis, Germany, and marketed in the EEC and North America. General Motors now produces its 'world car', the Chevette, in the USA, West Germany, the United Kingdom, Japan, Australia, Brazil and Argentina (Jones, 1981: 19–22).

Yet another expression of global integration is *global sourcing* — taking advantage of lower costs and other opportunities provided by locating production in export platforms based in third countries. For example, Ford followed the Fiesta with the Fiera — a car made in the Philippines, Taiwan and Thailand. The Fiera's engine, transmission, and brakes came from Ford subsidiaries in England; its light rear axles and differentials from Argentina; its heavy duty axles and some engine parts from Australia; and its steering gears, windshield wipers, and shock absorbers from Japan. Remaining Fiera parts were manufactured in the assembly plants of each producing country or purchased from local sources. Ford has thereby sought to develop an integrated manufacturing capability in Southeast Asia by producing individual components in different countries (Jones, 1981: 9).

General Motors has also moved towards the global integration of components production. For example, the company is developing new engine plants in Australia, Brazil, Mexico and Austria. These plants will reap the advantages offered in local markets, while surplus production will be exported to assembly sites in Western Europe and the USA. Some two-thirds of the Australian and Brazilian engines will be exported to Europe while Mexican engines will go to the USA (Jones, 1981: 22).

The transnational auto corporations, therefore, are building more assembly and manufacturing facilities in Third World nations, at least in those that have government-protected markets and some promise of growing demand. But these Third World nations are not likely to become full producers; rather they are more likely to serve as extensions of the global sourcing strategy; that is, as export platforms or production niches for components, like engines and gear boxes, produced primarily for export.

The world car, global sourcing, and export platforms support the NIDL diffusion and global factory hypotheses. But there are other tendencies that do not, as evidenced in Japan's formidable challenge to the rest of the world industry.

*Toyota's Total System*
Between 1960 and 1980, the Japanese auto industry grew from the smallest to the largest in the world.[8] Did the Japanese auto corporations create such phenomenal growth by becoming master organizers of the new international division of labour? Or, short of that, but still consistent with the NIDL argument, is the reason to be found in the low wages paid to auto workers in Japan? Neither is correct. The Japanese advantage came primarily from a home centred, export oriented, production system which generated higher productivity and therefore allowed domestic companies to produce cars for much less than their international competitors.[9]

Of all the auto companies in Japan, Toyota is the most successful. Despite stiff export barriers in Western Europe and the voluntary restraint agreement with the United States, Toyota made big profits while western companies made big losses during 1979–82.[10] Japanese competitors now call the company the 'Toyota bank', because its profits have been so large that it can finance most of its spending on plant and equipment from internal funds (Lohr, 1983).

Toyota's advantage is its ability to manufacture and ship a small car to foreign markets for substantially less ($1,300 to $1,700 in the USA, for example) than domestic manufacturers in other producing countries can make them. The Toyota advantage derives from the 'Toyota system' — an approach to manufacturing whose basic elements depend neither upon sophisticated technology nor upon cheap labour.[11] Yet when taken as a whole, the Toyota system is remarkably efficient and has been copied by many other Japanese companies much as Ford's mass production techniques and General Motor's administrative structure became models for US auto manufacturers in earlier eras. The Toyota system also departs from the tenets of mass production and assembly line work originally applied to the auto industry by Henry Ford and Frederick Winslow Taylor and projected onto the globe by the NIDL theory.

The Toyota system maximized manufacturing efficiency by keeping inventory to an absolute minimum; by making sure each step of the manufacturing process is done correctly the first time even though the assembly line runs slower as a result; and by continually reducing the amount of human labour that goes into each car. But Japan's most important manufacturing innovation is the just-in-time, production control system known as *kanban*.

Kanban, named after small cards used to order more parts, is a resource conserving approach to mass production which synchronizes delivery of parts to the assembly line. As often as 20 to 25 times daily, trucks are dispatched from suppliers with loads of parts to keep production and assembly lines running. The kanban approach reduces waste and removes cumbersome storage areas from assembly plants, allows factories to be smaller and more compact, groups plants into industrial complexes, and builds closer ties to suppliers (Lienert, 1983). Kanban imposes discipline on a manufacturer's supplier network. Production problems are exposed and quality is maintained because faulty parts shut down the assembly line, and when that happens the supplier risks losing the business. In essence, kanban is a way of keeping 'indirect' labour, or 'non value added work' to a minimum (Holusha, 1983).

In striking contrast to the global geography of the NIDL, the integrated kanban system requires factories clustered together and Toyota has followed this logic to the limit. All nine of its major production plants and most of its major suppliers are located within a few miles of one another in the vast urban–industrial complex, Toyota City, on the outskirts of Nagoya, 150 miles west of Tokyo. In Japan, the corporation is also a kind of community, and this suggests cultures as well as corporations are clashing in today's international competition.

Toyota City bears the unmistakeable imprint of Japan's largest auto maker, just as it bears the company name. Of Toyota Motor Company's 48,000 employees, more than 35,000 work here. In Toyota City married workers live in row after row of look-alike houses, purchased at cut-rate prices subsidized by the company. Toyota dormitories can house 20,000 men, and another 1,500 units are available for single women. Recreation is provided by a company stadium seating 30,000; company baseball fields, company gymnasiums, company swimming pools, company tennis courts, and company sumo rings. Toyota City looks like the ultimate company town.[12] There

> workers leave subsidized housing, gather obediently early in the morning to do calisthenics together, sing the company song, participate in calls for higher productivity, troop off to their tasks ... some executives are expected to spend part of their career as union officials, firings are rare, and over one-half of Japanese auto workers have guaranteed lifetime jobs. (Smith, 1983)

The Toyota advantage in time, space and money was graphically illustrated in a recent study of Ford Motor Company. When Ford compared Toyota plants with similar manufacturing facilities in Western Europe and North America, the corporation discovered that:

due to inventory saving techniques, Toyota's production per worker was three times that of Ford; a Toyota engine plant takes up 300,000 square feet compared to 900,000 at a comparable Ford facility; from 80 to 85 percent of the Toyotas coming off the line had no defects as compared to an average of seven to eight defects per car at Ford; due to Toyota's heavy investment in back-up tooling, the time required to change a standard die took five to ten minutes at Toyota, as compared to three to four hours at Ford (Lohr, 1983).

**Global Factory and Company Town**
The contrast between US and Japanese methods of organizing auto production suggest two competitive tendences in the division of labour in the world auto industry today.

The NIDL tendency is a deskilling strategy whereby productivity is enhanced by annexing workers to a single operation; labour control is maintained by fragmenting workers' skills; and wage costs are reduced by replacing skilled with simple labour. Advances in transportation and communication allow companies to project the detailed division of labour within the factory across the face of the globe, and the pressure of intercapitalist rivalry turns this possibility into an imperative. As a consequence, industry is diffused from centre to periphery, the production chain is subdivided among nations like it is among individuals, all in the quest to maintain profits by relocating production to sites where wages are lower and labour more malleable.

The NIDL tendency in the international auto industry is best evidenced in the world car and global sourcing strategies and has advanced the furthest in US-based multinationals. But the phenomenal success of Japanese auto companies suggests there may be limits to dispersing assembly plants and to global sourcing. Like emperors, corporate monopolists tend to overextend themselves until the sheer weight and complexity of their imperial operations makes them vulnerable to enemy attack.

The NIDL scenario, played out fully in the auto industry, requires immense logistical pipelines, as assembly plants are supplied with metal stampings, engines, transmissions, cloth or vinyl for seats, windshields, radios, and the thousands of other items making up a car that come streaming in from low-cost production points around the globe. Tens of thousands of people are required just to manage the material flow, load and unload it, and inspect it for damage. It is also necessary to have big stockpiles in storage for security against easily disrupted supply lines and that way more damage is sustained. So, half of the space in the average assembly plant is a warehouse. Since many parts are damaged or require recleaning, more repair labour is needed. Moreover, platoons of workers are needed just to gather and dispose of cardboard packaging. Plants grow to immense size to accommodate the billions of dollars tied up in inventory storage; and they require enormous energy outlays for heat and light. These are the disadvantages that must be weighed against the competitive advantages in labour costs and labour control that accrue from subdivided, far flung production sites linked together in a global factory.

It is the Toyota City system that brings the NIDL's competitive disadvantages most to light. In contrast to the NIDL relocation imperative, Toyota's rationalization strategy benefits greatly from the economic efficiencies and possibilities for controlling suppliers and workers that can come from concentrating economic activity in a company town environment.

Ironically, Toyota City was patterned after Henry Ford's Rouge complex built half a century ago. Ford's ideal was a totally integrated production system: steel, glass, engines, car bodies and components, all produced in one place. Even today, iron ore is loaded from Ford ships at one end of the Rouge complex facing the Detroit River and Mustang cars roll out the other. This may suggest that the Toyota City system is anachronistic, a throwback to the more primitive, 'classical' phase in the international division of labour. But that is not the case. A better way of looking at the contrast between the global factory and the company town is to suggest there is a sort of dialectical relationship between relocation and rationalization; it is not so much that one supersedes the other as that they define each other's limits.

The Toyota City system is also a strikingly different method of organizing the labour process than that suggested by the deskilling model. At the root of the Toyota system is a conception of the corporation as community, and therein rests Toyota's success in generating productivity, controlling its workforce and keeping labour costs in line. But the boundaries of community can only be stretched so far, and therein too lies the vulnerability of Toyota's total system.

Japan's successful development strategy — protecting its domestic market against imports while exporting finished vehicles from a highly efficient, home-based manufacturing system — has angered its trading partners and led to many restrictive actions against its exports. By 1981, for example, Japanese finished vehicle imports were restricted in markets accounting for '77 percent of non-Communist world demand, up from 20 percent in 1980' (Hervey and Cole, 1983: 2). In the face of national resistance, Japanese companies must change strategy. Now they must invest directly in assembly and manufacturing facilities in other lands, not for reasons of cost competition as one would expect from the NIDL theory, but to protect their markets in a world system characterized by increasing national protectionism.

So the extent to which Japanese companies can transplant their production system abroad is now being put to the test. Nissan is producing pickup trucks in the USA, and cars in the United Kingdom, Italy and Spain. Honda is assembling cars in the USA, and has reached a licence agreement with the British Rover company to produce a car in the UK for sale throughout the EEC. Toyota now has operations in 19 countries (Stokes, 1981).

But even as the Japanese companies are carving out an NIDL in the face of mounting political pressure, US transnationals are beginning to emulate the Toyota City system. In February 1983, General Motors and Toyota Motor Sales Company, Ltd. announced they had signed a joint venture agreement to produce 200,000 subcompact cars annually in Fremont, California. The General Motors–Toyota agreement was the culmination of two years of complex negotiations involving dozens of cross-Pacific flights and thousands of details.

Production is at GM's Fremont plant, a 411-acre suburban site on the southeastern rim of San Francisco Bay. Fremont is an attractive site because it is on the Pacific Rim and is the centre of the largest import market in the United States (Hayes, 1983). The new venture employs some 3,000 workers, half the typical GM workforce in an assembly plant with comparable production. The car is Toyota's front wheel drive replacement for the Corolla. 50 percent of the content is of US origin (including body, seats, most of the interior trim and many components); and 50 percent comes from Japan (including the design, engine and transmission). The joint venture has formed a new company. Toyota is in charge of production, employs its own labour-management techniques, and uses much of its own equipment. Beyond providing the assembly plant, General Motors is co-ordinating output and managing distribution. The new cars are now being sold by Chevrolet dealers as a replacement for GM's world car, the Chevette. The agreement is to last up to 12 years. General Motors and Toyota each own half of the new company and they are splitting profits equally. Each partner has appointed the same number of directors to the board. Toyota selected the chief executive officer (Smith, 1983).

General Motors approached Toyota with a joint venture proposition because the company wanted Toyota assistance in designing a small car; because it wanted to buy a 'prepackaged' Toyota system to make up part of Japan's current cost advantage; and because GM wanted to experiment with more 'flexible' Japanese models for organizing the labour process, and the joint venture provided a port of entry against the United Auto Workers (UAW) — a way to pressure the union for concessions on work conditions, seniority and wage determination that GM probably could not have obtained otherwise (Hill, 1983a).

For their part, Toyota officials explained the Fremont pact as 'offering salt to our enemy' — as a way of helping out an opponent in the Japanese tradition (Holusha, 1983). But Toyota's manoeuvre had less to do with rules of warfare in medieval Japan (when warlords gave essential supplies to peasants on the opposing side despite hositilities) than it does with the exigencies of Japan's international trade conflicts today. For Toyota, the Fremont agreement was a good way to establish manufacturing operations in the USA at a minimum cost. It was also an opportunity to learn more about GM's global strategy through closer access to corporate management and closer contact with parts suppliers in the USA.

General Motors' own divisions are now mimicking the Toyota system too. GM's Buick Division, for example, is grouping plants into a 'Buick City' complex around the division's headquarters city of Flint, Michigan. The Buick city complex in Flint is the first phase in a company master plan for a reorganized urban–industrial hub in Michigan (Job, 1985). This manufacturing hub is projected to include six assembly plants and a variety of major suppliers — all within a 100-mile radius of one another. GM is attempting to forge closer links with its suppliers and hopes to attract satellite operations around the assembly plants, including some of its own components divisions, to build parts and subassemblies. The aim is to increase profits by lowering inventory and manufacturing costs, thus improving efficiency and productivity.

However, it is General Motors' recently announced Saturn project which will come the closest to cloning Toyota's corporate community concept. Saturn is a new GM subsidiary charged with making a new car with new methods to boost the company's share of the world's small car market. Saturn adds up to as much as five billion dollars worth of plant and equipment, and the project will create perhaps 6,000 new production jobs and 14,000 more spun-off to parts and service suppliers. Saturn's design follows the kanban system and blueprints a close-knit manufacturing complex for engines, metal stampings, plastics fabrication and for soft trim items like seats. These operations are to feed an assembly plant with two lines, capable of producing 2,000 cars a day (Higgins, 1985).

Saturn will have a computer for a heart; robots will perform most tasks; work stations will be linked by computer-guided vehicles; and fancy software of all sorts will guide the design, engineering, production and distribution of the vehicle. But since the inner workings of this electronic factory are fragile and easily sent awry, workers have to be committed to the enterprise to make it work.

So the Saturn project calls for a big move in the Japanese direction in GM's style of management and the way the company organizes work. Saturn extends some principles established in recent UAW–GM labour negotiations, but the new corporation will also have its own special labour contract. Base wages will be lower, job classifications greatly reduced, and work rules relaxed. Technical expertise will be more widely distributed, reducing distinctions between blue and white collar work. Work will be organized by production teams. Teams will compete against one another and will share in Saturn's successes and failures since wages will be tied to team productivity and corporate profitability. Saturn will probably have less inequality and less separation between mental and manual work; more worker access to corporate information and more social benefits (including childcare and recreation facilities) than any previous method of organizing heavy industry in the United States. It will also cut by half the size of the workforce necessary to produce automobiles (Hill, 1985).

## Conclusion

In the final analysis, just how well does the NIDL theory capture the changing division of labour in the international auto industry today?

The auto industry is certainly *diffusing* to many nations around the world as implied by the first NIDL hypothesis. But the major tendency in direct foreign investment today is cross penetration: companies based in wealthy countries are investing in the markets of other wealthy countries largely to get behind tariff walls and protect their markets; and that kind of internationalization of production is not explained by the NIDL theory.

Direct foreign investment in the poorer nations is still a small percentage of total outlays by transnational auto corporations. The auto giants are unlikely to locate major export platforms in very poor countries. The commitment of capital is great, and without a relatively assured home market, too heavy dependence on exports harbours many economic and political risks. Because the car companies depend upon a spectrum of suppliers, they are unlikely to develop big export-oriented production complexes without a pre-existing manufacturing base of sufficient magnitude to produce some of the required materials and components at competitive prices. So, auto production will increase in the Third World but mainly in larger countries with growing markets which require domestic manufacture in return for market access.

Is the global factory the wave of the future in the international auto industry? Harley Shaiken (1984) in his recent book on microelectronic technologies and the labour process in the auto industry certainly thinks so. According to Shaiken:

> Computer technology combined with telecommunications makes it possible for management to recast the shape of production on a world scale. Paradoxically, this more integrated managerial control leads to a more fragmented production. Multinational companies are already defining a new

worldwide use of labour, based on where wage rates are lowest and local conditions most favourable, in what is rapidly becoming a global factory. (1984: 234)

Yet a recent study on the future of the automobile by some of Shaiken's own colleagues at the Massachusetts Institute of Technology reaches a different conclusion (Altschuler et al., 1984). These authors downplay the world car and global sourcing trends and see a future geography for auto production that conforms more to 'a philosophy of manufacturing at integrated assembly sites', that is, a tendency towards the Toyota City system. The MIT researchers also predict that most elements of the auto production chain, particularly major mechanicals and finished parts, will be located at the point of assembly in the future; some vehicle systems will be produced by specialist firms at their own centralized production sites; and only minor parts will be outsourced to a significant degree.

What seems to be taking shape is a kind of blend of global factory and company town into integrated regional production complexes with some cross-regional, international linkages and co-ordination. George Maxcy captured this scenario best when he suggested that the typical transnational auto company of the future:

> . . . will have a world-wide network of subsidiaries and affiliates made up of an integrated group of firms in each of the major regions — North America, Europe, Latin America, Asia–Pacific and Africa — with each regional bloc being more or less self-sufficient. But there will be production as well as technological links between firms in different regions because of world-wide sourcing of components and built-up models in short supply or missing from the range of an individual subsidiary. (Maxcy, 1981: 162)

This scenario makes sense out of the global net Toyota may eventually weave with General Motors. Toyota executives have indicated they anticipate possible joint ventures with GM affiliates in South Korea and in the United Kingdom. South Korea's Sehan Motor Company is owned equally by GM and the local Daewoo group. Sehan produces the subcompact, Rekord, and faces strong rivalry from another major Korean automaker, Hyundai Motor Company, which is tied to Japan's Mitsubishi Motor Corporation. A joint venture with Sehan would provide Toyota with a competitive base against foreign companies intending to use South Korea as a platform to penetrate the Asian regional market. In addition, GM's British subsidiary, Vauxhall Motors, which has suffered from continous deficits over the past few years and is attempting to revitalize its management, would provide Toyota tariff-free access to the market of the EEC.

The global marriage of convenience between General Motors and Toyota also illustrates other important features of the international auto industry today: how cross-national equity holdings and joint ventures are changing the very nature of international competition in the industry; how poorly the NIDL wage cost thesis captures the complexities of transnational collaboration and rivalry in a 'world of competing sovereign states with national, often conflicting goals' (Maxcy, 1981: 159); and how the imperatives of accumulation — productivity, labour control, and wage cost containment — may be met through methods other than deskilling: automation, just-in-time manufacturing systems, changing corporate cultures and social relations at work, and profit-sharing.

Even so, the social consequences implicit in the NIDL thesis are still present: trade deficits, structural unemployment and fiscal contradictions in the centre; poverty and export dependency in the periphery.

## Notes

1. Car production accounts for 5 to 10 percent of manufacturing output, investment and employment in advanced capitalist societies today, and if the raw materials and capital goods which feed the auto industry are taken into account, the influence of auto production mounts higher still (United Nations Centre on Transnational Corporations, 1983).

2. In the late 1970s, for example, cars accounted for 12 percent of world trade in manufactured goods, and from 11 to 12 percent of manufacturing exports in the producing countries (Jones, 1981: 3). Even this understates the auto's importance because it excludes trade in engines, electrical components and tyres.

3. In the late 1970s, the world's nine largest firms, based in five countries, accounted for 83 percent of the world production; the largest two accounted for 39 percent (Jones, 1981: 30).

4. Auto suppliers provided 1.4 million jobs in the USA in 1979; by 1983, one-third of those jobs had disappeared (Flynn, 1984).

5. Some 4,800 companies account for 85 percent of US auto supply sales, and just 120 account for 45 percent. But the largest suppliers in value of production usually have a small percentage of their total sales in the auto sector, while smaller suppliers tend to be much more dependent upon car manufacture (Flynn, 1984).

6. What follows in this section is a brief synopsis of a much longer research report. For more empirical detail, see Hill (1983b).

7. General Motors began taking on a heavy commitment in Europe by spending 30 to 50 percent of their investment funds in the United Kingdom and West Germany.

8. By 1980, Japanese companies were producing 11 million cars and trucks to North America's 7.8 million (Stokes, 1981).

9. This section, too, is a synopsis of a longer research report. For more documentation see Hill (1983a).

10. Between 1976 and 1982, the Toyota Motor Company's profits rose 33 percent, and its marketing arm, Toyota Motor Sales, registered a profit rise of 83 percent. But this actually understates the company's profits because it does not include net income from partly owned affiliates. Between 1975 and 1981, Toyota's production of cars and trucks rose 38 percent (from 2.3 million to 3.2 million); while employment rose 8 percent (to 48,180) (Lohr, 1983).

11. According to the widely cited James Harbour study, hourly wages and benefits of US auto workers averaged $19.95 at General Motors and $11.00 at Toyota in 1982, and accounted for at best $500 a car. That sum was nearly offset by the shipping and duty costs of transporting cars from Japan to the United States. He estimated Japan's advantage was still $1500 a car taking labour costs into consideration (Lohr, 1983).

12. I can attest to the accuracy of these observations, after doing field work in Toyota City in December 1983.

## References

Altschuler, A., M. Anderson, D. Jones, D. Roos and J. Womack (1984) *The Future of the Automobile*. Cambridge, Mass.: MIT Press.

Braverman, H. (1974) *Labor and Monopoly Capital*. New York: Monthly Review Press.

Flynn, M.S. (1984) *The Competitive Status of the U.S. Automotive Industry*. Testimony before the Subcommittee on Trade, Finance Committee, United States Senate, Washington, DC reprint.

Frobel, F., J. Heinrichs and O. Kreye (1980) *The New International Division of Labour*. Cambridge: Cambridge University Press.

Hainer, M. and J. Koslofsky (1979) 'Car Wars', *NACLA Report on the Americas*, XIII: 3-9.

Hayes, T.C. (1983) 'GM Turns to the Japanese', *New York Times*, 31 May.

Hervey, R.P. and R. Cole (1983) 'Notes on the Internationalization of the Auto Industry'. Paper presented at the Annual Meetings of the Society of Automotive Engineers, Detroit, Michigan.

Higgins, J. (1985) 'Saturn: Auto Plant of the Future', *Detroit News*, 10 January.

Hill, R.C. (1983a) 'A Global Marriage of Convenience: General Motors and Toyota at Fremont'. Paper presented at the Annual Meetings of the Society for the Study of Social Problems, Detroit, Michigan.

Hill, R.C. (1983b) 'The Auto Industry in Global Transition'. Paper presented at the Annual Meetings of the American Sociological Association, Detroit, Michigan.

Hill, R.C. (1985) 'Astronomy for the Unemployed', *Detroit Metro-Times*, 16-23 April.

Holusha, J. (1983) 'GM—Toyota Deal Set', *New York Times*, 11 February.

*Japan Economic Journal*, (1982) 'Toyota Shows Readiness to Work with GM's Offshoots', March.

Job, A. (1985) 'GM Halts Flint Lines for Buick City Shift', *Detroit News*, 8 February.

Jones, D.T. (1981) *Maturity and Crisis in the European Car Industry*. Brighton: Sussex European Papers No. 8, University of Sussex.

Lienert, P. (1983) 'Kanban', *Detroit News*, 30 January.

Lohr, S. (1982) 'The Company that Stopped Detroit', *New York Times*, 21 March.

Maxcy, G. (1981) *The Multinational Automobile Industry*. New York: St. Martins Press.

Mutlu, S. (1979) 'Interregional and International Mobility of Industrial Capital: The Case of the American Automobile and Electronics Companies', Ph.D. dissertation. Berkeley: University of California.

Shaiken, H. (1984) *Work Transformed: Automation and Labor in the Computer Age*. New York: Holt, Rhinehart & Winston.

Smith, R. (1983) 'Toyota—GM: A Glimpse into the Future', *Los Angeles Times*, 3 March.

Stokes, H.S. (1981) 'Japan's Amazing Auto Machine', *New York Times*, 18 January.

United Nations Centre on Transnational Corporations (1983) *Transnational Corporations in the International Auto Industry*. New York: United Nations.

Updike, J. (1985) 'The Artist and His Audience', *The New York Review of Books*, 18 July.

# 3
# US–Japanese Competition and the Worldwide Restructuring of the Electronics Industry: a European View

## Dieter Ernst

I propose to review current patterns of US–Japanese competition in the worldwide restructuring of the electronics industry and to assess how this affects Europe's scope for upgrading its own electronics industry. Given the vast canvas of the topic, but limited space, I shall focus on one particular sector of the electronics industry: semiconductor manufacturing. This is in fact an industry which is widely considered to be of crucial importance for future structural transformation and international competitiveness.

Developments in the semiconductor industry, especially in the design and manufacture of integrated circuits (ICs), condition to a very large degree the future shape of the world electronics industry. In fact, as microprocessors, memories and input–output devices have become increasingly powerful, computer and communication and control technologies, which used to be strictly separated, are being increasingly linked together into integrated information systems. This technological convergence in turn is bound to impose fundamental changes on the market and on industrial structures and the patterns of competition, not only for the electronics industry, but for industrial manufacturing at large.

The scope for automating industrial manufacturing and related services has certainly increased drastically. Of even greater importance, however, is that previously separate information flows can be integrated today, irrespective of spatial boundaries. Consequently, worldwide networks of information are being established, leading to a proliferation of data networks and data communication services. It is in this sense that information technologies are becoming an important vehicle for new rounds of the internationalization of industrial manufacturing. It is now technically feasible for multinational corporations to install captive worldwide information networks, through which headquarters' managements can link together production facilities around the world as if they were divisions within one factory. Thus, it has become possible today to synchronize, on a worldwide scale, decentralized production with a strictly centralized control over strategic assets (Ernst, 1983, 1986a, 1986b, 1987).

Furthermore, the development of the semiconductor industry contains nearly all the ingredients of our more general concern: how newly emerging patterns of conflict and cooperation between the US and a select group of Asian countries, particularly Japan, is likely to influence Europe's position in the world economy. By focusing on the microcosmos of semiconductor manufacturing, I intend to raise some doubts, if not more, about the validity of some widely quoted interpretations of the driving forces behind US—Japanese competition and behind the ascendancy of East Asia.

According to some observers (Borrus et al, 1983) today's drama of the US electronics industry has a clearly identifiable culprit: an unholy alliance of private firms and governments, particularly in Japan (but increasingly also in countries like South Korea and Taiwan), whose unfair competitive practices have succeeded in bypassing US technological superiority and thus have inflicted major damage on American semiconductor merchant firms. Fighting for survival, these companies, as with much of the US electronics industry at large, are said to have no choice but to 'pay-back' in kind. In other words, unfair competitive practices introduced by Japan and some East Asian 'newly industrializing countries' (NICs) are claimed to be the primary cause of the rapid erosion of free trade in electronics.

In contrast to such positions, I suggest that global competition in semiconductors, as much as in any other industry, is a somewhat more complex and contradictory affair. In a period of pervasive internationalization of trade, production and finance, it would be surprising if clearcut and watertight delineations were still possible between *the* US, *the* Japanese and, for that matter, *the* European electronics industries. It would also be surprising if the implementation of trade and industrial policies, derived from a diagnosis such as the one described above, were not to be confronted with major trade-offs and conflicts, and if it were not to add further to the already very high instability of the world economy. If Europe wants to avoid being trapped in reductionist concepts of industrial policy, then a careful re-reading is urgently required of how technology, crisis-induced structural transformation and new patterns of global competition are reshaping the balance of power in world industry.

I have structured this chapter to reflect such an agenda. I begin with a brief assessment of the current state of US—Japanese competition in the semiconductor industry. I then assess how crisis-induced re-structuring is likely to change the nature of global competition in this

industry. Further, I discuss some key aspects of a worldwide rationalization of industrial structures and competitive strategies: the shifting
balance between US captive and merchant firms[1], the global race into
strategic alliances, a redeployment of wafer fabrication to Asia, and,
last but not least, the proliferation of neo-mercantilist policies. I
conclude with a few remarks concerning the possible implications for
Europe.

**An Assessment of the Current State of US—Japanese Competition**
The United States still dominates to a considerable degree the
worldwide production of semiconductors and in particular of ICs: 56
percent of all semiconductors and 62 percent of ICs originate from
production in the US. Japan, which certainly has increased its
importance as a location for semiconductor manufacturing, is still
running a distant second, except for discretes. The role of Europe, apart
from discretes, is close to insignificant, with less than 9 percent of all
semiconductors being produced in this region and only 6 percent of ICs.
Finally, the rest of the world (excluding the COMECON) so far still
plays only a very marginal role in the production of semiconductors
(Table 1).

TABLE 1
The structure of worldwide semiconductor production:
a comparison of country/regional shares, 1985

| Country/Region | Proportion of Worldwide Production (percent) |
|---|---|
| *United States* | |
| Semiconductors | 56.0 |
| Integrated circuits | 62.0 |
| Semiconductor production by US merchant firms | 41.0 |
| Semiconductor production by US captive firms | 21.0 |
| Discretes | 35.0 |
| *Japan* | |
| Semiconductors | 33.0 |
| Integrated circuits | 30.0 |
| Discretes | 42.0 |
| *Europe* | |
| Semiconductors | < 9.0 |
| Integrated circuits | 6.0 |
| Discretes | 19.0 |
| *Rest of the world (excluding COMECON)* | |
| Semiconductors | 2.3 |
| Integrated circuits | 1.8 |
| Discretes | 4.0 |

*Source:* ICE (1986).

Statistics such as those produced by the Integrated Circuit Engineering Corporation (ICE, 1986) on the geographic distribution of semiconductor production (and expressed in Table 1) are, however, somewhat misleading, as the figures are assigned to regions by the headquarters location of the producing firm. In other words, they specifically do not allow us to understand the importance of the internationalization of semiconductor manufacturing and are thus only of limited value for assessing fundamental transformations in the structure of supply.[2]

It is common knowledge that Japanese firms have succeeded in eroding the position of US merchant firms in key segments of the IC commodity market. By 1984, for instance, the Japanese were reported to control between 70 and 90 percent of the market for certain memory devices. Since then, however, the computer market has collapsed. As a result sales, for instance of MOS memory products, which had accounted for 62 percent of total Japanese semiconductor exports to the United States in 1984, had dropped to 22 percent by the first half of 1985 (Tatsuno, 1985a).

While public debate has focused almost exclusively on competition in the IC memories market, the key issue today is that Japanese firms are already making substantial inroads into areas that were previously the exclusive arena (for reasons of technological superiority) of US merchant companies. This applies to a growing variety of state-of-the-art ICs, such as very large scale (VLSI) and ultra large scale (ULSI) integrated memories, ASICs (both gate-arrays and standard cells)[3] and 32-bit microprocessors. Furthermore, as Japanese companies are heavily investing in R & D projects for next-generation ICs, they are well positioned for future rounds of the global technological race associated with optoelectronics, three-dimensional ICs, superlattices, biochips and so on (Tatsuno, 1985b).

A key area of debate is whether Japanese firms are capable of achieving in sufficient time the technological advances necessary for them to compete effectively in the 32-bit microprocessor markets. Current wisdom in the United States has it that '... Japanese participation (in these markets) will be virtually non-existent through at least the mid-1990s' (Cole and Cohen, 1986: 41), and Table 2 indicates the projected market shares that support this claim.

The projection represented by Table 2 is based on the assumption that current trends will continue unchanged. There are indications, however, that this may not be the case. NEC, Hitachi and Toshiba, among other Japanese firms, are engaged in extensive microprocessor-related R & D and have built a sophisticated network of strategic alliances to assist technological development. As a result, some knowledgeable observers expect these firms to be able to introduce profitable 32-bit microprocessors by 1987 (see for instance, Tatsuno, 1986a).

TABLE 2
Market shares for 32-bit general purpose microprocessors:
projection for 1990

| Company | Country | Proportion of Worldwide Production (percent) |
|---|---|---|
| Motorola | USA | 27[1] |
| Intel | USA | 25[1] |
| National Semiconductor | USA | 18[1] |
| AT&T | USA | 11 |
| Zilog | USA | 9 |
| *Others* | | |
| Fairchild | USA ⎫ | |
| INMOS | UK ⎬ | 10 |
| Leading Japanese firms, etc. | Japan ⎭ | |

[1]Including sales of second-source suppliers, both US and Japanese companies.
*Source:* M.L. Bader, President, Bader Associates, Mountain View, California, as quoted by Cole and Cohen (1986: 41).

These conflicting assessments seem to be a product of different methodological approaches. The first group of observers tends to stress technology to the detriment of organizational innovation and assumes that US companies have a quasi-natural technological supremacy. The second group, however, takes a somewhat more differentiated approach and acknowledges the importance of organizational innovations such as strategic marketing and selective strategic alliance-building. In my own view, Japanese firms still have sufficient chances to become strong players in the 32-bit microprocessor markets.

Turning to another state-of-the-art semiconductor technology, that associated with ASICs, we find that companies like Fujitsu, NEC, Toshiba, and Hitachi already have a sound position in these markets. For instance, by 1985, these companies were amongst the ten leading gate-array producers, and indeed Fujitsu was the market leader by a considerable degree (Table 3).

Thus while Japanese firms clearly dominate important segments of the memory market, they also have developed a strong presence in gate-arrays and are beginning to move into microprocessor production. These latter two areas until quite recently were supposed to be the invincible strongholds of US merchant firms.

But to claim that Japanese firms are about to achieve dominance in the world semiconductor markets would seem to be premature. This

TABLE 3
Principal gate-array IC manufacturers (value in $ million[1])

| Company | Country | Bipolar | MOS | Total |
|---|---|---|---|---|
| Fujitsu | Japan | 130 | 74 | 204 |
| LSI Logic | USA | — | 130 | 130 |
| Ferranti[2] | UK | 75 | 10 | 85 |
| Motorola | USA | 70 | 15 | 85 |
| Toshiba | Japan | — | 47 | 47 |
| NEC | Japan | 45 | — | 45 |
| Siemens | Germany | 13 | 22 | 35 |
| Texas Instruments | USA | 2 | 33 | 35 |
| Hitachi | Japan | 4 | 20 | 24 |
| GE Semiconductor[3] | USA | — | 22 | 22 |

[1]Estimates, November 1985.
[2]Including Interdesign.
[3]Formerly Intersil.
*Source:* ICE (1986: 95).

would apply even more so for the computer and telecommunications markets. After all, '...since personal computers are a major source of demand for the memory chips in which Japanese producers hold a 70 to 90 percent market share, Japanese firms that export chips to the US were far more devastated than US producers when computer demand slowed' (Federal Reserve Bank of San Francisco, 1985: 2). This is reflected in a drastic decline in Japanese IC exports to the US. In 1985 they dropped by 40 percent relative to 1984, down from $1.6 billion to $900 million. For memory chips themselves, Japanese exports declined even more dramatically. In late July 1985 they were projected to decline for the whole of 1985 by 65 percent. All this was relative to a then projected reduction of 'only' 20 percent in total US semiconductor sales (Neely, 1986).

In other words, the profit squeeze due to the declining sales of memories combined with drastic price falls has already reduced considerably the scope of Japanese companies for capital formation. In addition, the recent steep appreciation of the yen, together with increasing trade pressures from the US administration have also had constraining effects. As a result of these developments, Japanese firms have started to rely increasingly on offshore sourcing in East Asia. In order to ward-off US Commerce Department dumping rulings, Hitachi, for instance, has decided to produce in Malaysia most of its 256 K memories destined for the US market. Similar developments have been reported for NEC, Toshiba and Matsushita.

But even worse problems are already looming large for the Japanese electronics industry more generally. A crisis is already emerging in the strategically important video (VCR) market which is likely to be much more dangerous than the one currently experienced in the memory chip market (*Global Electronics*, January 1986). At some point soon, supply of home VCRs should exceed demand in the US market. This market has always been dominated by machines made in Japan (including all 'American' brand names). Should this happen, prices will crash and business will become unprofitable. What is more, newly emerging competitors in this market, particularly South Korean firms, are likely to exert increasing pressure on Japanese profit margins.

## Crisis-induced Restructuring and the Changing Nature of Global Competition

It is impossible to understand the nature of global competition in the semiconductor industry without referring to its current crisis. Since autumn 1984, the world semiconductor industry has experienced its worst ever recession which has played havoc with sales and profits on a global scale. Tables 4 and 5 present some of the basic indicators.

These tables show that in 1985, worldwide sales of semiconductors fell by 13 percent relative to 1984, while global sales of ICs fell by 14 percent. In terms of their overall sales of semiconductors, US merchant firms registered a particularly large fall in value terms: 16 percent. As a result, 'creative destruction' (to use Schumpeter's term) took place on a massive scale, involving both capital invested and human labour. Capital devaluation applies as much to physical capital (the 'fixed capital' embodied in equipment and production facilities) as to financial capital (shareholder and venture capital investments). By 1985, for instance, an enormous amount of surplus capacity had been built up, with between 60 to 70 percent of the high-volume worldwide DRAM (memory) capacity sitting idle, prior to the withdrawal from the market by all the leading US merchant firms except Texas Instruments. In terms of finance capital, the losses declared by US semiconductor merchants in 1985 went considerably beyond the half billion dollar mark, much higher than in the 1981–82 IC recession.

More than anything else, the current crisis has led to a massive devaluation of 'human capital' (or the value of human labour), and this has affected nearly everyone in the industry, from unskilled female assembly workers to the 'heroes' of the previous 'high tech' boom: the circuit designers, computer engineers and systems analysts. For the US semiconductor merchant firms in particular, there is ample evidence of the heavy social costs imposed by the current crisis, in terms of shorter workweeks, enforced wage reductions and sweeping redundancies. According to recent *Dataquest* figures, employment in

TABLE 4
Current crisis of the semiconductor industry:
basic indicators (value in $billion)

|  | *1984* | *1985* | *Change, 1984–85 (percent)* |
|---|---|---|---|
| *Sales*[1] |  |  |  |
| Worldwide sales of semiconductors | 32.895 | 28.685 | – 13 |
| Worldwide sales of integrated circuits | 26.245 | 22.550 | – 14 |
| Sales of semiconductors by US merchant firms | 19.115 | 16.137 | – 16 |
| *Japanese exports* |  |  |  |
| Japanese integrated circuit exports to the US[2] | 1.6 | 0.9 | – 40 |
| Japanese memory exports to the US[3] |  |  | – 65 |

[1]ICE (1986).
[2]*Electronics*, 6 January 1986.
[3]July 1985 projection for the whole of 1985, quoted in *Electronics*, ibid.

TABLE 5
Devaluation of capital and labour

| *Capital* |  |  |  |
|---|---|---|---|
| Capacity utilization in high-volume memory ICs, 1985 |  | 30 – 40 percent[1] |  |
| Losses declared by leading US merchant firms, 1985 |  | >> $500 million[2] |  |
| *Labour* | *December 1984* | *October 1985* | *Change (percent)* |
| Employment in the US semiconductor industry[3] | 280,000 | 226,000 | – 19 |
| Permanent employment in the Japanese semiconductor industry[3] |  |  | – 5.5 |
| Reduction of non-permanent workers in the Japanese semiconductor industry[4] |  | November 1985: Toshiba refuses to renew the six-months contracts for > 2000 temporary workers | |

*Sources:*
[1]Author's interviews, Californian electronics industry, April–May 1986.
[2]*Fortune*, 6 January 1986: 20.
[3]Semiconductor Industry Association, based on figures generated by *Dataquest*.
[4]*Global Electronics*, January 1986.

the US semiconductor industry between December 1984 and October 1985 fell by 19 percent from 280,000 to 226,000 (Table 5). Japanese firms, due to their long-established dual workforce structure, may still have some leeway to avoid such drastic reductions in their permanent workforce. Reductions in the temporary workforce, however, have been quite substantial. Toshiba, for instance, in November 1985, refused to renew the six-monthly constracts for 2000 of its temporary workers. (*Global Electronics*, January 1986).[4]

It needs to be stressed that the present crisis in the semiconductor industry is structural rather than cyclical in nature. The crisis is the result of understandable and predictable structural changes in supply and demand that have been developing for more than a decade. Two factors are of particular importance. Firstly, there has been strong pressure to generate enormous surplus capacities which is the logical outcome of the current structure of the industry, the prevailing patterns of competition and the dominant approaches to corporate strategies and public policies. Secondly, there have emerged very severe limitations to a rapid and pervasive proliferation of viable applications for IC devices, which are less of a technological but more an economic and social nature, and thus cannot be overcome at short notice. Neither of these constraints on sustained growth in the semiconductor industry is likely to change substantially in the foreseeable future. If that is so, surplus and oversupply are bound to change drastically the nature of competition, the structure of the industry and the underlying relations of power.

Unlike the tidy oligopoly that the US semiconductor industry enjoyed up to the mid-1970s, new powerful actors have entered the game, all of whom are ruthlessly increasing their capacities as rapidly as possible. As a result, the patterns of competition have fundamentally changed. The semiconductor industry has become a 'global industry' in the sense defined by Michael Porter (1986) in which '. . .the rivals compete against each other on a truly worldwide basis'. Further, one should add, competition today cuts across established sectoral boundaries so that in order to understand the nature of global competition in the semiconductor industry, it is necessary to analyse the patterns of conflict and cooperation underlying the current worldwide restructuring of the electronics industry at large (Ernst, 1983: chapter 4). As for the dominant segment of the semiconductor industry, namely the production of commodity ICs, such as memories and microprocessors, about 25 transnational companies from the US, Japan and Europe since around 1982–83 have been involved in an enormous expansion of capacity. In addition, new 'hotbeds of IC production' (ICE, 1985: 10) have emerged in a great variety of geographic locations, either at the periphery or even outside the OECD region, including South Korea, Scotland, Ireland, Israel, China, India, Australia, Taiwan, Singapore and Brazil. As a result, the world IC commodity production capacity has experienced a massive expansion. This applies in particular to memory devices. Today, existing production capacities in this major market segment surpass by far the existing demand potential, let alone effective demand. Small wonder then that memory prices have fallen drastically.

The current price falls are, in fact, the steepest in the history of the semiconductor industry. What is of particular interest is that for the first time, prices are approaching the variable costs of the industry's most efficient producers: the Japanese firms.[5] This is very much in contrast to traditional patterns of price setting. In times of reasonable balances of supply and demand, prices were generally set at the point where a good competitor would get returns sufficient to encourage him to add capacity (the 're-investment price'). As long as US merchant firms dominated this industry, the price of a memory IC generally hovered near this mark. In the infrequent short periods of slack demand, prices would drop to the full cash manufacturing cost of a marginal competitor, below which the higher cost competitors would have to close down some of their capacity, at least temporarily. Although these periods were sometimes agonizing, as for instance during the downturn of 1981–82, there was sufficient scope for all but the highest cost competitors to survive.

Today, however, the rules of the game for price-setting have changed fundamentally, as has the capacity of different firms to generate sufficient funds for reinvestment in competitive memory IC production capacity. Since the autumn of 1984, the free fall of memory prices has forced all leading US merchant firms, with the sole exception of Texas Instruments (TI), to leave the memory market altogether. But even for TI, the chances of success in memories are not very bright, and this applies despite the aggressive investments which this company has made in recent years in Japan and East Asia in order to fight the memory IC battle head-on. In fact, the experience of Motorola, the other major so-called 'broadline memory supplier' of the US merchant industry, is hardly convincing. Despite similar aggressive moves in Japan and East Asia, it recently had to quit the DRAM segment of the memory market.

## Towards a Worldwide Rationalization of Industrial Structures and Competitive Strategies

Consider the following scenario. If present trends continue, there is likely to be a substantial decline of US semiconductor merchant firms relative to the huge, diversified electronics systems companies: the 'captive' producers. Secondly, strategic alliances built around a few major system corporations will become a key feature of global competition. Thirdly, there will be a major shift of wafer fabrication capacities to Asia, particularly for the principal fabrication technology, CMOS. Finally, neo-mercantilist policies will continue to proliferate.

If such a scenario were to materialize, it would have considerable implications for corporate strategies and government policies. In particular, it would imply that some established interpretations of US–Japanese competition in microelectronics would have to be seriously reconsidered. In what follows, I will comment on each of these prospective structural transformations.

### The Shifting Balance between US Captive and Merchant Firms

There has been an important change in the semiconductor industry's global competition, which however, has received fairly limited attention in the public debate. I refer to the shifting balance between US captive and merchant firms (Table 6).

TABLE 6
US captive integrated circuit production:
basic indicators (proportion by value: percent)

|  | 1984 | 1985 | Change 1984/85 |
|---|---|---|---|
| US captive IC production as proportion of total US IC production | 27 | 33 | + 6 |
| *Growth of output by value* | | | |
| Merchants | | | − 24 |
| All captives | | | + 9 |
| IBM | | | + 7 |
| AT&T | | | + 10 |
| Delco | | | + 11 |
| Hewlett Packard | | | − 9 |
| Commodore | | | − 40 |

*Source:* ICE (1986).

In 1984 captive firms accounted for about 27 percent of total US IC production. In the recession year of 1985 however, when the output value of US merchant firms dropped by 24 percent, captives increased production by a healthy 9 percent in value. As a result, they now account for more than one-third of total US IC production.

It is worth mentioning that the term 'captive IC producer' covers a small band of unequal characters. In fact, IBM with its estimated $3 billion worth of IC production accounts for nearly two-thirds of US captive production, with AT & T, GM's Delco, GE's RCA, DEC and Hewlett Packard being other important producers. US captives thus are part of diversified conglomerates with a predominant focus on electronic systems.

Any casual reading of recent corporate reports in the financial press shows that these companies, in contrast to the dire situation of merchant firms, are often reporting good and rising profit margins. In fact, such diversified systems corporations clearly have had a superior capacity to weather the impact of the current IC commodity crisis. It is important to note, however, that in contrast to the gospel of 'high tech', technological superiority has not been a primary factor. What mattered instead was access to cheap finance (frequently from the growing in-house financial services of such conglomerates) and well-established distribution and logistics networks. In addition the capacity to define and control major application needs and system requirements, together with a capacity to impose standards, was also of significance.

US semiconductor merchant firms, which in 1985 were responsible still for around 41 percent of worldwide semiconductor production (see Table 1), are in a much more awkward position. This type of firm, which once was the pride of the US 'high tech' revolution, is now losing its importance and this applies as much in relation to the main US systems companies (IBM, etc.) as in relation to the leading Japanese competitors.

A major shake-out is imminent in the US semiconductor industry, with US merchant firms bearing the brunt of the current crisis. Basically, there are two forces at work. First, the enormous surplus capacity accumulated in all kinds of commodity ICs has had a disproportionately negative impact on US merchant firms. While the large captive suppliers such as IBM, AT & T, Fujitsu, and Hitachi can all minimize the burden of surplus capacities by supplying their own needs internally, independent merchant firms cannot fall back on such a protective cushion. This is why US merchants are finding it increasingly difficult to compete in the main IC commodity markets, such as high-volume memories. Secondly, a growing number of large systems houses are implementing aggressive penetration strategies into high value-added market niches, which once were supposed to be the main terrain for US merchant firms to implement their product innovation counter-strategies against Japanese competition. In particular, more systems companies are involved in backward integration, and are beginning to produce their customized IC demand (such as ASICs) in-house, thus exacerbating the situation for merchant vendors.

As a result of these developments, US component suppliers, not owned or protected by large, diversified corporations, find it more and more difficult to compete in the markets for low-volume 'value-based' products. Similarly, their attempts to build strategic alliances with the major global systems companies (whether for computers, telecommunications or automobile electronics) are frequently frustrated.

Take the example of Intel which, for some time, has been hailed as the most glamorous success story of the US semiconductor merchant community. Despite a general improvement in US semiconductor orders, Intel is currently making heavy losses. In April 1986, it reported a net loss of $22 million, or 19 cents per share for the first quarter of that year (*Financial Times*, 11 April 1986). This loss was all the more problematic, as it occurred in a situation when, due to the yen's appreciation and heavy trade restrictions imposed by the US Department of Commerce, the international competitiveness of Japanese exports was under increasing pressure. Further, this loss occurred despite the fact that Intel in March 1986 was able to increase considerably the price of its EPROM devices which the company considers to be one of its leading future growth products.

Intel's problems highlight a basic strategic dilemma confronting nearly all US merchant firms. On the one hand, demand for products which were expected to become major 'engines of growth', has been vacillating if not stagnating. On the other hand, the previous rush into special relationships with huge powerful systems houses, in which nearly all major merchant vendors have been participating, may have privileged the 'Goliaths' rather than the 'Davids'. In the case of Intel's arrangements with IBM, it led to an over-dependence on this all powerful corporation. In the words of Intel's PR spokesperson: 'IBM, our largest customer, bought less because it is working-off inventory acquired under its 1985 contract with Intel' (*Financial Times*, 11 April 1986).

Intel's experience seems to indicate a general pattern. Take, for instance, 'market niche strategies' based on high value-added ASICs, notably 'gate-arrays'. As the market for gate arrays shows, low-volume markets are not immune to surplus capacity and drastic shake-outs are already under way (Cole, 1985). As a result gate-array markets are becoming highly concentrated and the proportion of US merchants producing for them is beginning to decline. In other words, speciality market niches as much as large volume commodity markets have become an uncomfortable place for US merchant firms, and successful latecomer entry is becoming more and more unlikely.

As for 'special relationships', senior management in US electronics systems firms seem to have decided that building alliances with US merchants hardly makes sense when these IC producers are the likely losers in the global IC commodity battle. In addition, the huge electronics systems houses do not want to lose their control over system design, and have made aggressive moves to internalize circuit design and silicon foundry activities. Thus, merchant firms are losing much of their previous attractiveness as independent partners to systems companies.[6]

In short, it seems that whichever way US merchant firms are trying to move, they are stuck with unsolvable dilemmas. While this is an under-researched topic, the available evidence strongly indicates that the decline of the US semiconductor merchant firms is not just conjunctural but a fundamental and long-term development.

### The Global Race into Strategic Alliances

In the future, strategic alliances built around a few major systems corporations will play an increasingly important role in the global electronics industry. Giant corporations such as IBM, GM, GE-RCA, AT & T, Matsushita, Philips, Hitachi, NEC and Siemens, to name but the most prominent ones, have been experimenting now for some time with the most unconventional and often contradictory forms of strategic alliance. This applies in particular to two crucial areas: the convergence of computer and communications technologies and the design and implementation of integrated computer-based automation systems for the office and the factory.

So far, most of these moves have been fairly ad hoc. It is my impression, however, that companies will try to apply strategic cooperation in a much more flexible and selective manner to all the main business functions, namely, finance, design skills, human resources development, equipment, R & D capabilities, production facilities, and marketing plus distribution. As a result, concentration and the hierarchization of global trade and investment flows are likely to increase.[7]

### Shifting Wafer Fabrication to Asia

There is likely to be a major shift of MOS wafer fabrication capacities for memory devices to Asia, particularly to Japan, South Korea and perhaps some other East Asian countries. According to one observer, 80 percent of such capacity is expected to be in Asia by around 1990 (Neely, 1986: 90). There are four basic reasons for such a shift:

1. The predominance of Japanese firms in MOS and in particular in CMOS ICs is likely to increase substantially. That this is a realistic projection, can be seen from Table 7. It shows that, by 1984, Japanese shipments of CMOS ICs, that is, the leading-edge process technology, exceeded US shipments for the first time by $267 million. It documents in addition that in 1985, out of the top ten CMOS manufacturers, six were Japanese, with the two leading Japanese firms having substantially higher sales figures than the leading US CMOS producer, Motorola.

TABLE 7
Growing importance of Japanese CMOS integrated circuit
manufacturers, 1984–85

|  | Country | Sales ($ million) |
|---|---|---|
| *Total shipments, 1984* | Japan[1] | 1,787 |
|  | US[1] | 1,520 |
| *Principal manufacturers,* |  |  |
| *1985 (rank order)* |  |  |
| Toshiba | Japan | 549 |
| Hitachi | Japan | 357 |
| Motorola | USA | 282 |
| NEC | Japan | — |
| National Semiconductor | USA | — |
| RCA | USA | — |
| Oki Electric | Japan | — |
| LSI Logic | USA | — |
| Sharp | Japan | — |
| Fujitsu | Japan | — |

[1] Japanese shipments exceed US shipments for the first time.
*Source: Dataquest*, March 1986.

2. A few East Asian NICs (such as South Korea and Taiwan) will stick stubbornly to their attempts at 'high tech-latecomer industrialization'. As a result, they will spend enormous amounts on infrastructure and human resource development, as much as on equipment and technology imports and on investment incentives. All of that is bound to continue for some time despite the fact that the chances for successful latecomer entry into the worldwide IC commodity markets have become quite low. The basic problem is how to enter a market which is already crowded by many tough and powerful competitors and which has already seen the demise of firms which used to play a pioneering role in developing it (for details see Ernst, 1986a, 1986b).

3. US systems houses do not have much choice but to increase, often substantially, their sourcing arrangements for MOS memory devices with Asian firms. Often they may face the prospect of placing most of this vital business with their Japanese competitors. At least for the 'second-tier' system firms, internalizing the design and manufacturing of MOS memories will be possible only on a limited scale, simply due to the high investment threshholds and fixed costs burdens involved. On the other hand, building alliances with US merchant firms is not a very attractive option either, for the reasons mentioned previously.

4. Finally, consequent to the shift of memory IC manufacturing to

Asia, there is likely to be a shift also in the location of the design and manufacture of the production equipment required. Japanese companies have already started to build up prominent positions in a number of key market segments for lithographic and assembly equipment.

A shift in the locus of wafer fabrication for memory ICs to Asia (especially Japan) is bound to have important strategic implications. What it points to is a clear trend towards an increasing multipolarization of global competition in semiconductor manufacturing. From its early stages, the semiconductor industry has been among the most internationalized industries in terms of geographic decentralization of its investment and location. Until the early 1980s, however, such internationalization has had a clearly discernable dual structure. Typically, the so-called front-end activities, such as design and wafer fabrication, have been restricted to the OECD region, whereas assembly and, to some degree, final testing, have been shifted primarily to a select group offshore locations in East Asia.

Today, however, the delineation between the internationalization of production *within* the OECD region and the redeployment of production facilities to a few Third World growth poles is becoming blurred. On the one hand, offshore assembly, once predominantly a manual or semi-automated business, is currently experiencing fundamental transformations due to recent developments in circuit design, packaging technology and the proliferation of computer-based automation. In contrast to earlier expectations, this has not led to a redeployment back to the North of such activities (Ernst, 1983).

On the contrary, some first steps have been made towards more integrated patterns of semiconductor manufacturing. Design and wafer processing activities have recently developed in countries such as South Korea, Taiwan, China, Singapore, Malaysia, Brazil and India. As a result of these developments, the internalization of production in the semiconductor industry has become a much more complex and multifarious affair with substantial implications for international flows of trade, investment and finance (for details see Ernst, 1986b).

*The Proliferation of Neo-Mercantilist Policies*
In terms of trade and industrial policies, it is safe to predict a continuous proliferation of neo-mercantilist policies in nearly all major countries involved in the global race in microelectronics. Japan, an early pioneer of such policies, hardly has much scope today for retreating to more accommodating positions for the reasons already mentioned (for discussions see Okimoto et al, 1984; Borrus et al, 1983).

In the case of the US, my reading of the current industrial policy debate leads me to the following assessment. Aggressive policies with regard to export promotion and import restrictions are likely to gain in importance, both in the semiconductor and in the electronics industry at large. In addition, restrictions on foreign investment, particularly from Japan and South Korea, have recently also been put onto the agenda by prominent spokesmen of the US semiconductor merchant industry.

For instance, Charles Sporck of National Semiconductor suggested in 1986 that investment by Japanese and Korean semiconductor companies in the United States was motivated primarily by the need to avoid protectionist pressures. In Sporck's view, such investment was a further unfair attack on the competitiveness of US merchant firms: '. . . by manufacturing in the US, they [the Japanese and Korean firms] gain access to our workforce, our talent base and our markets without setting up any R & D facility that we could benefit from . . . . Many countries, such as Singapore, don't allow the establishment of a foreign manufacturing plant without an R & D facility' (quoted in Tsantes, 1986). Whether the call to restrict foreign direct investment in the US will find a powerful enough political constituency remains to be seen. Undoubtedly, however, the sort of views expressed by Sporck are gaining in currency (see, for instance, the widely quoted article by Reich and Mankin, 1986).

As for longer-term policies, a new global rush into policies geared to improve the international competitiveness of national companies can be expected (for the US, see Borrus, 1985). This relates as much to monetary policies that decrease the cost of capital, to fiscal policies that provide incentives for productive investment and R & D outlays, as it does to drastic modifications of existing anti-trust laws designed to open up new possibilities for mergers and strategic alliances. While lip-service is being paid to policies for strengthening human resources, R & D and engineering capacities, I doubt whether viable policies can be formulated to tackle such topics. If anything, the current obsession with military-oriented R & D, centering in particular on the Strategic Defence Initiative (SDI), would seem to be a clear cause for concern. According to recent National Science Foundation figures, three-quarters of the US budget's R & D outlays are military-oriented, with the largest segment being absorbed by SDI (US Academy of Science, 1986).

Overall, then, public policy interventions are likely to increase rather than decrease the already powerful trends towards a growing concentration and uneven development of the world semiconductor and electronics industries.

**Final Remarks: Implications for Europe**
More than in any other industry, competition in the world

semiconductor industry is dominated to a considerable degree by two actors, namely US and Japanese companies and the patterns of conflict and cooperation prevailing between them. European companies, even the most powerful ones, have been reduced to playing a secondary role. Apart from discrete devices, required primarily for consumer applications, European electronics companies have had an insignificant impact, particularly in the main market segments: memories and microprocessors. In addition, they have been unable to translate their strength in applications into a strong position in the increasingly important market for ASICs. In short, global competition in the semiconductor industry is still close to an exclusive US–Japanese affair.

We have argued however that there are strong reasons to believe that this situation will change considerably during the next decade or so, with a clear trend towards an increasing multi-polarization of global competition in semiconductor manufacturing. On the other hand, spatial concentration and an increasing hierarchization of production, trade and investment patterns will characterize more than ever before the world semiconductor industry and the electronics industry at large.

What are the implications for Europe? While this is not the place to engage in detailed policy suggestions, I would like to present some observations which, in my view, urgently deserve further attention and clarification.

First of all, policy formulation and implementation in Europe on these issues has been characterized so far by ad hoc improvisation, excessive reductionism, and a hectic vacillation between often contradictory positions. There is no need to be hypnotized by the threats of 'Japanese competition' or of an alleged 'US–Asian Alliance', as much as there is no reason for being intoxicated by the glamour of US technological supremacy. Europe must overcome this strategic indecisiveness if it wants to avoid falling into the trap of new forms of dependence, whether of a technological or, in some cases, even of an economic and political nature. While it is true that, for new information technologies, barriers to entry and risks involved are substantial, this neither legitimates political fatalism nor technocratic *fuite-en-avant* strategies.

There is no doubt that Europe is capable of coping with new information technologies, and that it can build up the necessary scientific, technological and industrial base. This requires, however, that the social carriers who would be willing to back up such policies are identified and mobilized from the beginning. In my view, doing this as a technocratic exercise from above will lead nowhere. What is required is a broadly based social learning process. This is the only way to reduce the unequal distribution of costs and benefits involved in such policies. Apart from upgrading the manufacturing capacity and the related infrastructure and back-up services, the development of human resources should become a third major strategic area.

Secondly, European firms will need to build strategic alliances. In my view, the choice of alliances has to take into account some of the afore-mentioned structural transformations. While US semiconductor merchant firms have suggested on various occasions the possibility of building strategic alliances with European systems firms against the 'Japanese threat', the current decline of US merchant firms should raise some doubts about the benefits and viability of such an approach. After all, building alliances with the main losers in the global competition in microelectronics is hardly an attractive option.

In this context, the following issues need to be urgently addressed. How can Europe (companies and governments) best utilize the pervasive US–Japanese competition for its own purposes? Is there room for establishing strategic alliances with US systems companies, and, if so, in which areas and under what conditions? Can European companies engage in selective strategic alliances with Japanese companies, and what are the risks involved? To what degree can Europe make use of some newly emerging actors in Asia and Latin America? And, finally, how can selective and flexible approaches to strategic co-operation for key business functions, including finance, marketing networks, design, R & D and production engineering know-how be devised?

Only when some of the afore-mentioned questions have been sorted out, will it be possible in Europe to tackle seriously issues like the 'memory debate' (whether or not to stay in the memory IC business) and the options for building up viable capabilities in ASICs. It can, in fact, be argued that for the European semiconductor industry, a strategy based on high value-added market niches such as ASICs is feasible and would help to improve its competitiveness (Blackwell, 1985).

Yet, while such issues are of great practical importance, they have to be tackled in the context of a much more fundamental debate. This brings me to my third and last observation. What is at stake is the nature of European industrial policies and their underlying goals. So far, regaining international competitiveness has been the over-riding concern, while re-establishing full employment has become a neglected topic: '. . .saving labour by capital deepening is a half-welcome, half-unwelcome by-product of the real purpose, i.e. to stay in the top league of technological excellence' (Hager, 1985: 6). Such unfettered neo-mercantilism is based on the belief that only those nations that are willing to adjust and subordinate their societies to the requirements of the 'Third Industrial Revolution' will survive.

'Invest, innovate and re-adjust' is the credo of this new industrial policy doctrine.

Neo-mercantilism establishes a radical break with the post-war Keynesian growth model. For the time being at least, it abandons internal mass consumption as a major engine of growth. It is argued that the resultant fall in final demand can be easily compensated by a quantum jump in investment and an increasing reliance on export-led growth. In short, modernization is to be achieved via investment, which is to be stimulated by higher profits on the supply side, and exports on the demand side.

Investment is expected to rise in proportion to the fall in final demand engendered by reduced government spending and the squeeze on consumption caused by increased private taxes and lower wages. The catalyst for such a new investment boom is claimed to be the availability of new technology, particularly in the field of information, automation and communications. In theory at least, such a closure of the model could be achieved, if there was a once and for all shift in the relative shares of consumption and investment in GNP, with both terms of the equation growing at a higher and equal rate after that.

Reality, however, is different. Neo-mercantilist policies are medium, if not long-term, in concept, implying a slow and steady squeeze on wages and mass consumption. Moreover, such policies are already showing disastrous consequences for the world economy, in terms of stagnation, financial crisis, and the, at least partial, blockage of trade and capital flows.

As for export-led growth, its historical pattern in the OECD region has been aptly described by Kaldor (1964). Incomes in the exporting countries rose more slowly than productivity and world income. Exports thus gave firms surplus capital which enabled them to increase productivity, before being confronted with rising wages. It is unlikely, however, that this harmonious model of export-led growth could be repeated again. In fact, a '. . . slow-down of US growth or a fall of the dollar or increased protectionism in the US (and potentially all three) will throw Europe back on its own resources for demand creation with a vengeance' (Hager, 1985: 9–10).

To conclude, re-vitalizing final demand within Europe should become a major guideline for restructuring and upgrading Europe's electronics industry. Blindly following the whims of global competition is certainly not sufficient anymore today.

## Notes

1. 'Captive' semiconductor firms are those whose product is for use substantially by the parent companies. Typically, less than 25 percent of production is for the open

market (ICE, 1985: 89). The semiconductor branches of IBM and AT & T are examples. 'Merchant' firms are those who produce for the market at large. Examples include Motorola, Intel and National Semiconductors.

2. Take for instance some widely quoted figures on the market share of US semiconductor firms in Japan. According to the Semiconductor Industry Association, in 1984 this share was 11 percent while the Electronics Industry Association of Japan computed a 20 percent share. The second figure, in my view, makes more sense, as it includes semiconductors produced by US affiliates in Japan and other Far Eastern countries.

3. Application Specific Integrated Circuits (ASICs) is the generic term of state-of-the-art customized devices such as gate-arrays, standard cells and programmable logic circuits.

4. Pressures are also likely to increase for reductions in the ' permanent' workforce. The longer the crisis in the semiconductor industry drags on and the more the VCR market (the main 'cash-cow' for Japanese electronics companies) is confronted with demand saturation, the more likely redundancies become.

5. Author's interviews in the Californian electronics industry, April–May 1986.

6. Based on author's interviews in the Californian electronics industry, April–May 1986.

7. Typical examples, claimed to be models for such selective strategic alliance-building, include: the formation of Counterpoint Computers of San Jose, California, by AT & T, Kyocera and British and Commonwealth Shipping Inc; and the establishment of European Silicon Structures (ES 2), backed by Philipps, ICL and Olivetti (Duffy, 1986).

## References

Barney, C. (1986) 'How a New Venture Started Up: Big-Counterpoint Computers May be the Ultimate Strategic Alliance', *Electronics*, 27 January.

Blackwell, N. (1985) 'European Semiconductor Industry: Focus on ASICs — A Last Chance?', in 'European Electronics', a special report of *Electronic Business*, 1 October

Borrus, M. (1985) 'Reversing Attrition: A Strategic Response to the Erosion of US Leadership in Microelectronics'. Working Paper. Berkeley Roundtable on the International Economy. Berkeley: University of California.

Borrus, M., J. Milstein and J. Zysman (1983) 'Responses to the Japanese Challenge in High Technology: Innovation, Maturity and U.S.–Japanese Competition in Microelectronics'. Working Paper. Berkeley Roundtable on the International Economy. Berkeley: University of California.

Cole, B.C. (1985) 'Innovation Spurs Market for ASICs', *Electronics*, 22 July.

Cole, B.C. and C.L. Cohen (1986) 'Can Japan Catch Up in 32-Bit Microprocessors?', *Electronics*, 12 May.

Duffy, H. (1986) 'A Eurocompany Takes Wing', *Financial Times*, 9 April.

Ernst, D. (1983) *The Global Race in Microelectronics: Innovation and Corporate Strategies in a Period of Crisis.* Frankfurt am Main and New York: Campus Verlag.

Ernst, D. (1986a) 'Automation, Employment and the Third World: the Case of the Electronics Industry' in R. Gordon and L. Kimball (eds.), *Automation, Work and Employment.* Berkeley: University of California Press.

Ernst, D. (1986b) 'The Impact of Microelectronics on the Worldwide Restructuring of the Electronics Industry: Implications for the Third World'. IDPAD Final Report. The Hague: Institute of Social Studies.

Ernst, D. (1987) *Innovation, Industrial Structure and Global Competition: The Changing Economics of Internationalization*. Frankfurt am Main and New York: Campus Verlag.

Federal Reserve Bank of San Francisco (1985) *Weekly Letter*, 18 October 1985.

Hager, W. (1985) 'Adjustment to the World Economy: Is Self-Taiwanisation the Answer?: Macro- and Micro-Policies under Neo-Mercantilism'. Presented at the Conference on Securing National Prosperity in a Changing World Economy. Friedrich Ebert Foundation, Bonn: 28–29 May.

ICE (1985) 'Status 1985: Report on the Integrated Circuit Industry'. Scottsdale, Arizona: Integrated Circuit Engineering Corporation.

ICE (1986) 'Status 1986: Report on the Integrated Circuit Industry'. Scottsdale, Arizona: Integrated Circuit Engineering Corporation.

Kaldor, N. (1964) 'Foreign Trade and the Balance of Payments', in N. Kaldor, *Essays on Economic Policy*, Vol. II. London: Duckworth.

Neely, R.J. (1986) 'A Restructured IC Economy Needs a Restructured Strategy', *Electronic Business*, 1 March 1986.

Okimoto, D.I., T. Sugano and F.B. Weinstein (eds.) (1984) *Competitive Edge: The Semiconductor Industry in the U.S. and Japan*. Stanford: Stanford University Press.

Porter, M. (1986) 'Changing Patterns of International Competition', *California Management Review*, XXVIII(2).

Reich, R. and E. Mankin (1986) 'Joint Ventures with Japan Give Away Our Future', *Harvard Business Review*, 86(2).

Tatsuno, S. (1985a) 'Turning the Tide: U.S. Semiconductor Activities in Asia', *Dataquest Research Bulletin*, 5 September.

Tatsuno, S. (1985b) 'Japanese Technology: The Future Wave', Presented at the CAD/CAM Focus Conference. Dataquest, Palo Alto: December.

Tatsuno, S. (1986a) 'Matchmaking Japanese Style: The Surge in Japanese Strategic Alliances Continues', *Dataquest Japanese Research Newsletter*, 23 January.

Tatsuno, S. (1986b) 'How to Succeed in ASICs: Industry Leaders Share Their Thoughts', *Dataquest Japanese Research Newsletter*, 14 February.

Tsantes, S. (1986) 'Charles Sporck: Champion of Competitive Advantage', *Electronic Business*, 1 March.

US Academy of Science (1986) *Proceedings, National Science Foundation Conference on R & D Budgets*, Washington DC: US Academy of Science.

# 4
# Issues of Core and Periphery: Labour Migration and Global Restructuring

*Saskia Sassen-Koob*

Since the middle of the 1960s, three major new migration flows have developed. Two of these are intra-periphery migrations, one to the oil-exporting countries and the other to rapidly growing industrial zones producing for the world market. The third flow is the migration from Southeast Asia and the Caribbean Basin, directed mostly to large urban areas in the developed countries at a time of high unemployment and severe urban decay, as was the case with London and New York.

This chapter posits that all three labour flows are associated with worldwide trends in the recomposition of capital.[1] This association is probably most evident in the case of the domestic and international intra-periphery migrations to the new industrial zones. The rapid growth of jobs in these zones is the result of considerable relocation of capital — particularly labour-intensive types of production — from the highly industrialized countries to several areas in the Third World in order to gain access to vast supplies of low-wage labour.

The association is rather less evident in the case of the labour migration generated by accelerated industrialization in OPEC countries. I posit that the rise in the international price of oil made possible a massive concentration of capital into a few selected targets. The decision to invest this capital into large-scale industrialization projects generated both a large demand for workers supplied by migrations, and a reinjection of this capital into the world economy where it could function as financial capital contributing to the subsequent push to sell loans to Third World countries.

Thirdly, this association is least evident in the case of the Caribbean Basin and Asian migrations to the old capitalist centres at a time usually seen as one of economic decline. Here my argument is that the dispersion of industrial capital has generated new forms of concentration of managerial and specialized servicing operations in major urban centres. Besides generating a large supply of high-income professional jobs, this new economic core also needs, directly and indirectly, a wide array of low-wage jobs. Immigration has been a supplier of low-wage and typically powerless workers, a not insignificant fact in these strategic centres for control and management of the world economy.

Finally, this chapter posits that the availability of a large supply of immigrant labour in highly developed countries, in combination with more purely technical/locational constraints, is inducing today a reconcentration of industrial capital in those countries. Notable cases are southern California and the New York metropolitan area which have emerged as competitive for certain kinds of manufacturing, particularly electronics and garments, with Southeast Asia and the Caribbean.

This chapter will focus particularly on the last two instances and discuss the first two only briefly. My intention here is not an exhaustive description of either these labour migrations or of the components of capital recomposition. The intention is rather to identify strategic economic processes that set the patterns and rhythms for the formation and directionality of labour migrations. Within these overarching contexts there are pronounced differences among and within the major migration flows. For the purpose of the analysis in this paper, the differences matter only insofar as they represent differences in modes of labour utilization and in the role of immigrant labour in the recomposition of capital.

## The New Industrial Zones in the Periphery and Capital Recomposition

The restructuring of the world economy assumes specific forms in locations losing manufacturing and in those receiving it.[2] There has been a tendency to look at the specific areas involved separately, thereby usually losing a world perspective and reducing the unit once again to the nation- state: those who focus on the devastating effect of manufacturing losses at the core and those who look at the 'newly industrializing countries'.

In order to disaggregate the very abstract formulation of a restructuring of the world economy without losing the worldview, I posited elsewhere a capital migration circuit which contains both the locations that have lost manufacturing and those that have received it (Sassen-Koob, 1981b). This overcame the tendency to see 'capital emigration' as a one-way process which, once accomplished, is over. On the contrary, once a location has experienced a severe economic decline it has also potentially re-established the conditions for profitable investment if it contains resources that can be conceived of as use-values for capital, e.g., a certain level of development of the physical infrastructure and of public services, a skilled workforce that has lost political power due to factory closures; and a local government eager to draw investment. These constitute a sort of reserve of unemployed use-values which under certain conditions can become employed by capital and generate profit. The fact that 60 percent of German, British and Swiss direct investment in the US from 1977 to 1979 was in declining northeastern urban areas is suggestive in this regard (Bauer, 1980). Equally so are the proposals for 'enterprise zones' in these areas.

At the same time, the relocation of manufacturing to other areas of the country or world may spawn a whole array of economic activities for locations with highly developed specialized services, as is the case in the old centres of the world economy. The pronounced increase in the share that services represent in total US exports, paralleling the increase in direct investment in manufacturing abroad, points in this direction. I will return to these issues in my discussion of New York City.

The new labour migrations to the core (see Table 1 below for changing composition and entry levels) and the new migrations within the periphery are articulated with different moments of the capital migration circuit. The first are articulated with the recomposition of the economic structure of old centres of the world economy now in decline. The second are articulated with the relocation of manufacturing and clerical activities to select periphery areas (Sassen-Koob, 1984b, 1987) where the regional concentration of these activities and their labour-intensive character maximizes the impact on people, promoting internal migration to the new industrial zones.

Export processing zones (EPZs) represent an institutionalization of key patterns underlying the new industrialization in select areas of the periphery.[3] While they account for only a part of the process, more exhaustive data available on EPZs can be used to obtain a profile. Though an increasing number of countries are developing zones, most EPZs are in Hong Kong, South Korea, Singapore, Mexico, Indonesia, the Philippines, Taiwan, Malaysia, Colombia, El Salvador and Haiti. A new series of EPZs is being developed in the Middle East (Syria, Egypt and Jordan) and Africa as well as in Asian countries such as Sri Lanka and India.

Besides geographic concentration, zones have a very high industrial concentration. Electronics, textiles and garments account for up to 80 per cent of all production in zones (UNIDO, 1980). These two types of industries represent very different characteristics of production. Yet both are labour-intensive and need abundant supplies of cheap labour; one because it is technologically backward, the other because its technological sophistication has permitted the incorporation of tasks into machines and a fragmentation of the production process that allows for the use of unskilled workers. Other industries located in zones are toys, footwear, leather, sports goods, plastic articles, miscellaneous light consumer goods, assembly of scientific and medical instruments and of optical and photographic equipment. In one way or another they all represent a type of production or assembly that allows for the use of unskilled labour even when the components being worked on are the result of high capital intensity and high levels of technical expertise. These activities generate additional clerical and service jobs.

In addition to geographic and industrial concentration, zones are also characterized by a very high concentration of women workers (Lim, 1982; Safa, 1981; Salaff, 1981; Wong, 1980; Fernandez-Kelly, 1983; Grossman, 1979). About 70 percent of all workers in zones are women and up to 80 percent of all production and assembly workers in zones are women. This level varies among countries but is uniformly high. Women constitute 95 percent of all workers in zones in Malaysia. Indeed, the expansion of these industries is beginning to result in changes in the sex composition of rural to urban migration streams in areas of Asia and the Caribbean where males used to be prevalent (World Bank Staff, 1975; Standing, 1975; Arrigo, 1980; Kelly, 1984).

The relocation of manufacturing, the associated intra-periphery migrations and the new migrations to the core can be shown to be interdependent occurrences when we introduce the set of explanatory variables that can be summarized under the notion of class struggle. Insofar as the relocation of manufacturing is a response to the gains made by labour at the core, the intra-periphery migrations generated by this relocation represent an incorporation of low-waged, unorganized, and highly controllable workers into capital's struggle against labour at the core, that is, against the most powerful sectors of labour. Ultimately, it is a struggle against labour everywhere. The fact that a large share of the workers employed in the EPZs and in world market factories are women can then be seen as part of the process of disenfranchisement of the working class rather than simply a victory for women workers (but see also Lim, 1982, for an opposing view). Women from very poor families with no formal education are targeted for the sweatshops and women from lower-middle class families with high school degrees are targeted for the semiconductor assembly plants and clerical work.

It would seem that these three occurrences represent a victory for capital, though one charged with contradictions. Two factors have facilitated this victory. In a context of increasing pauperization in the periphery, the possibility of migrating to industrial zones in the periphery or the core emerges as a survival strategy, or as an option for maximizing opportunities in the case of migrants with considerable human capital. Furthermore, we can also see a convergence between capital's interest in relocating manufacturing in countries with low-waged and highly controllable workers and the developmentalist interests of the ruling sectors in these countries. These ruling sectors have come to view export-led industrialization as an effective strategy to replace import-substitution industrialization, once the latter's exhaustion as a model for development became evident in the late 1960s. These two factors which, together with many others, at one point facilitate capital's readjustment to the accumulation crisis, eventually feed into this crisis by further adding to the growing pauperization at the periphery and therewith to the overproduction–underconsumption dynamic.[4]

## OPEC: A New Circuit for Surplus Capitalization

The sharp increases in the price of oil starting in 1973 can be, and typically are, understood as a victory for OPEC and a redistribution of wealth from core to peripheral areas. In many ways this is correct: there was a struggle by OPEC against the international oil companies (and their home governments) and there was a victory that resulted in a massive flow of money from the core to OPEC members. The interpretation of post-1978 developments as reflecting OPEC's loss of power and a 'failure in its mission' is rooted in that same type of understanding. But what was the nature of OPEC's victory and power after 1973 which allowed it to set huge increases in the price of oil, to impose participation agreements, and to implement early nationalization of the oil fields?

The magnitude of the money flow, its direction from core to periphery, and the hardships it caused in most core countries have overshadowed the role this money flow came to play as part of a new strategy for accumulation for transnational capital. Here, as with export-led industrialization, we see a convergence of the nationalist interests of the governments of most OPEC members, with the interests of transnational capital, especially the energy industry. This convergence further confuses the issues.

Very briefly, my argument is as follows (see Sassen-Koob, 1981a). The magnitude of the cumulative money flow from core oil-importing countries to OPEC countries in the post-1973 period makes it qualitatively different from the pre-1973 period. This flow makes possible the launching of vast industrialization programmes on a scale and at a pace that render it significant for the world economy. The value of imported goods and services necessary for the realization of these programmes eventually reaches and surpasses the value of oil revenues in all OPEC countries except the Gulf states. From 1973 to 1978, oil revenues were $700 billion, compared with $80 billion in the decade preceding 1973. Imports increased by an average of 60 per cent in the first few years after 1973. From 1973 to 1978, the cumulative value of imports was $530 billion, representing about 76 percent of oil revenues.

Accelerated industrialization in OPEC countries can be seen as a mechanism for the reinjection of oil revenues back into the world accumulation process. Luxury consumption in OPEC countries could not have generated this level of reinjection of oil revenues. Most imports came from core countries. West Germany amassed a large trade surplus with OPEC, notwithstanding the huge increase in its oil bill. The US increased its exports to OPEC five-fold. By 1977 exports to OPEC represented 11 percent of US exports worldwide. In addition, OPEC reinjected oil revenues through direct financial placements, most of which went to core countries. For example, in the US there was a $38 billion capital account surplus with OPEC from 1974 to 1977. Major components in the capital inflow were investment in the US, treasury obligations and commercial bank liabilities. OPEC's foreign assets in the US were $796 million in 1972; they increased by $1.8 billion in 1973 and then jumped by a further $11.8 billion in 1974, with fluctuations since then. Finally, it is worthwhile noting that receipts in the service accounts of core countries increased significantly after 1973. OPEC members accounted for about one-third of US worldwide receipts on contracts from 1972 to 1977. These are mostly contracts for construction, engineering, consulting and other technical services. In sum, if we add the value of direct financial placements to that of imports, then the level of reinjection of OPEC's oil revenues is remarkably high.

The increased oil revenues were paid largely by core countries through additional increases in inflation, cost of living, and cost of production for national fractions of capital. (Though peripheral countries were much harder hit by the increase in the price of oil, they contributed a relatively small share of total oil revenues.) Given an historically developed need for imported oil, the international price of oil operates as a mechanism generating forced savings and concentrating these diffuse expenditures in one massive flow of money directed to OPEC countries and to the international oil companies. I can think of few systems that would have been so effective in extracting additional surplus and concentrating it into a few highly select targets. Furthermore, the size of the increase in the price of oil, far from being arbitrary, can be seen as linked with the costs at which alternative sources of energy become profitable.

What were the immediate consequences of a huge increase in the price of oil after 1973? Tanzer (1974: 124–30) has briefly described these as follows. First, it promptly raised the per-barrel revenues of the oil-exporting countries by 60 percent. Second, it promptly raised the per-barrel revenues of the oil companies by 400 percent. Third, it consolidated monopoly control by the top seven companies, which had been severely threatened by the entry of newcomers during the 1960s and by the willingness of oil-producing countries to grant concessions to any company that would weaken the position of the top seven. Ironically, the new power of OPEC, in satisfying nationalist interests in the OPEC countries, diluted opposition to the top seven companies, as these were seen as having received a major blow. Fourth, a belligerent and powerful OPEC facilitated the ideological task of legitimizing in the US the huge profits made by the oil companies after 1973 in a context of growing inflation and unemployment. Fifth, it increased the political leverage of the oil companies over Congress in the US and facilitated the suspension or defeat of various environmental measures. Sixth, it contributed to the profitability of other oilfields, most especially the North Sea and US fields. In sum, 1973 was a victory for OPEC and redistributed wealth away from the population and national capital in core countries. But it was a victory that worked to the advantage of the oil companies as well.

The unusually high need for imported labour in order to carry out the vast industrialization programmes after 1973 can be seen as another indicator (in addition to the high level of reinjection of oil revenues) of the extent to which those programmes responded to requirements for world accumulation. Did the OPEC countries need to industrialize on such a scale and at such a pace that importing between 40 and 80 percent of the labour force was the only way to build, operate and manage these 'new' economies? This question becomes particularly important if we consider that by 1976 many of the OPEC countries were beginning to show deficits and had to borrow on the international money market in order to finance imports needed for the industrialization programmes.

In 1975 the proportion of foreign workers in the labour force was 39 percent in Bahrain, 70 percent in Kuwait, 42 percent in Libya, 81 percent in Qatar, 48 percent in Saudi Arabia, and 85 percent in the United Arab Emirates. The bulk of these workers came from other Arab nations and from India, Pakistan, Bangladesh, South Korea and the Philippines. Other oil-exporting countries also rely heavily on foreign workers, though not as much as those cited above. For example, Iraq lifted all requirements, except a valid passport, for the entry of Arab workers and became the main importer of Egyptian workers in the late 1970s. Unusual for Latin America, Venezuela after 1973 arranged for labour imports with several countries and incorporated such imports in its Fifth Development Plan (1976–80).

Though there are no accurate figures, it is generally accepted that the size of the foreign labour force continued to increase in the Arab oil-exporting countries during the late 1970s. Official figures put the foreign labour force in Saudi Arabia at 813,000. Yet the *Financial Times* (28 April 1980) reported that Saudi government officials informally estimated it to be 1.5 million, representing 75 percent of the labour force. In Kuwait, illegal residents were estimated to number 300,000 by 1979, far above the official count. Similar discrepancies between official figures and estimates of the foreign population and labour force can be found in all the oil-exporting countries.

In sum, on a more speculative note, one could say that oil revenue-financed industrialization represents a systemic equivalent, in terms of world accumulation, to the sharp increase in middle-class consumption in the US in the post-World War II period. At that time, middle class consumption (of homes, cars, college educations, etc.) was an important factor for surplus realization. Now it no longer has that central a function, and indeed we see the shrinking of the 'middle class' and its loss of political clout (Bluestone et al., 1984; Sassen-Koob, 1984a). The new circuit for capital *extracted* additional surplus value via inflation during the 1970s and *concentrated* a large share of it via the increase in the price of oil and OPEC industrialization.

Most recently, we are beginning to see the exhaustion of oil revenue-financed industrialization as a mechanism for surplus generation. As the OPEC countries begin to face the limitations and contradictions of their industrialization boom, transnational capital has consolidated a new structure for accumulation. OPEC countries, on the other hand, have become dependent on a high level of oil revenues for the reproduction of their industrialized economies, dependent in a way and to an extent that they were not before 1973. Suggestive here is the fact that a much larger share of the oil revenue surplus is now deposited in the form of non-income earning liabilities mostly with commercial banks, as prepayments on future purchases in core countries.

### The Centralization of Management and Control at the Core

The above two sections describe processes which can be conceived of as a relocation of growth poles to selected areas in the periphery. Similar relocations have occurred within the core countries. In the US there has been a pronounced spatial dispersal of manufacturing and clerical activity and the development of major new investments in less developed areas. These processes not only bring about changes in the organization of production, they also generate a demand for types of production needed to ensure the management, control and specialized servicing of this new organization of production: what I refer to as the *production of global control capability* (Sassen-Koob, 1987). The production of management, control and service operations is concentrated largely in major urban centres at the core and a few in the semiperiphery. I refer to them as *global cities*. These have become the sites for this particular kind of production. In reorganizing production, increased capital mobility also brings about a reorganization of the capital–labour relation. This is a subject that has received considerable attention in some of its aspects: for example, the increased unemployment among well-paid workers and the weakening of their position vis-a-vis employers in locations losing capital, and the employment of young women from backgrounds that promote discipline and obedience in locations receiving capital in the periphery.

But there are aspects of the capital–labour relation that have not been recognized as linked to economic restructuring. Notable among these are certain aspects of the new immigration to the United States, specifically its magnitude, timing and main destinations. These aspects need to be examined in terms of the emergence of several key cities as centres for the management, control and servicing of the global economy. For a number of reasons to be discussed below, these new sites of production generate directly, and indirectly via agglomeration effects, a large supply of low-wage jobs that are a function of this restructuring, and hence are not marginal or a distortion of the normal pattern. In this context the politicization of supplies of native low-wage workers in many large cities since the 1960s is particularly threatening. This is not class struggle as it is usually manifested. It is struggle in a moment of restructuring and in locations that are sites of key control and management operations in the new global economy. Global cities can be seen as one location in the broader process of the reorganization of the capital–labour relation.

The current phase in US immigration (see Table 1) needs to be understood against this background. While it shares a number of general conditions with past migration phases, it is also rooted, as are all migrations, in a more specific set of conditions. Changes in immigration legislation, the existence of old immigrant communities in the receiving countries and unemployment in sending countries, are general conditions in the migration process that assume their specific weight through a particular spatio-temporal configuration. The current restructuring of economic activity, with its associated transformation in the job supply, contains factors that play a central role in the continuation of today's immigration. Of particular interest here is the creation of low-wage jobs induced directly and indirectly by the restructuring. That is to say, besides the generation of low-wage jobs in declining sectors of the economy or the reproduction of a traditional set of low-wage jobs, what is of concern here is the generation of low-wage jobs in highly dynamic sectors and localities.

TABLE 1
Immigrants admitted to the United States by area: Caribbean,
Hispanic and Asian

| | Caribbean | Central America[1] | South America | Asia | Total |
|---|---|---|---|---|---|
| 1955–59 | 78,557 | 26,825 | 42,278 | 98,856 | 246,516 |
| 1960–64 | 120,337 | 43,658 | 100,131 | 117,140 | 381,266 |
| 1965–69 | 351,806 | 51,344 | 119,219 | 258,229 | 780,698 |
| 1970–74 | 318,680 | 44,159 | 104,676 | 574,222 | 1,041,737 |
| 1975–79 | 413,715 | 73,794 | 155,745 | 879,178 | 1,522,432 |
| 1980 | 73,296 | 20,968 | 39,717 | 236,097 | 370,078 |
| Total | 1,356,391 | 260,748 | 561,766 | 2,163,702 | 4,342,621 |

[1]Excludes Mexico.
*Sources:* INS, 'Tabulation of Immigrants Admitted by Country of Birth, 1954–79'
(1981, Unpublished); INS *1980 Statistical Yearbook of the Immigration and
Naturalization Service*; INS, 'Tabulation of Immigrants Admitted by Country or
Region of Birth' (US Department of Justice, 1983).

When we consider the evidence on different occupational and
earnings distributions for various industries in combination with the
locational patterns of such industries, it becomes rather clear that
major cities like New York and Los Angeles have a high incidence of
industries with considerable income and occupational polarization.
The core economic sector in these cities consists of a wide array of
producer services. These accounted for respectively 31 and 25 percent
of all employment by 1981 (see Table 2).

The high incidence of producer and other services in the employment structure of major cities contributes to the generation of low-
wage jobs directly and indirectly. The data on earnings classes show a
very high incidence of the next to lowest earnings class in all services,
except distributive services and public administration (Stanback et al.,
1981). Only 17 percent of workers in manufacturing and 18.8 percent
in construction were in the next to lowest earnings class, compared
with almost half of all workers in the producer services (Stanback and
Noyelle, 1982: 33). The other half of the workers in producer services
were in the two highest earnings classes. Only 2.8 percent of the
workers in these services were in the middle earnings class, compared
with half of all workers in construction and manufacturing.

The consolidation of this economic core of top-level management
and servicing activities needs to be viewed alongside the general move
to a service economy and the decline of manufacturing. New economic
sectors are reshaping the job supply. However, so are new ways of
organizing work in both new and old sectors of the economy.
Components of the work process which even 20 years ago took place

TABLE 2

Employment share of producer services in all industries, New York City, Los Angeles and Detroit, 1977 and 1981[1]

|  | New York City | Los Angeles | Detroit |
|---|---|---|---|
| *1977* | | | |
| Employment share | 28.1% | 22.7% | 11.3% |
| Employment in | | | |
| all industries ('000s) | (3,188) | (1,367) | (490) |
| *1981* | | | |
| Employment share | 30.7% | 24.9% | 12.6% |
| Employment in | | | |
| all industries ('000s) | (3,340) | (1,398) | (395) |

[1]Producer services include SIC 60-67, 73, 81 and 89.

*Sources:* Based on US Bureau of the Census, *County Business Patterns* (Various Issues); *Advance Estimates of Social, Economic and Housing Characteristics*, California (1983); *Advance Estimates of Social, Economic and Housing Characteristics*, New York (1983); *Advance Estimates of Social, Economic and Housing Characteristics*, Michigan (1983); City of Detroit, Planning Department, *Annual Overall Economic Development Program Report and Program Projection* (1983).

on the shop-floor and were classified as production jobs, today have been replaced by a combination of machine/service-worker/engineer. Activities that were once all consolidated in a single service/retail establishment have now been divided between a service delivery outlet and central headquarters. Finally, a large array of activities which were being carried out under standardized forms of organizing work a decade ago, are today increasingly characterized by informalization, e.g. sweatshops and industrial homework (Sassen-Koob, 1984c). In brief, the changes in the job supply evident in major cities like New York are a function both of new sectors and of the reorganization of work in both new and old sectors.

At the national level, the general trends shaping the job supply have brought about a greater inequality in the earnings distribution of workers over the last decade. The shift to a service economy is, first of all, generally recognized to result in a greater share of low-wage jobs than is the case with an economy dominated by a strong manufacturing sector (Singelmann, 1979; Stanback et al., 1981; Bluestone et al., 1984; Jacobson, 1978). Second, some of the fastest growing service industries are characterized by larger than average concentrations of lowly and of highly paid jobs (Stanback et al., 1981; Appelbaum, 1984). Third, there has been what I call a downgrading of manufacturing jobs: major new industries, notably electronics, have a high incidence of low-wage jobs in production and assembly, while several of the older industries have undergone a social reorganization of the work process characterized by a growth in non-union plants and a rapid increase in sweatshops and industrial homework (New York State Department of Labor, 1982; Wolff, 1984; Sassen-Koob, 1981b; Balmori, 1983; Morales, 1983; Marshall, 1983). Fourth, the technological transformation of the work process, in part underlying the above trends, has further added to earnings polarization by either upgrading or downgrading a vast array of middle-income jobs. Mechanization and computerization have transferred skills to machines and have shifted certain operations from the shop-floor to the computer room or designer's studio.

Various kinds of evidence document aspects of this growing polarization. Using 1970 and 1980 census data on earnings organized by industry-occupational cells, I found the two highest earnings classes increased their total share from 32 percent to 37 percent while the two lowest ones increased their share from 32 to 38.5 percent. Correspondingly, the two middle earnings classes reduced their share by 11 percentage points (see Table 3). Estimates made by the Bureau of Labor Statistics (US Department of Labor) show that the highest absolute growth in jobs will occur in low-paying occupations. Using unpublished data and forecasts from the Bureau of Labor Statistics, Bluestone, Harrison and Gorham (1984) examined the 1969–82 growth performance of 136 manufacturing and non-manufacturing sectors monitored regularly by the Bureau and categorized them by their mean annual wage in 1980. They found that from 1969 to 1982, the sectors with the largest net growth in jobs were those which in 1980 paid the lowest average wages.

In addition to generating a demand for immigrant workers, it is my hypothesis that this form of economic polarization contains conditions that promote informalization in a wide range of activities (Sassen-Koob, 1984c). Linking informalization and growth takes the analysis beyond the notion that the emergence of informal sectors in cities like New York and Los Angeles is due to the large presence of immigrants and their supposed propensity to replicate survival strategies typical of Third World countries. It suggests, rather, that basic traits of advanced capitalism may promote conditions for informalization. The presence of large immigrant communities, then, can be seen as mediating in the process of informalization, rather than directly generating it: the demand side of the process of informalization is therewith brought to the fore.

The fact that about half of all immigrants are in the 10 largest cities in the United States, in contrast to only 11 percent of the total US population, can partly be explained by the large concentration of low-wage jobs in major cities. New York and Los Angeles have the largest

TABLE 3
Distribution of US labour force among earnings classes, 1970 and 1980[1]

Distribution of total US labour force (%)

| *Earnings classes*[2] | *1970* | | | *1980* | | |
|---|---|---|---|---|---|---|
| | *Total* | *Female* | *Male* | *Total* | *Female* | *Male* |
| 1.60 and above | 11.3 } 32.2 | 7.5 | 9.4 | 12.9 } 37.0 | 4.8 | 11.0 |
| 1.59 to 1.30 | 20.9 | 18.6 | 18.9 | 24.2 | 14.5 | 20.7 |
| 1.29 to 1.00 | 18.9 } 35.8 | 21.5 | 23.1 | 12.8 } 24.5 | 12.8 | 15.6 |
| 0.99 to 0.70 | 16.9 | 10.5 | 14.3 | 11.7 | 15.8 | 17.0 |
| 0.69 to 0.40 | 22.8 } 32.0 | 13.5 | 15.4 | 25.2 } 38.5 | 16.7 | 11.8 |
| 0.39 and below | 9.2 | 28.4 | 19.0 | 13.3 | 35.4 | 23.9 |

[1] Civilian workers 14 years and over by total money earnings.

[2] Earnings classes are derived from the application of 1975 average earnings for each major occupation within each industry group. A basic assumption is that the relative income at 1975 levels for each occupational industrial subgroup is constant — in this case from 1970 to 1980. I followed the method used by Stanback and Noyelle (1982) in their comparison of 1960 and 1975 earnings for industry-occupation cells (see Chapter 3). The total earnings distribution obtained is then divided into sixtiles. The major industry groups are Manufacturing, Construction, Distributive Services, Retail, Producer Services, Consumer Services, Nonprofit Services (Health and Education), Public Administration. Not included are Agriculture, Fisheries and Mining. The major occupational groups are Professional, Technical, Managerial, Office Clerical, Nonoffice Clerical, Sales, Craft Workers, Operatives, Service Workers, Labourers.

*Source:* Based on US Bureau of the Census, 1982. *Money Income of Households, Families and Persons in the United States: 1980* (Current Population Reports: Series P-60, No. 132); and US Bureau of the Census, 1972, *Money Income of Households, Families and Persons in the United States: 1970.*

Hispanic populations of all US cities, respectively 2 million and 1.5 million, a size significantly larger than that of the next, Chicago and Miami, each with about 580,000 Hispanics. New York City and Los Angeles also contain, together with San Francisco, the largest concentration of Asians. Finally, New York City is the major recipient of West Indians. The expansion in the supply of low-wage jobs, particularly pronounced in major cities, can be seen as creating employment opportunities for immigrants even as middle-income blue-and white-collar native workers are experiencing high unemployment because their jobs are being either downgraded or expelled from the production process. Furthermore, a large immigrant population, especially if organized into fairly complex immigrant communities, generates its own demand for immigrant workers from professionals to unskilled labourers (Marshall, 1983; Wilson and Portes, 1980).

In sum, the existence of major growth sectors, notably the producer services, generates low-wage jobs directly, through the structure of the work process, and indirectly, through the structure of the high income life-styles of those therein employed and through the consumption needs of the low-wage workforce. Even a technically advanced service industry such as finance generates a significant share of low-wage jobs with few skill or language proficiency requirements. High income residential and commercial 'gentrification' is labour intensive. And so is the massive array of low-cost service and goods-producing firms selling to the low-wage work force.

**The Reconcentration of Industrial Capital at the Core: Preliminary Findings**

The larger argument organizing the materials here presented is that recent technical, economic and political developments have made certain regions within the US highly desirable industrial zones for native and foreign investors (Sassen-Koob, 1987).[5] Southern California is a good example. So are Texas and the New York–New Jersey metropolitan region. These regions are beginning to function partly as alternatives to the industrial zones developed in low-wage Third World countries over the last decade and a half. But they also represent a response to a set of locational constraints inducing a new spatial organization of production and requiring a combination of resources well represented by regions such as southern California, the focus of this section (see Sassen-Koob, 1987). Among the key factors inducing the development of such new industrial zones within the US are the following. First there are new technical and economic factors that promote agglomeration economies and disincentives towards vertical integration. Notable among these are the requirements for production in the most advanced sectors of high-technology industries, and in the expansion of commercial applications of microelectronics. Both, even if involving at times very different kinds of production, require proximity to centres of research, control and design, as well as to intermediate buyers. The overall result is a tendency towards a clustering arrangement of a broad range of firms, some specializing in similar lines and others in complementary ones. This clustering arrangement presupposes access to a rather large, somewhat contiguous territory. Space only becomes a resource on the collective level. In this context the whole southern California region can be seen as one massive base for this new territorial organization of production. Proximity to Mexico and the development of the Otay Mesa Mexico—US industrial zone acquire added significance in this context. And so does the availability of vast supplies of cheap labour along with an abundance of research centres and highly trained technical personnel.

Second, the emergence of a number of constraints in the industrial zones (export processing, or free trade zones) in the Third World may make investment in these relatively less attractive than it was in the 1970s. These constraints involve, among others: pressure by the governments on foreign companies operating in their territories to transfer more advanced technologies and more capital-intensive production, while it is precisely the more labour-intensive and simpler segments of production that have typically been located in these zones; labour shortages in some of the better established zones, largely due to the marked preference for employing young women and to high turnover rates; growing militancy among workers employed in these zones and export industries generally, notwithstanding the ruthless disciplining of workers and various repressive measures; a consistent trend towards rising wages which may be reducing the relative desirability of locating plants off-shore, especially given a growing supply of immigrant workers in the US and the severe defeats suffered by organized labour.

A third factor of considerable weight to foreign investors is access to the US market and, in the case of certain industries, access to high-level technologies through the acquisition of US firms. The US is still the largest single market in the world and one which a range of foreign firms want to secure in the face of rising pressures towards protection against imports. Acquisition by foreign investors of US manufacturing firms as a way of gaining access to the US market and to advanced technology has accelerated since the late 1970s if we use the figures on acquisitions as an indicator. There may of course be a number of other reasons inducing such acquisitions, including the relative decline in the attractiveness of investing in the Third World. I

TABLE 4

Foreign-owned manufacturing firms, selected states and US total, 1980

| | Cumulative total through 1975 | 1976 | 1977 | 1978 | 1979 | 1980 | Cumulative total through 1980 | % US | Net increase 1976–80 |
|---|---|---|---|---|---|---|---|---|---|
| New York State | 222 | 42 | 45 | 36 | 50 | 23 | 418 | 11.4 | 196 |
| New Jersey | 178 | 13 | 21 | 16 | 17 | 18 | 263 | 7.2 | 85 |
| NY–NJ Metropolitan Region | (234) | (9) | (17) | (18) | (28) | (16) | (322) | | (88) |
| California | 103 | 16 | 22 | 43 | 50 | 30 | 264 | 7.2 | 161 |
| Texas | 82 | 6 | 14 | 16 | 31 | 20 | 169 | 5.8 | 87 |
| N. Carolina | 90 | 6 | 11 | 16 | 25 | 36 | 184 | 5.0 | 94 |
| Pennsylvania | 125 | 10 | 16 | 14 | 19 | 30 | 214 | 4.6 | 89 |
| Georgia | 68 | 5 | 5 | 20 | 22 | 23 | 143 | 3.9 | 75 |
| Illinois | 92 | 10 | 5 | 6 | 10 | 13 | 136 | 3.7 | 44 |
| All other | 1006 | 137 | 135 | 191 | 210 | 194 | 1873 | 51.2 | 867 |
| US total | 1966 | 245 | 274 | 358 | 434 | 387 | 3664 | 100.0 | 1698 |

*Source:* The Conference Board, Inc., The Port Authority of New York and New Jersey Planning and Development Department, Regional Research Section.

would add to these, the new locational constraints as a factor inducing investment in manufacturing in the US (see table 4).

One question raised by this analysis and of interest to this study concerns the mobility of capital. It is possible that capital is less mobile and more subject to locational constraints than is generally assumed. Another, more particular question is whether this current stage represents a distinct phase in the 'product cycle' of high technology, and once standardization sets in, these locational constraints will cease to operate. This would, however, not address such issues as the increase in direct foreign investment in manufacturing in certain regions of the US. Nor would it address the emergence of constraints making investments in Third World industrial zones relatively less attractive for certain economic sectors.

These general developments and questions provide the context for the more detailed examination of the case of southern California. A hypothesis derived from this general argument is that the massive growth in this region's high-technology and other manufacturing branches over the last decade is not simply a function of an expanding market for the products, but is also a function of technical, economic and political constraints that have promoted the development of a new spatial organization of production. The combination of resources entailed by this new spatial organization of production shows southern California and other such regions to be suitable locations: simultaneous access to highly trained workers and to an abundant supply of low-wage labour, simultaneous access to abundant supplies of industrial space and to centres for research and control, and a regional development geared towards expanding manufacturing capacity in high-technology and other branches. In the case of southern California and Texas, proximity to Mexico and its abundant resources of space, labour and energy, is a key ingredient in the combination of necesssary resources. The new locational constraints raise a question as to the possibility of a new articulation with Mexico, one to be distinguished from the ongoing one existing between Mexican and US economic activities. That is to say, the new spatial organization of production entails not simply a quantitative expansion of the Border Industrialization Programme, but a qualitative transformation in some of its components. One way of conceptualizing this transformation is to link it with the issue of capital mobility: while the earlier phase represents an instance of capital mobility, this new component represents an instance of capital immobility — the new locational constraints. Correspondingly, two processes that have accelerated over the last decade are the influx of foreign capital and of foreign labour into the US. Discussing these is one way of capturing the new trend.

*The Rise of Foreign Investment in the United States*
Since 1983 the US has become a net borrower for the first time in 50 years. Foreign investment in the US began to increase rapidly in the late 1970s, reaching average annual rates of about 30 percent in the 1980s. The acceleration in the pace of investment is evident in the doubling of total investment in five years, from $416 billion in 1979 to $833 billion in 1984. While the absolute level may not be extremely high in an economy with a GNP of $3.6 trillion, it is worth noting. Indeed, it has led some analysts to maintain that, barring this influx of foreign investment, the recent economic recovery would not have been as pronounced as it has been.

Foreign direct investment more than doubled in the five-year period from 1979, reaching $140 billion by 1984. This is a remarkable increase if we consider that as recently as 1970 it stood at $13 billion. Much of this direct foreign investment is coming from the highly industrialized countries. In 1960 the US accounted for a little over 2.4 percent of all direct investment abroad by such countries. By 1980 it accounted for 30 percent, with highly increased absolute levels. These figures, though fraught with measurement problems, do point to a significant trend. Particular aspects illustrate this significance. For example, Data Resources Inc. has estimated that foreign investment financed 26 percent of US corporate capital spending in that country in 1984. Not only is this an unprecedented level, it also represents a doubling from the 1980 share.

Of particular interest to this study is the increase and distribution of direct foreign investment (DFI) in the US. Until the middle of the 1970s, US direct investment abroad grew more rapidly than direct foreign investment in the US. From 1954 through 1966, such investment in the US grew from $4.6 billion to $11.8 billion, or by 257 percent, while US DFI abroad grew from $17.7 billion to $67 billion, or by 379 percent. This trend began to reverse in the 1970s. US DFI grew from $67 billion in 1969 to $148.8 billion in 1977, or by 222 percent, while DFI in the US grew from $11.8 billion to $34.1 billion, or by 285 percent. After 1977 there was a rapid acceleration in the rate of growth of DFI in the US, quadrupling from 1977 to 1984. In 1981 DFI in the US for the first time exceeded US direct investment abroad, after more than 30 years of net outflows. In the early 1980s the rate of growth of US DFI declined considerably — to 5 percent in 1981, the lowest in the post-World War II period (Whichard, 1982: 11). In contrast, the rate of growth of DFI in the US reached 31 percent annually, a level at which it remains (Howenstine and Fouch, 1982: 32).

The geographic distribution of direct foreign investments in manufacturing, which accounted for about one-third of all such investment in the last few years, shows some changes over time. The largest numbers of foreign plants had been located in the mideast, southwest and Great Lakes regions prior to 1976. In 1977–78, most announcements of new facilities were in the mideast, southeast and far west regions. Recent foreign investments in new facilities have gone largely to the southeast and far west regions. Most acquisitions by foreign investors affect facilities located in the mideast, New England and Great Lakes areas.

While total foreign investment in manufacturing has been concentrated primarily in the mideast, New England and Great Lake regions, largely because of sizeable acquisitions, most new plants have been built in the southeast and far west regions. By state, nearly 60 percent of the number of foreign investments had been made in distressed states, both prior to 1975 and during 1977–78. Yet the value of foreign investments in distressed states has fallen off considerably, with 83 percent of the total prior to 1974 and 64 percent of the announced value of investments in 1977–78. In actual numbers of foreign investments, New York and California have been the major recipients and continued to be in the early 1980s. If one distinguishes between new constructions and acquisitions, New England has been at the top in acquisitions per thousand manufacturing employees, while the southeast and the southwest lead in new constructions per thousand manufacturing employees (Little, 1983).

The most prominent foreign investors in manufacturing are large, multinational firms. They invest in the US for a number of reasons. These include: the exploitation of important innovations, import substitution to avoid tariff restrictions, problems with domestic market regulations, and a desire to gain access to US technology and management expertise (US Department of Housing and Urban Development, 1979).

Investment in the United States may have been more attractive because production costs there grew more slowly than in most other major industrialized countries during the 1970s.[6] Between 1965 and 1975 average compensation of US manufacturing workers increased 80 percent. In Canada, Japan, Germany, the Netherlands, Sweden and the United Kingdom, the increases were 109 percent, 307 percent, 150 percent, 213 percent, 162 percent, and 207 percent, respectively. The Bureau of Labor Statistics estimated that in 1975, hourly compensation in three countries — Belgium ($6.60), the Netherlands ($6.53) and Sweden ($7.18) — was above that in the United States ($6.35).

Foreign investors base regional and state locational decisions largely upon the availability and skills of labour, proximity to port facilities and to markets, the availability of investment incentives and the fiscal stability of state and local government. Little (1983) estimated the relative dependence of different regions on foreign investments in selected industries. The far west region shows a very high dependence on foreign investment in the Electric and Electronic Equipment category as well as in that of Instruments and related products. The southwest shows a much lower dependence in the first industrial sector and zero dependence in the second sector. Dependence on investment by a given country shows the far west to have one of the highest levels of dependence on a given country's investment, in this case on Japan. The southeast shows high levels of dependence on the Netherlands and France and very low levels on Japan. These data point to a certain weight of direct foreign investment in manufacturing in certain regions and in certain industrial sectors.

The distribution of foreign owned manufacturing firms in the US by industry shows rather high increases in the share accounted for by non-electrical and electrical machinery going from about 9 percent of all firms in 1975 to about 17 percent in 1981 (Conference Board, 1981; US Department of Commerce, 1980). Primary Metals and Instruments also showed marked growth in their shares. Fabricated Metals and Food and Chemicals showed some of the largest declines in their shares. These declines in shares do not however mean a decline in absolute levels of foreign investment given the sharp overall growth in such investment.

## *The Immigrant Workforce in California*

The available evidence shows that a large share of all immigrants entering the US over the last decade live in California, that the level of entries is increasing in the 1980s compared with the annual average for the 1970s, and that the occupational and industrial distribution of immigrants is characterized by much higher concentrations in manual jobs and in transformative industries than is the case for natives. If we add to this the information on income and educational levels prevalent among immigrants, particularly Hispanics, then immigrants can be seen to constitute an abundant supply of low-wage workers for some of the major growth industries in the state. The flexibility of this supply, both in its capacity to expand and in its powerlessness, is probably not insignificant given the types of jobs that prevail in several major growth industries and the locational constraints that make an overseas shift of plants less feasible and less attractive than a decade ago. This kind of immigrant workforce represents yet another resource that attracts investment to the region.

From 1980 to 1983, California received 730,000 new residents, a high figure for a period of three years considering that total net legal immigration into the state was 782,000 for the 1970–80 decade. Given the tendency for undocumented immigrants to settle in areas with high concentrations of legal immigrants of the same national origin, we can assume that California has also received a large share of the undocumented immigration. Almost 70 percent of all immigrants who arrived in the state after 1970 settled in Los Angeles County and in the rest of southern California. For Mexicans this figure reached 75 percent. This pattern of regional distribution within the state can be expected to hold for the undocumented population as well.

The vast majority of all immigrants in California are Mexicans and Asians. While Mexicans are the single largest nationality group, the Asians' rate of entry is higher than that of Mexicans. Inclusion of undocumented entries would probably change this relation. The arrival of Indochinese refugees after 1980 has also contributed to the fact that 40 percent of all entries since 1980 have been Asians compared with a 30 percent share for Hispanics (including Mexicans). A lowering in average educational levels for Asian immigrants and the information we have about a rising presence of Asians in manual jobs suggest that Asians may increasingly be contributing to the supply of low-wage manufacturing and service workers in the state alongside their ongoing participation in higher occupational levels. Of particular significance is the growing number of Asian women employed in high-technology production and assembly facilities.

The occupational distribution of immigrants nationwide differs considerably from that of native workers. The evidence suggests that immigrants are a significant labour supply for manual jobs, particularly in California and in New York. California is one of the states with the highest index of dissimilarity of the five states that account for most immigrants (Bach and Tienda, 1984: 18). Using 1980 census data, Bach and Tienda (1984) found that almost half of all women in these five states hold service and operative jobs, compared with 25 percent of native women and between 20 and 30 percent of immigrant men. The industrial distribution shows immigrant women to be disproportionately concentrated in transformative industries — particularly food, textile and garment production — compared with native women who are disproportionately concentrated in social services. Among men, immigrants are more highly represented in personal services than native men, and in transformative and extractive industries (particularly in California, Texas and Illinois). There has been a considerable decline in the number of professional jobs held by the foreign born and a corresponding increase in the share of blue-collar and service jobs.

In California, the occupational and sectoral distribution of immigrants diverges even more from that of natives than is the case nationwide and in the other four states with the largest share of immigrants. About 25 percent of the immigrant female experienced workforce hold operative jobs, compared with 7 percent of native women. On the other hand, about 38 percent of native compared with 25 percent of immigrant women hold clerical jobs. Among men, the greatest differential is in operative jobs, held by 20 percent of immigrants compared with 14 percent of native men, and in farm jobs, held by 7 percent of immigrant compared with 1.3 percent of native men. Generally, immigrants have lower shares in the more desirable jobs and higher shares in the lower-paid jobs.

The most pronounced difference between immigrant and native women in the sectoral distribution is the 30 percent share of immigrants in transformative industries compared with 15 percent of native women. Further, almost 33 percent of native compared with 23 percent of immigrant women are in the social services. Native women are more heavily represented in distributive and producer services than are immigrants. Only New York and Illinois have such high shares of women immigrants in transformative industries. Among men, almost 40 percent of immigrants compared with 33.6 percent of native men are in transformative industries. Immigrant men are more highly represented in extractive industries and in personal services than are native men.

Though incomplete in coverage, the EEOC (Equal Employment Opportunity Commission) data offer some information worth noting on the incidence of immigrants, both Hispanics and Asians, in a whole range of mostly low-wage jobs. The data for Los Angeles–Long Beach — a region that accounts for about half of all manufacturing employment in California — showed that almost 57 percent of Hispanics were labourers, service workers or operatives. The 39.6 percent share of Blacks in these jobs, though high, was lower than that of Hispanics. Less than a quarter of Asians held these jobs. A breakdown by industry shows that in service industries the share of Hispanics in low-wage jobs is even higher at 65 percent, while that of Asians remains the same. In manufacturing industries, about 68 percent of Hispanics held such jobs. It is worth noting the 43 percent share of operative jobs held by Hispanics, a level associated with the massive industrial growth in the Los Angeles region. The share of Asians holding operative and labouring jobs, 33.3 percent, is also relatively high.

In general immigrants emerge as an important labour supply for the growing manufacturing sector in California. Furthermore, immigration is providing a type of labour supply that is in demand at a time of rapid growth in certain sectors and numerous plant closures in others, notably those that are heavily unionized. Alongside the high-technology explosion there have been thousands of plant closures. From 1980 to 1983 alone over 145,000 workers in California lost their jobs as a direct result of 1,385 plant closures (Shapira, 1983). There were, furthermore, thousands of jobs lost due to shrinking operations. The 100 percent growth rate from 1970 to 1980 for the electronics industry in several key counties of California obscures the simultaneous massive loss of a lot of unionized jobs.

In brief, the massive influx of direct foreign investment and of foreign labour can be seen as preliminary indications of the larger process of industrial reconcentration alluded to. This influx of foreign capital and labour acquires its significance in the context of technical, economic and political constraints that make such investment in peripheral locations either less competitive or less feasible.

**Conclusion**

The new industrial zones in selected peripheral areas and the massive industrialization projects in OPEC countries can be conceived of in more abstract terms as instances of the spatial dispersal of growth poles taking place from the mid-1960s onwards. This dispersal of growth poles is part of a new territorial organization of economic activities associated with the recomposition of significant components of capital. It is the concentration and sudden implantation of conditions creating an equally sudden demand for a large supply of labour which gives migration its specificity as a process crucial to the formation of the needed labour supply. A less sudden and concentrated demand for labour can conceivably correspond to a whole range of processes inducing the formation of the needed labour supply. The complexity of migration, which is always the migration of *people*, cannot be reduced to this specific aspect. But it is this specific aspect which contains the articulation of the new labour migrations with the recomposition of capital as it takes place in these peripheral areas.

The new territorial organization characterized by the dispersal of certain manufacturing and clerical activities entails, in turn, new forms of concentration for the control and servicing of the global production apparatus. The strong tendency for such activities to be located in major cities makes these into strategic nodes in the organization of the world economy. The direct and indirect generation of low-wage jobs induced by the new core economic sector gives the demand for low-wage workers in these sectors its specific character, one that distinguishes it from the demand for low-wage workers in declining or non-strategic sectors. The context within which this demand for low-wage workers occurs, however, is one of political disaffection and the remnants of 1960s militancy in the minority populations who constitute the mass of low-wage workers in major cities. The specificity of labour migration in this instance is derived from its capacity to meet the demand for low-wage, politically disciplined workers in what are strategic sectors in strategic locations of the world economy. Again, the process of migration cannot be reduced to this specific capacity. Furthermore, migration also provides workers for declining and marginal sectors. But it is the specific capacity to meet the demand in strategic sectors which provides the central articulation with the process of capital recomposition as it takes place in these core locations.

These processes of relocation and consolidation of new core economic sectors, together with other major components of the recomposition of capital, contribute to the emergence of new conditions. These new conditions are not necessarily conducive to the reproduction of the arrangements that engender them. For example, growing political pressures and declining economic returns in the periphery make the continuing relocation of capital to these areas somewhat less attractive today than 10 years ago. At the same time, there has been a consolidation of a large supply of immigrant workers in core areas, along with a weakening of the politico-economic position of native workers and a general context more favourable to capital than was the case in the 1960s.

Alongside more purely technical constraints, these political and economic trends have begun to induce a reconcentration of industrial capital in core areas. This process can be conceived of as the development of new investment zones for world capital. The specificity of immigration in this case is the capacity to provide a large supply of low-wage, disciplined manual workers in a social context characterized by middle-class aspirations or a degree of political disaffection that becomes problematic in the eyes of employers searching for low-wage workers.

One question at this point is what are the political implications of incorporating immigrant workers in growth sectors? History suggests that workers in growth sectors — who in the US were typically immigrants — have possibilities for organizing which those in declining or marginal sectors lack. The possibility of raising the economic and political cost of immigrant workers would then put in motion conditions that would, again, not be conducive to reproducing this new arrangement over time. It would create new diseconomies from the perspective of capital in a way similar to the growing militancy of workers in the new industrial zones of the periphery after a decade of disciplined hard work — a militancy that is one of the conditions contributing to the reconcentration of industrial capital in core areas.

## Notes

1. As this chapter is a synopsis of several research projects, extending over many years, it is quite impossible to give full references for each major topic. Detailed descriptions of the analyses, the evidence, and references to the pertinent literature can be found in Sassen-Koob, 1987.

2. The actual closing and moving of factories is only one component of the relocation of manufacturing, probably a relatively small one. More significant in terms of actual job losses are various kinds of disinvestment that amount to a gradual contraction of the manufacturing base: (a) the shift of profits and savings of a given plant to other plants in other locations, or their investment in other types of activities; (b) gradual moving of equipment and jobs, without necessarily closing the plant; (c) no new investments for plant maintenance or new equipment acquisitions. These can all lead to factory closing without the 'runaway' syndrome. I refer to all of these processes in speaking of the relocation of manufacturing or capital emigration.

3. The most extreme form of the large-scale transfer of manufacturing plants to the periphery is the development of export processing zones and world market factories. In both of these production is mostly for export to the core countries where the capital originated. This phenomenon began on a large scale only in the late 1960s. By 1975, there were 79 export processing zones, most of them concentrated in Southeast Asia and the Caribbean. In other words, they emerge once the decentralization of industrial production from core to periphery acquires a massive scale.

4. The exhaustion of export-led industrialization as a development strategy is suggested by the most recent developments in South Korea and Puerto Rico. There is evidence, not much publicized, that Japanese capital is moving out of some of the export processing zones in South Korea once the incentive period granted by the government runs out. In Puerto Rico, some of the more labour-intensive components in the garment industry are being exported for assembly to other countries in the Caribbean and then reimported into the island for final shipment to the mainland. At the same time, 'enterprise zones' are being promoted for declining core areas. (On Puerto Rico see Bonilla and Campos, 1982.)

5. This section is based on the research reported more fully in Sassen-Koob, 1987.

6. This statement is based on data for 1970–80 on unit labour costs in manufacturing in the United States and 10 foreign industrialized countries, published in 'International Comparisons of Manufacturing Productivity and Labor Cost Trends, Preliminary Measures for 1981', US Department of Labor, Bureau of Labor Statistics, June 1982.

# References

Appelbaum, E. (1984) 'High-Tech and the Structural Employment Problems of the Eighties', in E. Collins (ed.), *American Jobs and the Changing Industrial Base.* New York: Ballinger.

Arrigo, L.G. (1980) 'The Industrial Workforce of Young Women in Taiwan', *Bulletin of Concerned Asian Scholars*, 12(2): 25–37.

Bach, R.L. and M. Tienda (1984) 'Contemporary Immigration and Refugee Movements and Employment Adjustment Policies', in V.M. Briggs, Jr. and M. Tienda (eds.), *Immigration Issues and Policies*, pp. 37-82. Salt Lake City: Olympus Publishing Co.

Balmori, D. (1983) 'Hispanic Immigrants in the Construction Industry: New York City, 1960–1982'. *Occasional Papers*, 38. New York: Center for Latin American and Caribbean Studies, New York University.

Bauer, D. (1980) 'The Question of Foreign Investment', *New York Affairs*, 6: 52–58.

Bluestone, B., B. Harrison and L. Gorham (1984) 'Storm Clouds on the Horizon: Labor Market Crisis and Industrial Policy'. Brookline, MA: Economic Education Project.

Bonilla, A.F. and R. Campos (1982) 'Imperialist Initiatives and the Puerto Rican Worker: From Foraker to Reagan', *Contemporary Marxism*, 5: 1–18.

Conference Board (1981) *Announcements of Foreign Investments in U.S. Manufacturing Industries* (First Quarter, Second Quarter and Third Quarter). New York: The Conference Board, Inc.

Fernandez-Kelly, M.P. (1983) *For We are Sold, I and My People: Women and Industry in Mexico's Frontier.* Albany: State University of New York Press.

Grossman, R. (1979) 'Women's Place in the Integrated Circuit'. *Southeast Asia Chronicle*, 66/*Pacific Research*, 9 (joint issue): 2–17.

Howenstine, N. and G.G. Fouch. (1982) 'Foreign Direct Investment in the United States in 1981', *Survey of Current Business*, 62(8): 30. Washington, DC: U.S. Department of Commerce, Bureau of Economic Analysis.

Jacobson, L.S. (1978) 'Earnings Losses of Workers Displaced from Manufacturing Industries', in W.G. DeWald (ed.), *The Impact of International Trade and Investment on Unemployment.* Washington, DC: Government Printing Office.

Kelly, D. (1984) 'Hard Work, Hard Choices: A Survey of Women in St. Lucia's Export Oriented Electronics Factories'. Unpublished Research Report.

Lim, Y.C. (1982) 'Capitalism, Imperialism, and Patriarchy: The Dilemma of Third-World Women Workers in Multinational Factories', in Nash and M.P. Fernandez-Kelley (eds.), *Women, Men, and the International Division of Labor.* Albany: State University of New York Press.

Little, J.S. (1983) 'Locational Decisions of Foreign Direct Investors in the U.S.', *New England Economic Review*: 43–63. Federal Reserve Bank of Boston.

Marshall, A. (1983) 'Immigration in a Surplus-Worker Labor Market: The Case of New York'. *Occasional Papers*, 39. New York: Center for Latin American and Caribbean Studies, New York University.

Morales, R. (1983) 'Undocumented Workers in a Changing Automobile Industry: Case Studies in Wheels, Headers and Batteries'. Presented at the Conference on Contemporary Production: Capital Mobility and Labor Migration. Center for U.S.–Mexican Studies, University of California, San Diego (February).

New York State Department of Labor (1982) *Report to the Governor and the Legislature on the Garment Manufacturing Industry and Industrial Homework.* Albany: New York State Department of Labor.

Safa, H.I. (1981) 'Runaway Shops and Female Employment: The Search for Cheap Labor', *Signs*, 7: 418–433.

Salaff, J. (1981) *Working Daughters of Hong Kong*. New York: Cambridge University Press.

Sassen-Koob, S. (1981a) 'The Role of the State in Oil-Exporting Countries'. Presented at the Conference on the Political Economy of the World System. University of Wisconsin, Madison.

Sassen-Koob, S. (1981b) 'Exporting Capital and Importing Labor: The Role of Caribbean Migration to New York City'. *Occasional Papers*, 28. New York: Center for Latin American and Caribbean Studies, New York University.

Sassen-Koob, S. (1984a) 'The New Labor Demand in Global Cities' in M.P. Smith (ed.), *Cities in Transformation: Capital, Class and Urban Structure*, pp. 139–171. Beverly Hills: Sage Publications.

Sassen-Koob, S. (1984b) 'Notes on the Incorporation of Third World Women into Wage-Labor through Immigration and Off-shore Production', *International Migration Review*, 18: 1144–1167.

Sassen-Koob, S. (1984c) 'Growth and Informalization at the Core: The Case of New York City', in *The Urban Informal Sector: Recent Trends in Research and Theory*, pp. 492–518. Conference Proceedings. Baltimore: Department of Sociology, Johns Hopkins University.

Sassen-Koob, S. (1987) *The Mobility of Labor and Capital*. London and New York: Cambridge University Press.

Shapira, P. (1983) 'Shutdowns and Job Losses in California: The Need for New National Priorities'. Testimony Prepared for the Subcommittee on Labor Management Relations, U.S. House of Representatives, Hearings on HR 2847. Los Angeles, July 8.

Singelmann, J. (1978) *From Agriculture to Services: The Transformation of Industrial Employment*. Beverly Hills and London: Sage Publications.

Stanback, T.M. Jr., P.J. Bearse, T.J. Noyelle and R. Karasek. (1981) *Services: The New Economy*. New Jersey: Allanheld, Osmun.

Stanback, T.M. Jr. and T.J. Noyelle (1982) *Cities in Transition: Changing Job Structures in Atlanta, Denver, Buffalo, Phoenix, Columbus (Ohio), Nashville, Charlotte*. New Jersey: Allanheld, Osmun.

Standing, G. (1975) 'Aspiration Wages, Migration and Female Employment'. World Employment Programme, *Working Paper* 23 of the Population and Employment Project. Geneva: International Labour Office (November).

Tanzer, M. (1974) *The Energy Crisis: World Struggle for Power*. New York: Monthly Review Press.

UNIDO (United Nations Industrial Development Organization) (1980) *Export Processing Zones in Developing Countries*. Working Papers on Structural Change No. 19. New York: UNIDO.

US Department of Commerce (1980) *Selected Data on U.S. Direct Investment Abroad, 1966–1978*. Washington, DC: US Department of Commerce, Bureau of Economic Analysis.

US Department of Housing and Urban Development (1979) 'The Impact of Foreign Direct Investment on U.S. Cities and Regions'. Washington, DC: Office of Community Planning and Development. Contract HUD 5193-79.

Whichard, O.G. (1982) 'U.S. Direct Investment Abroad in 1980', *Survey of Current Business*, 61 (8 August): 20–39.

Wilson, K.L. and A. Portes (1980) 'The Immigrant Enclave', *American Journal of Sociology*, 86: 295–319.

Wolff, G. (1984) 'The Decline of Unionization and the Growth of Employment in the Los Angeles Region', Los Angeles: Graduate School of Architecture and Urban Planning, University of California, Los Angeles.

Wong, A.K. (1980) 'Economic Development and Women's Place: Women in Singapore', *International Reports: Women and Society*. London: Change.

World Bank Staff (1975) 'Internal Migration in Less Developed Countries', *Bank Staff Working Paper* 215. Prepared by Lorence Y.L Yap. Washington, DC: International Bank for Reconstruction and Development (September).

# 5
# Policing the Frontiers:
# The State and the Migrant in the International Division of Labour

*Robin Cohen*

> In capitalist society, the state is charged with the primary responsibility of defending the interests of the dominant classes: of managing the affairs, of mediating the needs, of capitalism and the capitalist class. These ends are accomplished through the removal or erection of obstacles which benefit or inhibit the functioning of a capitalist economy. The degree of relaxation, selectivity or stringency involved in the formation and enforcement of boundary regulations is illustrative. (Petras, 1980: 174)

The evolution of national boundaries is relatively new. Natural boundaries (rivers, mountains, oceans) inhibited intercourse between peoples and regions but, with odd exceptions like the Great Wall of China, artificially constructed political borders did not exist before the seventeenth century. Political geographers show how the evolution of boundaries accompanied the development of the modern nation-state. Where natural boundaries did not exist, treaties, laws and contracts created 'paper walls' to divide land, sea and air into legally defined domains 'belonging to' legally recognized states (Prescott, 1965; Petras, 1980: 159). The older school of political geographers, much influenced by liberal economic doctrine, lamented the gradual hardening of political boundaries. In a passionate denunciation of modern boundaries, Boggs (1940: 110) claimed:

> Today the barriers to trade in Europe rise like walls between nations, slow the pulse of industry, rob artisans and labourers of a chance to earn a living, impoverish peoples whose ample capacities are thwarted, and instil fear and despair.

Radical political geographers are nowadays more dispassionate as they weld spatial divisions onto the international division of labour and uneven development theories. The connection between space, state and economy is thus considered the primary focus of research while, as one geographer expresses it, nationalism can 'in one sense be seen as the cultural fallout from the economic explosion of capitalist uneven development' (Short, 1982: 125).

While contemporary analysis undoubtedly yields fruitful work on international restructuring and industrial relocation (see Massey, 1984), Boggs' moral outrage is not entirely inappropriate. He wrote as war clouds loomed in Europe and tightening frontiers prevented millions of innocent people from escaping the Nazi juggernaut. Now we see boat people from Vietnam or Haiti brutally clubbed by the minions of the state, aspirant emigrants denied passports by states in the Comecon bloc and long-standing residents of Nigeria told to pack up and return to their 'homes' in Ghana. In the 1980s as in the late 1930s, the state's restrictive practices deny workers the opportunity to earn a living. The doctrines of 'deregulation' and private initiative are applied selectively in our contemporary political order. Whereas the international mobility of workers is controlled and restricted, the international mobility of capital is comparatively unfettered. Where exchange control regulations obtain, they are frequently and easily evaded by transfer pricing, dummy registrations in tax-havens and the capacity of many transnationals to dictate terms to most of the modern world's nation-states. By contrast, non-state-sanctioned mobility by people is deemed illegal and undocumented workers are unable to benefit from uneven spatial distribution of the world's productive forces in the manner perfected by the owners of capital. Currency speculation, foreign investment, repatriation of profits and the development of global communications networks are just four ways in which transnational capital supersedes the historic bounds of the nation-state.

While capital's horizons expand, workers' physical and psychological frontiers are corralled into narrower pens, policed by the national state. This trend has altered the context of academic debates about the frontier's role in history. For Turner (1962) the frontier signified free land, freedom from restraint and the possibility of recapturing the innocence of Arcadia, lost in the march of industrial civilization. This provided an attractive prospect for many. 'For European peasants burdened by feudal obligations, the West was the lure of free land, for workers penned in by industrial cities it provided the illusion of carefree life, perhaps echoing a recently lost rural past'. But this dream cannot be sustained. 'In Latin America there is no West, no Frontier, there are only frontiers' (Hennessy, 1978: 6). In earlier days the borderlands were inhabited by folk heroes like Kitt Carson, Daniel Boone and Davy Crockett, or romantic bandits, runaway slaves and gauchos; now they are peopled by pathetic work seekers (Hennessy, 1978: 158).

I shall take examples from the American, European and South African political economies to show how the most powerful regional states engineer and refine the regulatory apparati directed against free worker mobility. In conclusion, I will discuss how far such controls have been evaded by illegal entrants.

### US Immigration Policy: Haitians and Cubans

Despite its immigrant heritage, since it established effective national boundaries the United States has always controlled immigration. As Martin (1981: 4) notes, immigration law was predicated on an ever lengthening list of 'undesirables', starting from the 1880s. Prostitutes, convicts, Chinese, lunatics, idiots and contract labourers (1885) were followed by quantitative (1907) and national origins (1921 and 1924) restrictions. There are now over 30 classes of undesirable aliens and a sophisticated seven-tier system of preferences, ceilings and quotas for various categories of would-be immigrants.

With such a battery of legislation one might assume a controlled and predictable pattern of migration to the US, yet for over a decade the system has been widely perceived as ineffective. In one poll, 91 percent supported an 'all out effort' to control illegal immigration, while 80 percent wanted further restrictions on the entry of legal migrants and refugees. This popular reaction was set in a context where the authorized number of 450,000 migrants for 1980 had been superseded by a further 358,000 legal immigrants, refugees and special entrants and perhaps half a million illegal migrants (Martin, 1981: 1). In the 1980s, total annual immigration is thought to be exceeding the all-time high of 880,000 per annum achieved in the period 1901 – 10.

Why is the US unable to impose restrictions like its European and South African counterparts? Some of the difficulty arises from the practical problems of policing so large a country. With the sheer volume of passenger movements for trade, study and tourism, 'overstayers' are neither quickly nor easily detected, especially when internal state boundaries are crossed. But more important than these problems is the certainty that any decisive political action will be opposed by pressure groups wanting to exploit cheap labour-power to the full. In addition to the state versus big business conflict, politicians are cross-pressured by the need to appease voters who may feel challenged by an undiscriminating drive against their illegal co-ethnics. Many politicians also wish to sustain the ideology that, unlike the Eastern bloc, the US provides a haven for the tired, poor or those seeking 'freedom' from 'totalitarianism'. The contradictions of these cross currents are shown by the thus-far doomed attempts of successive presidents to tackle the immigrant question, and well illustrated in recent years by the experience of trying to develop a consistent policy towards Haitian and Cuban migrants.

Concern over immigration became particularly acute during Nixon's presidency, which was characterized by virtual militarization of the undocumented worker 'problem'. General Chapman (head of the Immigration and Naturalization Service) and Charles Colby (then head of the CIA) regarded the US–Mexican border as 'the greatest threat posed to US national security' (NACLA, 1977: 4). Massive deportations of one million a year did not significantly slow the level of illegal immigration. Moreover, Hispanic communities were outraged at the selectivity of INS arrests, which were disproportionately directed against Mexican nationals. Only 45 percent of undocumented migrants are of Mexican origin, yet 95 percent of the pick-ups are Mexicans. Again, whereas European undocumented aliens are given two to three months to leave 'voluntarily', Hispanic migrants are deported within five to six hours (Pandya and Schey, 1981). Attacks on undocumented workers served only to radicalize and politicize groups that had remained tangential to mainstream US politics. To his credit, President Carter recognized that employers were as much a party to illegality as employees, but provided little in the way of practical sanctions in his 1977 proposals. The penalties for employers of illegal workers were small ($1,000); they would be charged with a civil rather than criminal offence, and the obvious 'let-out' had to be 'knowingly' hiring illegal workers. Carter's 1977 immigration plan also combined a hard-line commitment to stopping illegal entry (he proposed a $100 million increase in the INS budget to provide for military equipment and a further 2,000 border guards) with a limited 'amnesty' for undocumented aliens (those who could prove seven years' uninterrupted residence could apply for legal recognition). Finally, Carter's plan also offered a package of aid and loans, aimed principally at Mexico, to reduce population growth, create employment and stabilize the border region (NACLA, 1977).

There is little point in detailing the largely ignominious collapse of these proposals as they were dragged through the mire of public and Congressional debate. Agribusiness mobilized against fining employers, while sections of organized labour felt the proposals would lead to the non-hiring of non-white workers, even where they were legal. Minority communities mobilized against the second-class citizenship implied in the amnesty proposals, civil rights groups directed more fire at the militarization of the border area, while the Mexican aid and loans package ended up in the boardrooms of major US corporations.

In 1978 Congress established yet another commission, the Select Commission on Immigration and Refugee Policy, 'to study and evaluate ... existing laws, policies and procedures governing the admission of immigrants and refugees to the US'. Martin (1981) summarized the no less than 57 major recommendations in a 453-page report taking three years to complete. Fines against employers, a one-time amnesty for illegal aliens in the US and an increase in legal quotas, combined with stronger enforcement procedures, all made a reappearance. What was new was the Commission's narrow vote (8–7) in favour of a counterfeit-proof social security card to identify legal workers. The analogy with the South African pass system was perhaps too uncomfortable for the dissenting commissioners. The Commission also proposed major changes to refugee policy, some of which were anticipated in the Refugee Act of 1980.

The Select Commission's proposals, the Refugee Act and the sudden 'refugee crisis' in summer 1980, together exposed the paradoxes and problems of US immigration and refugee policy. Though not solely responsible, the political difficulties of trying to ride the refugee tiger damaged Carter electorally. The official total of refugee admissions for 1980 was 50,000, but during the spring and summer of 1980 alone, 125,000 Cubans and 20,000 Haitians sought asylum in the US. In both cases, the mix of ideology, economics and state policy proved explosive. At first Carter endorsed the 20-year-old policy of welcoming refugees from communist countries and offered Cubans an 'open heart and open arms', though carefully qualified by adding, 'in accordance with American law' (Bach et al., 1981–82: 31). Somewhat to Carter's surprise, Castro did not try to deter the would-be emigrants, but instead announced that the revolution was voluntary and that anyone who wished to leave was free to do so. But unlike the 'aerial bridge' of the 1960s or the prisoner releases a decade later, the Cuban government refused to discuss a *controlled* departure programme unless the agenda included talks on the economic boycott, the continuing US occupation of Guantanamo and the end to spy flights over Cuba (Bach et al., 1981–82: 31).

Castro then turned the tables by proclaiming, 'You are the showcase of an opulent society whose keys you refuse to surrender. Agree to face the real problems, or we will unleash the starving pack' (*Guardian Weekly*, 15 June 1980). The electorate decided that Carter showed an unusual capacity for shooting himself in the foot, but it was perhaps unexpected that beating the customary anti-communist drum would have so little effect. Three factors turned what might have been Carter's propaganda victory into Castro's moral coup.

First, Carter failed to take into account the xenophobia that always appears during a recession. With high unemployment, inflation and bleak economic prospects, many Congressmen and large sections of public opinion interpreted Carter's statements as an open-door policy, imposing another burden on the taxpayer and another set of competitors for housing, jobs, education and health facilities.

Second, the mood was fanned by reports that many Cuban entrants were 'socially undesirable', that the Cuban authorities were emptying their jails and mental asylums and rounding up street criminals to load into the boats at Mariel Harbour. One Democratic politician claimed that 'Just about every adult male . . . admitted to having been in prison in Cuba' (quoted in Bach et al., 1981–82: 31), an image reinforced by the riot of 300 Cuban internees at a transit camp in Arkansas. However, as Bach et al. show, the level of criminality was vastly exaggerated and the 1980 entrants did not differ significantly from earlier waves of migrants. They did, however, tend to be younger, with a higher proportion of blacks and mulattoes, were more working class and more likely to be unemployed than earlier waves of Cuban migrants. About 16 percent had been incarcerated in Cuba (Bach et al., 1981–82: 46:47), but although regarded as 'anti-social' there, it is doubtful that many of their activities (minor corruption, petty trading in the shadow economy) would have landed them in jail in the US. There were equally few full-blown political dissenters. While many learned political slogans for opportunistic reasons, it is doubtful that more than a handful held strong anti-socialist convictions.

Third, the Cubans landed and mostly stayed in that hotbed of urban politics, Miami — the closest urban concentration to Cuba and traditionally the Cuban community's major point of settlement. In 1960, when Cubans first started arriving in significant numbers, the city had a fairly typical southern ethnic mix — 80 percent white, 14 percent black and 6 percent Hispanic. Twenty years later, 47 percent were Hispanic with a nearly equivalent proportion of whites. In a *Miami Herald* poll, only 17 percent of 'non-Latin whites' regarded the arrival of Cubans as 'a good thing'. The black minority was so alarmed that sustained rioting began, ostensibly occasioned by the miscarriage of justice in the trial of a black man, but in fact, according to a Harris poll, by the arrival of the Cubans (*Guardian Weekly*, 4 June 1980). A Florida businessman closely mirrored local public opinion by declaring, 'We're Castro's hostages!' (*Guardian Weekly*, 15 June 1980).

Policing the frontier between the US and Haiti was also politically embarrassing for the US administration. Between 1953 and 1976, 745,815 Haitians legally entered the US (Buchanan 1979: 19), fleeing both severe economic impoverishment and the political depredations of Papa Doc and his son, Baby Doc Duvalier, so brilliantly captured in Graham Greene's novel, *The Comedians*. But despite the random violence, beatings and executions perpetrated by the informal arm of government, the Ton-Ton Macoutes, the Haitian government nonetheless gained staunch support from the US — with half its revenue coming from foreign, overwhelmingly US, aid. While permitting some legal migration from Haiti, the US authorities clamped down severely on illegal migration from the island. Legally and ideologically, it was nigh-impossible to admit that a state dedicated to capitalism and heavily supported by US aid, investment and tourist receipts could generate *refugees*. Yet refugees many undoubtedly were — 20,000 Haitians risked their lives in 1980 in overcrowded and leaky boats attempting the boats attempting the 700-mile journey to Miami. To INS officials, Haitians are no different from the illegal Mexican aliens who cross the border on foot (Bogre, 1979: 9), but to many Haitians they are folk heroes making desperate bids to save their plots from ruination and their wives and children from starvation.

Haitian illegals were treated much like their Mexican counterparts until civic groups and attorneys began to publicize cases which clearly fell within the terms of the 1980 Refugee Act, designed to bring the US in line with international norms and defining a refugee as someone unwilling or unable to return to their country of origin 'because of a well founded fear of persecution on account of race, religion, nationality, membership in a particular social group or political opinion'. To legitimate the INS's treatment of Haitian refugees, the State Department commissioned a study which found that 'most Haitian migrants come to the US drawn by the prospect of economic opportunity and [are] not fleeing political persecution .... economic motives, however admirable, do not translate into a right under the Protocol to asylum' (cited in Bogre, 1979: 10). When I add that this conclusion was reached by a study team comprising four white men, in Haiti for three weeks and basing their findings on interviewees publicly recruited through the government-controlled radio station, it is understandable that at least one writer (Bogre, 1979) is sceptical of the report's validity. The political crises surrounding the admission of Cuban and Haitian refugees dramatize the US state's general incapacity to translate its ideological utterances and elaborate regulatory apparati into effective administrative practice. President Reagan has sought to wrestle with the same inconsistencies and has found a similar legislative impasse for his immigration proposals. As I shall show, the European and South African states were better able to match their immigration policy and practices to the racism of their electorates and to the labour-power needs of their industrial and service sectors. But even here, no complete consonance was possible.

**Guestworkers, Settlers and Citizens: European Variations**
In Europe, the state was more effective than in the US in insulating the metropolitan society from mass, uncontrolled migration from the edges of the regional political economy. But there were limits to the scope of state action in Europe too. State intervention took two major forms — policing outer frontiers, by tighter immigration regulations and better border controls, and policing the internal state, by subtler yet more pervasive measures, particularly when prompted to do so in the wake of riot conditions. Germany, France, Britain and Switzerland (the four major European importers of migrant labour) have all implemented both sets of control measures, though in somewhat different ways. As

my concern here is primarily with the labour supply question I have concentrated particularly on the variations in respect of immigration policy.

## Germany

The post-war German model consisted of temporary guestworkers filling immediate gaps in the labour market and then leaving when their services were no longer required. Though at first East German refugees filled all the vacancies at the bottom of the labour market, the German economy's rapid expansion in the 1950s meant an equally rapid expansion in the recruitment of foreign labourers — from 95,000 in 1956 to 507,000 by 1961 and 1.3 million by 1966 (Castles et al., 1984: 72). The foreign labour recruitment system was taken over, virtually intact, from wartime Nazi models, with the Federal Labour Office setting up labour bureaux in the Mediterranean countries. Selection, occupational testing, medical, criminal and political checks were all carried out before entry. The work of the Federal Labour Office was, however, soon supplemented by intergovernmental labour supply contracts with Greece (1960), Turkey (1961 and 1964), Morocco (1963), Portugal (1964), Tunisia (1965) and Yugoslavia (1968) (Castles et al., 1984: 72).

The guestworker system's final test came in 1973 when a ban was imposed on all recruitment from non-EEC countries. Ideally the model implied a permanently rotating labour force, so it should have been easy both to stop new entrants and to expel existing workers as the economy lurched into crisis. In fact the figures show an only moderate decline in foreign worker employment after 1973 and an increase in the number of unemployed foreigners, together with an overall increase in the foreign population. The numbers of foreign residents rose from nearly 3 million in 1970 to 4.1 million in 1974 and 4.6 million in 1982 (Castles et al., 1984: 76). In some ways this growth is surprising given that, in common with Switzerland, Germany had some of the harshest legislation against foreign workers settling with their families. The Foreigners Law of 1965 reinforced the rights of the 'foreigners' police', hardly the most sympathetic authority, to grant or withold residence permits. The instructions given to officials on how to operate the 1965 laws (cited in Castles et al., 1984: 77) are nothing if not explicit:

> Foreigners enjoy all basic rights, except the basic rights of freedom of assembly, freedom of association, freedom of movement and free choice of occupation, place of work and place of education and protection from extradition abroad.

When I add that foreigners have no vote and that birth in Germany does not automatically imply a right to citizenship, it becomes apparent that the post-war German state viewed its foreign workers, especially the Turkish who are most discriminated against, in much the same way as the ancient Spartan state viewed its subject population. Why then did the foreign population in Germany show such a marked rise? First, it should be remembered that at the end of the war the West German constitution-makers sought to distinguish *their* state from its communist counterpart, resulting in an unusually generous constitutional provision for admitting refugees. It was evident that this was intended mainly to benefit East Germans wishing to desert the joys of state socialism, an opportunity many seized until physically prevented from so doing. Apart from providing a useful moral contrast with the political practices of East Germany, the refugees also helped fuel the post-war West German economy with well-trained and compliant labourers. However, it was ideologically impossible to deny similar rights of admission to other refugees — who began to stream into West Germany in significant numbers. Some 300,000 Eritreans, Afghans, Indians, Pakistanis, Vietnamese, Chileans, Argentines and Turks have arrived as 'refugees' since 1979 and now constitute some 40 percent of the foreign population. I use the word 'refugees' in quotes, since there is little doubt that in many cases it was used with a view to circumventing West Germany's otherwise forbidding immigration regulations.

A second factor in the recent growth of the foreign population is that, as Germany sought to represent itself as a morally enlightened member of the EEC and as migrant communities' demands began to escalate, it became politically impossible to deny dependants the right to join their breadwinners in Germany. As this was a relatively recent concession in Germany's migration history (compared, say, with Britain where Commonwealth citizenship permitted family reunification in the 1950s and 1960s for West Indian and most Asian migrants), in Germany the baby boom associated with the reconstitution of families was in the 1970s and 1980s. Third, the numbers of foreign residents also increased because of adverse conditions in Turkey — a combination of economic collapse, brutal authoritarian government and arbitrary exercises of local administrative power made many Turks in Germany reluctant to return, and propelled those who had relatives in Germany to join them before legislative restrictions made this impossible.

In sum, German migration policy represents a combination of strong controls at the manpower planning level, relatively open access to refugees and some recent concessions on the question of family reunification. The result has been what some scholars describe as a dual policy. On the one hand, the migrant communities' social integration is pursued through easier provisions for family unification and naturalization of second-generation migrants. On the other hand, the

German government has fiercely restricted new entrants and in 1982 introduced a scheme for repatriation assistance (a policy even the Thatcher government in Britain has shied away from). The relaxations on naturalization should not, however, be seen in too benevolent a light: they are intended to defuse what is widely recognized as a 'social time bomb', the problem of alienated, sullen and rebellious migrant youth (Castles et al., 1984; Phizacklea, 1983: 99). All that the latest round of reforms in Germany really indicates is that, from an extreme model with no rights of settlement or citizenship, the West German state has been forced to accept the social reality of migrant settlement and has, therefore, begun to converge with its European counterparts.

*France*
During the d'Estaing presidency, the French authorities also systematically linked immigration to employment, social control and repatriation. In July 1979 the French Immigration Minister, Monsieur Stoleru, announced plans to reduce the immigrant population by 200,000 a year. First, the French government offered the equivalent of £1,000 to any unemployed migrant ready to go home — an offer accepted by an estimated 30,000 people per annum in the first years. Second, the National Assembly approved a law allowing the police to hold immigrants for up to 48 hours without charge and to expel any immigrant whose papers were not in order (potentially affecting some 300,000 aliens). Third, it was decided that work permits would be renewed only for periods of one to three years, except for those who had lived in France for a full 20 years, who still would not obtain permanent renewals, but 10 year ones (*Guardian Weekly*, 15 June 1979). Finally, the Interior Minister, Christian Bonnet, set up a system of computerized records which combined residence and work permits on one unforgeable document. About one million foreigners were forced to carry such documents, each of which contained 40 items of information about nationality, residence, employment and dependants. (This obviously enhanced the potential for police surveillance and ultimately mass expulsions.) As an article in *Le Monde* (17 February 1980) put it: 'Such a filing system is unprecedented in France, except perhaps for the register of Jews during the Occupation'.

Fortunately for the migrant community, some of these provisions were modified or expunged in the wake of Mitterand's election. Now, most migrants' children have rights of residence and can normally obtain a work permit, though not necessarily a job. The difficulty of finding employment in a recession has pushed many second-generation immigrants into the shadow (informal) economy, where there are perhaps as many as 400,000 illegal workers. The French government, rather like the US government, offered a one-off amnesty to legalize some of these workers, but the take-up was disappointing and would anyway have involved less than a third of the illegal workers (Verbunt, 1985). To the 400,000 illegal workers are added perhaps another 250,000 political refugees and their families whose fate is determined by the Bureau for the Protection of Regugees and Stateless Persons. France's distinguished record in offering hospitality to political refugees, since Article 120 of the 1793 constitution proclaimed that the French would 'give asylum to foreigners driven from their homeland in freedom's cause. They refuse it to tyrants', is now undermined by the sheer numbers of refugees involved. Senior officials in the State Secretariat regard 'the refugee problem [as] insoluble . . . France can't take charge of the world's 10 million refugees'. Since this shift in the official mood, border police have acquired considerable discretion in deciding who are 'true' refugees (*Le Monde*, 18 January 1981).

## Britain

Since 1962, Britain's immigration Acts have been directed towards slowly removing full British citizenship rights from colonial and Commonwealth citizens. The distinction between 'old' and 'new' Commonwealth was clearly based on racial criteria and intended to separate the white dominions (Canada, Australia and New Zealand) from the Caribbean, black Africa and the Indian subcontinent. White Rhodesians and South Africans of British descent had blotted their copybook by being associated with a Unilateral Declaration of Independence from British authority in the first case, and the creation of a Republic outside the Commonwealth in the second. So although residual Commonwealth rights remained for these two minority white groups, their sins were sufficient to link their fate to that of the so-called 'new' Commonwealth. These categories of 'new' and 'old' were cynically manipulated to discriminate against black entrants. Barbados, for example, had been British since 1627, Canada was only ceded to the British in 1763 — yet the logic of immigration control deemed that the first be designated new Commonwealth, the latter old.

The first attack on Commonwealth entry came in 1962 when the Commonwealth Immigrants Act established a voucher system, linking entry to a prior employment offer. Before this Act became law, immigration from the new Commonwealth rose steeply as dependants joined existing workers and others rushed to 'beat the ban'. The legislation thus served to precipitate family settlement, even when only temporary migration was contemplated. By 1964, only professional or highly skilled workers obtained work permits. In 1968, another Commonwealth Immigrants Act was passed whereby possession of a UK passport no longer entitled the holder to free entry. Three years later there was yet another Act, this time restricting the rights of dependants to join their families in the UK and further specifying the link between a work permit and permission to enter and reside. By 1982, so few work permits were being issued to potential entrants that 90 percent of those accepted for settlement were dependants still trying to struggle through the labyrinths of bureaucratic red tape strung out to impede their entry.

The Nationality Act of 1981 phased out the major remaining distinctions between Commonwealth citizens and aliens. Citizenship by registration was replaced by naturalization which takes five years, is discretionary, and subject to tests of language and good conduct (Castles et al., 1984: 46). Moreover, the principle of equating birthplace with nationality was changed, making nationality dependent on parental status irrespective of whether a child is born in the UK. The Nationality Act not only demotes Commonwealth citizens to the status of aliens at home, but also includes two new classes of citizenship for those with British connections abroad — British Overseas citizenship and citizenship of the British Dependent Territories. The first, mainly covering holders of dual citizenship in Malaysia, neither permits right of abode in any British territory, nor is transmittable to descendants. In short, it effectively invites the holder to take out local citizenship and abandon all hope of Britain retaining its colonial responsibilities (Layton-Henry, 1982: 30). The 'citizen of the British Dependent Territories' category is significant for possible future migratory patterns. This part of the Act was probably directed largely at residents of Hong Kong with the intention of excluding the three million Hong Kong Chinese, who might otherwise have been eligible, from entering Britain in the event of mass panic as 1997 approaches. (In 1997 China is due to repossess her territory ceded to the British under what the Chinese call the 'unequal treaties'.) At first, some obfuscation of this target was successful. For example, in Parliamentary debate the British government denied that the Act was 'racist' and, to demonstrate its impartiality, included the (white) residents of the Falklands/Malvinas in the same category of citizenship. When Thatcher went to war to defend the liberties of these British subjects in their struggle against the iron heel of the Argentine *junta*, it no longer became politically viable to deny the Falkland islanders the right to enter Britain. So, at the end of the war, this prohibition was quietly dropped from the Falklanders' passports, but retained for the Gibraltarians, St Helenians and Hong Kong Chinese.

## Switzerland

The fourth and final European country, Switzerland, has a long anti-statist, open-door tradition regarding tax matters and capital movements and had an almost equally long tradition of denying foreigners access to the material delights of its successful bourgeois civilization. Even in Switzerland, however, nearly half a million foreigners had by the 1980s managed to acquire residence permits (excluding the 10,000 *frontaliers* who commute across the frontier each day and the 110,000 'seasonal' workers on permits of nine months or less) (*Guardian Weekly*, 12 April 1981). Since 1931, when the Law of Foreigners was drawn up, the Swiss state has vigorously policed its frontiers. But so dependent were the post-war Swiss manufacturing and service industries on foreign labour that all the state could do was try to regulate labour movements as tightly as possible. The Swiss citizenry, for its part, was happy to benefit from foreign labour, but periodically activated plebiscites against 'over-foreignization', which has led to even tighter restrictions. Under Swiss law, a foreigner must possess a Permit of Abode, of Residence or of Tolerance. The Permit of Abode is the main instrument of control, and since 1970 the annual quota has been fixed at 10,000 a year. It is issued for a year and is subject to a labour market vacancy and good conduct. A migrant wishing to take up citizenship would have to wait for at least 12 years. Individual communes and cantons impose additional periods which are non-transferable from one canton to another, while many impose a further financial hurdle by charging naturalization fees of up to 70,000 Swiss francs (Hoffman-Nowotny, 1982).

**Influx Controls and Labour Bureaux: the South African Way**
In this section, I examine attempts, particularly recent attempts, by the South African state to manage and control supplies of labour-power to South African industry, agriculture and mining, as well as to control the growth of black urban townships.

At the heart of the control system is the 'pass' — an internal passport serving as an identity document indicating work, residence status, 'nationality' (including the fabricated 'homelands' nationality accorded to all blacks) and police record. White South African officialdom likes using the term 'influx' to describe the movement of African labourers. It suggests a natural process unassociated with the mines' almost insatiable historical demand for black gang labour. But insofar as an 'influx' suggests an inanimate phenomenon, akin to a rising tide, it would seem appropriate for the representatives of 'civilization' to erect dykes and canals to control this threat. In fact, the control measures are implemented on a huge scale. In one study, Savage estimated that since the turn of the century, 17 million blacks had been arrested under the South African pass laws. In another, West showed that about 10 percent of adult blacks in Cape Town are likely to be arrested *each year*. Women are particularly singled out as pass offenders as the authorities rightly see their presence as a harbinger for establishing black families in the area (*Lincoln Letter*, July 1984). Implementation of the pass laws depends on the arrestee's status under the provisions of the Bantu (Urban Areas) Consolidation Act of 1946. Section 10 of the Act stipulates that no African may remain in an urban or peri-urban area longer than 72 hours unless the 'visitor' 'qualifies' to be there. Qualification lies in continuous residence since birth (Section 10/1/a), continuous working for one employer for 10 years (Section 10/1/b) or a restricted possibility for immediate family to join a male breadwinner (Section 10/1/c). Those qualifying under these provisions are the permanent, stable, urban residents whom the post-1948 Nationalist Party government were forced to accept and could not 'endorse out' to the homelands or force into the contract labour system. Consequently, they constitute the core of the black urban working class in service, domestic and manufacturing employment. The terms 'Section 10 workers' or 'Section Tenners' are often applied to such residents who have gained an entitlement to live in a black urban township like Soweto (the South Western Townships) near Johannesburg.

Section 10 also provides for workers to stay in an urban area with permission from a local labour bureau. But since the bureaux invariably give permission only to short-term contract workers, it is a way of controlling migrant worker registrations rather than permitting another route into permanent urban residence. In 1968, the Regulations for Labour Bureaux stipulated that blacks could not qualify for urban residence by continually renewing short contracts until the 10-year period was fulfilled (Wages Commission, n.d.: 18–19). Nonetheless, this ruling was successfully challenged by a machine operator, Mehlolo Rikhoto, in a case which went to the Court of Appeal in 1983. The Minister of Co-operation and Development, who estimated that 143,000 migrant workers might benefit from the Rikhoto decision, decided to accept the judgement but block the loophole by insisting that such workers and their families be housed in 'approved housing'. As there was already an officially recognized shortage of 260,000 houses, this provided an immediately effective deterrent to any other workers wishing to emulate Mr. Rikhoto (*African Labour News*, August 1983).

The distinction between Section Tenners and contract workers hardened into a distinction between stable and migrant labourers, the latter being routed either through the mines' private system of recruitment or through the state's labour bureaux. These bureaux provide the institutional basis for classifying, funneling and further regulating labour power. They have existed in embryonic form since the turn of the century, but their number and powers increased sharply with the 1964 Bantu Labour Act, the 1965 Bantu Labour Regulations and the 1968 Regulations for Labour Bureaux. These measures provided a network of 1,300 labour bureaux to cover every city, town, village or rural area in the country — areas classified as 'prescribed' ('white' industrial and residential areas where Section Tenners are the predominant black labour force); 'non-prescribed', (where 'district' labour bureaux supply mostly agricultural labour to the farming communities); and 'homeland' areas. Two aspects of the homeland bureaux, hierarchized into 'territorial', 'district' and 'tribal' offices and constituting the effective base of the system, are important. First, they are directly accountable to the Central Labour Bureau in Pretoria, thus exposing the apartheid myth that these areas are in some measure 'independent' (Wages Commission, nd: 20). Second, they initiate the primary classification system. The 'Tribal Labour Office' is given responsibility for classifying every 'workseeker' into one of the 17 categories of employment — e.g. 'agriculture', 'mining', 'domestic', 'construction' or even 'unemployable'. Registration as a 'workseeker' is *compulsory* for all adult males over the age of 15 but in a classic demonstration of Orwellian logic, workseekers are not allowed to seek work, but must wait their turn at the tribal labour bureaux (Regulation 21 of 1968). This primary segmentation of the labour force is then reinforced by three further control meansures. First, there must be a contract, without which workseekers cannot be employed. Employees are not allowed to negotiate or enforce the terms of their contracts, even where these offer some modest protection. Characteristically, these terms are unkown to the worker and compliance is assumed after a process of mass thumb-printing. Second, the labour bureaux structure the *occupational* mix according to manpower demands by refusing to reclassify workers' categories of employment unless they select 'farming' or 'mining', the two most unpopular categories. Third, the labour bureaux control *geographical* destinations by registering workers only for zones with a shortage of labour-power. Again, changes of zone would always be made to the most unpopular area.

This system of labour regulation worked reasonably well until the 1970s when riots, boycotts, strikes and other forms of worker resistance began to shake the structures of the apartheid system. These protests were highlighted by a wave of strikes in 1973 (Dekker et al., 1975; Institute for Industrial Education, 1979) and an uprising in Soweto in 1976 (Hirson, 1979). The state tried to restore political stability by initiating a number of constitutional reforms with accompanying changes to the structures of industrial relations and labour control. Because commissions set up to review these structures were established in the wake of unrest and with a public rhetoric suggesting reform (see *South African Newsletter*), the extent of change was frequently exaggerated. Often the proposals sought to rationalize, consolidate and modernize existing state practices rather than provide genuine alternatives. In other cases, the Commissions recognized they could do little to reverse the level of class struggle and merely sought to channel it into acceptable directions.

The most relevant commissions here are the Wiehahn Commission — its recommendations resulted in the 1981 Labour Relations Act — and the Riekert Commission, which submitted its report in 1978. The Labour Relations Act permitted Africans to organize and join *registered* trade unions which, moreover, could be multi-racial. The qualifying adjective 'registered' was important because it subjected unions to financial and other checks by inspectors, aimed partly at ensuring that registered unions steered clear of political organizations and involvement, had no significant foreign links and would not grant strike pay to workers illegally on strike. These checks and restrictions were later also applied to 'unregistered' unions, which had to have ministerial approval to operate a 'check-off' system (Cooper, 1981). The new labour relations order was a recognition that in the wake of massive industrial unrest the state had no alternative but to accept unionization and, given this, it was better to talk to legally-sanctioned representatives who might be amenable to state control than to spontaneously generated leaderships, unknown to the Labour Inspectorate. Though the provisions of the new Act applied to all workers, migrant or Section Tenners, there is little doubt that stabilized workers benefited more from the Act, in that they were more likely to join and sustain trade unions.

The Riekert Commission (1978) not only reinforced the stabilized urban population's relatively privileged status, but also extended and refined the system of labour control in a number of important directions. Although not all the Commission's recommendations became legislation, its report is crucial in understanding the broad direction of change in the labour supply system upon which the major planks of apartheid rest. It represents a highly sophisticated attempt to design a segmented labour market by state intervention and therefore merits close attention by students of comparative labour regimes. On the supply of manpower, the report (Riekert, 1978: 24) states:

> The most important question is whether the right quantity of labour at the right *quality* will be available at the right *time* and the right *place* to satisfy the demand ... [its] availability is determined by ... (a) the optimal allocation of the available pool of artisan and technically skilled workers in accordance with demand conditions; (b) the *timely* training of an adequate number of workers ... (c) the horizontal and vertical mobility of labour. The horizontal and vertical mobility of labour is determined mainly by ... (a) statutory, administrative and traditional constraints, (b) the preferences of workers and employers, (c) wage differences and (d) the availability of housing.

The net result of this agenda was to rationalize and harden existing boundaries between the different labour markets by reinforcing discretionary and statutory differences. White and coloured (mixed race) workers in artisanal or supervisory positions would obviously retain their rights to organization and labour mobility (with the constraint for the coloureds of having to live in a designated group area). However, a new group was to enter these 'privileged' ranks (though at a lower level). Section Tenners would be given the right to join trade unions, more mobility in terms of influx control (e.g. the right to move between zones), higher wages and increased access to housing (Claasens et al., 1980: 34). The housing concession is interesting in that strict apartheid doctrine forbids blacks to *own* property in 'white areas'. The compromise effected by the Soweto riots permitted 99-year leases with an option to renew, thus satisfying apartheid doctrine on the one hand, and recognizing the need for labour stabilization and African demands on the other. The ideology will have to be readjusted again in the aftermath of the 1985 disturbances, when further concessions on property rights were presaged.

While Riekert undoubtedly strengthened the position of Section 10 blacks, he separated their fate from other categories of workers — migrants, foreign workers, commuters and the unemployed. In each case, the Commission recommended improving the organizational and institutional structures that policed these areas. For example, instead of closing the labour bureaux, Riekert argued that the South African system was fundamentally similar to employment services in the UK, the USA and West Germany. He acknowledged that 'the general image of local labour bureaux in the eyes of employers and workseekers is very poor for a number of reasons, including their link with: influx control, unpopular types of employers who cannot succeed in recruiting workers and workseekers who cannot find work for themselves, and staff who are not trained for this type of work' (Riekert, 1978: 140–144). However, he felt that these faults were not intrinsic. Staff had to be better trained, private employment offices should also be allowed (under the control of the Department of Labour) to offer their services and separate service points should be established for professional, clerical and unskilled workers. In one area the Commission even proposed that workseekers need not register at the bureaux, thus placing men in the same category as women. Riekert (1978: 144), however, was in no doubt as to the continued relevance of the bureaux:

> A programme of action should be initiated to ensure the efficient functioning of the labour bureau system ... because it fulfills an important role in connection with the olderly canalisation of labour and the supply of labour in accordance with the demand for it.

Along with improving the functioning of the labour bureaux, the report tidied up other 'anomalies'. For example, three of South Africa's major industrial areas are in Pretoria, Durban and East London, close to existing 'bantustans'. Many workers from Kwazulu, Bophuthatswana and the Ciskei tried to acquire Section 10 rights by commuting across these rather nominal boundaries, but Riekert put a stop to this by ruling that commuters could not quality for Section 10 rights. He also rationalized the interstate treaties regulating the supply of labour from foreign African countries. Finally, his report contained forceful recommendations designed to cut down on 'illegality', which is discussed in the next section on illegal workers.

The South African system of labour regulation essentially polices external frontiers through immigration checks and interstate foreign labour contracts, and internal frontiers (between racially defined residential and industrial areas) through influx control. What attracts such opprobrium to the South African system is that the state apparatus uses particularly brutal methods to enforce influx control and, in the past, used influx control to turn the indigenous (and voteless) blacks into a foreign population. The Riekert Commission's recognition that Section Tenners are irremovable has improved and stabilized conditions for long-standing urban blacks (10 to 15 percent of the black population as a whole), but for the majority, the apartheid state continues to present a brutal and unremitting face.

### Illegal Workers: Control and Evasion

In examining immigration and labour control policies in the US, Europe and South Africa, I indicated how each had a somewhat different capacity to police their frontiers and to enforce the central authority's will. In each case the state regulated the flow of labourers through a battery of immigration checks and other administrative means. The US at one point even tried to imitate the builders of the Great Wall of China by using barbed wire, dogs, infra-red scanners and helicopters along the Rio Grande. But this was soon whittled down to a few publicity-seeking, but ineffective, border control measures. Why do these states — even one as powerful and wealthy as the US or as authoritarian as South Africa — have so much difficulty enforcing their immigration and labour regulations? How widespread is illegal migration and how do we interpret its nature and significance?

I want to return first to the US, where the scholarly and political debate about illegal workers is more sharply drawn, before making brief comparisons with the other powerful states in the remaining regional political economies. In the US, illegal migration was estimated at between eight and twelve million in 1978, with a further half to one million illegals arriving annually. Illegal workers hold about a third of the full-time low-skilled jobs in the country (Wachter, 1978: 80). In particular sectors, notably agribusiness, the service sector, textile sweatshops and some manufacturing industries, illegal workers are numerically so significant that these industries would be unable to compete internationally without them. For example, in considering the competitiveness of the New York apparel industry in the face of cheap imports, deWind (1982: 12) writes:

> How have those garment manufacturers still in New York City survived? By producing short-run fast-moving goods and by cutting down labour costs — and that, very often, means hiring undocumented workers. Competing with international producers, New York employers have set wages too low to attract a full supply of American workers . . . . The undocumented workers who take jobs in the garment industry can hardly be accused of taking these jobs away from anyone else.

Such a depiction, which is common among US academics with a liberal political orientation (e.g. Priore, 1975, 1979; Cornelius, nd), assumes the existence of a dual labour market. Priore (1975), in effect, abolishes the problem of illegal migration insofar as immigration restrictions are concerned. If illegals are filling jobs in a separate labour market from that in which indigenous workers compete, cutting down illegal worker entry will not solve the domestic unemployment problem and may well damage sectors of US industry. Of course, even if we concede that the illegal workers' labour market is separable (or largely separable) from the legal one, this does not mean that the authorities can ignore illegal workers. As Rosberg (1978: 340) points out:

> Respect for the rule of law cannot be enhanced by the spectacle of widespread defiance of our immigration laws and the ineffectuality of law-enforcement efforts . . . and beyond the symbolic problem, the fact that many persons are now living outside the law as an underground labour force is itself troubling. To conceal their presence, illegal entrants may feel compelled to withhold payment of taxes, keep their children out of school, tolerate substandard wages and working conditions, decline to seek badly needed medical attention, and take other steps that may injure themselves as well as those around them.

Viewing illegal migration as economically beneficial (or at least not harmful) even with its consequential social problems is, however, unacceptable to US officialdom. Even if their logic is faulty, such officials have enormous public support in their campaigns against illegal workers. When, for example, General Chapman argued in a *Readers Digest* article (Chapman, 1976: 654) that 'the vast and silent invasion of illegal immigrants across our borders is reaching the proportions of a national disaster', he was undoubtedly articulating a common sentiment. Moreover, many US citizens would concur in

Secretary of Labour, Roy Marshall's statement (cited in deWind, 1982: 4) that:

> It is false to say American workers cannot be found for all the jobs filled by undocumented workers . . . no matter how undesirable the jobs may be . . . eliminating this displacement would bring unemployment down to 3.7 percent.

While the balance of logic and evidence backs a dual labour market rather than a displacement argument, dual labour market theorists should remember that the social conditions that determine job choice are not static. Workers with job security, good wages, a recognized skill and union protection are unlikely immediately to go down-market to a job characteristically occupied by an illegal migrant, even if faced with unemployment. If, however, conditions become sufficiently desperate, expectations can and do change and some job competition may arise. Apart from the problem of shifting expectations, both sets of theory largely ignore the institutional and sociological parameters that regulate and control the flow of workers and illegal migrants to particular job destinations. These include the policies and practices of labour-related agencies in both sending and receiving countries, the degree of a worker's attachment to an existing community, the activities of the *coyotes* (labour recruiters), union closed-shop norms, prior training, and many other factors making for an imperfect labour market.

But overriding shifting job expectations and the labour market's other non-economic determinants is the role of employers in shaping the extent and contours of the market for illegal labour. As Petras indicates in our opening quote, the state is responsible for enforcing or relaxing border controls in the interests of dominant classes *as a whole*. On the other hand, employers' sectoral interests do not necessarily correspond to the hegemonic and collective interests of their class, thus leading to constant wars of attrition between sectional employer interests and the state over the question of illegal migration. Now a blind eye is cast in the direction of agribusiness, now a threatening gesture is made to fine employers of illegal workers. But as long as this remains a subdued war of positions, illegal workers will be able to evade state controls (often in very precarious circumstances) with the effective connivance of employers ready to exploit a subordinate cheap labour force. Given the powerful lobbying capacity of agribusiness (in particular) and the non-interventionist and pluralist philosophy of government that legitimates the US state, it is doubtful, despite periodic ideological and short-term drives against illegal migrants, that the US government will ever be able to grasp the nettle of complete control over the traffic in illegal labour-power. Seen more analytically and comparatively, such total control implies five elements:

1. *A tight border*, possible in the UK since it has no contiguous land frontier, but difficult in the US with its shared borders with Mexico and Canada, its proximity to the Caribbean archipelago, and the sheer volume of passenger movements for trade, tourism and education.

2. *Public support* for a complete clamp-down. This existed in Switzerland where public plebiscites and action at the canton level against 'over-foreignization' forced the state into rigorously policing the system whatever the labour-power demands of Swiss employers. In the US, such support is periodically forthcoming, but cannot be universal given the bonds of co-ethnicity that significant sections of the electorate share with illegal workers.

3. *Employer penalties*. In the US, the employer invariably escapes attention from the law. Even the Carter and Reagan administrations' tenative moves to fine employers of illegal labour were frustrated or turned into such insignificant penalities that they do not act as a strong deterrent. In South Africa also, employer penalties have been weak historically and it is only because of the Riekert Commission recommendations that the government has moved more vigorously against employers of illegal labour. A bill before Parliament in 1982 raised fines for such employers from R500 to R5,000. The fine could be imposed as an alternative or in addition to a one-year prison sentence. The bill also provided for a R500 fine for anyone sheltering 'unauthorized' blacks (*Guardian Weekly*, 12 September 1982).

4. *Police enforcement* of laws against illegal workers is vital to the success of a state's campaign to restrict entry. Here the Europeans offer interesting contrasts. Traditionally, Britain relied on tight border controls and fairly weak internal police surveillance, whereas the French did the opposite. In France the local gendarmerie usually controlled the issue of residence permits and tended to know all about the foreigners in their district. Over the years a certain congruence has developed as France has strengthened her border controls and British local police constabularies have been amalgamated and brought more firmly under Home Office control. From the number of pass offenders caught, the South African police can be seen as shouldering a Sisyphean task with dogged and ruthless determination. But given the confusion of authority between city, state and federal policy and the variety of identification documents accepted in the US, it is doubtful whether the INS will ever be able to mount a campaign on the South African scale.

5. *State labour recruitment* is important in circumventing the employer's role in encouraging illegal work. In South Africa, mining companies have been allowed to organize their own private recruitment system since before the turn of the century and the Riekert Commission has further extended this privilege. However, these agencies are under relatively firm state control and the state plays an important role in

recruiting labour in its own right through the labour bureaux system. West Germany and, to some extent, France also recruited labour through intergovernmental contracts — with employers having to ask for labourers via government agencies. The Bracero Program in the US is another example of governmental labour recruiting, but it only covered a limited number of workers compared to the flow of undocumented workers recruited directly by employers. As Table 1 shows, only South Africa comes close to a complete control system.

TABLE 1
Control measures against illegal workers

|  | *Strong* | *Intermediate/ Intermittent* | *Weak* |
|---|---|---|---|
| (a) Tight Border | SA UK | Sw   WG | US   Fr |
| (b) Public Support | SA Sw | Fr   WG UK | US |
| (c) Employer Penalties | SA | WG Sw   UK | US   Fr |
| (d) Police Enforcement | SA Fr   Sw | WG US UK | |
| (e) State Labour Recruitment | SA WG | Fr   US | Sw   UK |

*Key:* US = United States of America
UK = United Kingdom
Sw = Switzerland
WG= West Germany
Fr = France
SA = South Africa

Illegal workers who evade the traps set for them by the state can be understood in a variety of ways. They can be depicted in heroic terms — as people refusing to allow their potential to be crushed by unjust governments, exploitative employers or adverse circumstances. Certainly, the gauntlet that has to be run by today's illegal migrants is far more formidable than that run by the immigrants of the turn of the century, whose stories have often been depicted in epic terms. Alternatively, the illegal worker can be seen more coldly, as a calculating economic being — weighing up costs and benefits, risks and opportunities, in a rational decision to beat the system. Undoubtedly there are such individuals among the millions of illegal workers who evade state control. Unfortunately, however, from numerous biographical and observational accounts, it seems that the mass of illegal workers are usually neither romantic heroes of the wild frontier, nor amateur micro-econometricians. Rather, they are sad, fearful, pathetic individuals desperate to escape intolerable conditions at the periphery of the regional political economy, thrown about by forces they at first only dimly comprehend, and forced to accept conditions of housing, employment and health care that permit a maximum level of exploitation. Such individuals, like many other migrant workers, are ideologically habituated into tolerating, even if not accepting, such conditions and are only slowly able to build the structures of personal and collective resistance to their fate.

## References

*African Labour News* (various issues), Brussels.

Bach, R.L., J.B. Bach and T. Triplett (1981 – 82) 'The "Flotilla Entrants": Latest and Most Controversal', *Cuban Studies*, 11(2) and 12(1): 30 – 48, July (1981) – January (1982).

Boggs, S.W. (1940) *International Boundaries: A Study of Boundary Functions and Problems.* New York: Columbia University Press.

Bogre, M. (1979) 'Haitian Refugees: (Haiti's) Missing Persons', *Migration Today*, 8(4): 9 – 11.

Buchanan, S.H. (1979) 'Haitian Women in New York City', *Migration Today*, 8(4): 19 – 25.

Castles, S. with H. Booth and T. Wallace (1984) *Here for Good: Western Europe's New Ethnic Minorities.* London: Pluto Press.

Chapman, L.F. (1976) 'Illegal Aliens: Time to Call a Halt', *Readers Digest*, 109(October).

Claasens, A., A. Sitas, P. Tobiansky and J. Yawitch (1980) 'The Reserve Army, Legislation and Labour Action in South Africa', *Africa Perspective*, 14: 34 – 46.

Cooper, C. (1981) 'Verdicts on South Africa's New Labour Act', *Africa Bureau*, Document Paper 27. London: African Publications Trust, November/December.

Cornelius, W. (nd) 'Briefing Paper on Illegal Mexican Migration to the US'. Prepared for the National Security Council. Cambridge: Massachussetts Institute of Technology.

Dekker, L.D., D. Hemson, J.S. Kane-Berman, J. Lever and L. Schlemmer (1975) 'Case Studies in Labour Action in South Africa and Namibia', in R. Sandbrook and R. Cohen (eds.), *The Development of an African Working Class: Studies in Class Formation and Action.* London: Longman.

deWind, J. (1982) 'Undocumented Workers and the Labour Market, the Impact of Employers'. Unpublished paper presented at the 44th Congress of Americanists. Manchester: University of Manchester, September.

*Guardian Weekly* (various issues), Manchester.

Hennessy, A. (1978) *The Frontier in Latin American History.* London: Edward Arnold.

Hirson, B. (1979) *Year of Fire, Year of Ash: The Soweto Revolt, Roots of a Revolution?.* London: Zed Press.

Hoffman-Nowotny, H.J. (1982) 'Immigration Policy in Switzerland', Draft Report for the Study of Swedish and European Immigration Policy. Zurich: Soziologisches Institut, University of Zurich.

Institute for Industrial Education (1979) 'The Durban Strikes: South Africa 1973', in R. Cohen, P.C.W. Gutkind and P. Brazier (eds.), *Peasants and Proletarians: The Struggle of Third World Workers.* London: Hutchinson.

Layton-Henry, Z. (1982) 'British Immigration Policy since 1945'. Mimeographed paper. Coventry: Department of Politics, University of Warwick.

*Le Monde* (various issues), Paris.

*Lincoln Letter: X-Ray on South Africa* (various issues). Periodic Newsletter issued by the Lincoln Trust, London and New York.

Martin, P.L. (1981) 'Immigration 1981: The US Debate'. Unpublished paper.

Massey, D. (1984) *Spatial Divisons of Labour: Social Structures and the Geography of Production.* London: Macmillan.

NACLA (1977) 'Immigration: Facts and Fallacies'. Pamphlet.

Pandya, A. and P.A. Schey (1981) 'Analysis of the Reagan Immigration/Refugee Plan', *Immigration Law Bulletin*, 2(3): July – August.

Petras, E. (1980) 'The Role of National Boundaries in a Cross- National Labour Market', *International Journal of Urban and Regional Research*, 4(2): 157 – 195.

Phizacklea, A. (ed.) (1983) *One Way Ticket: Migration and Female Labour*. London: Routledge and Kegan Paul.

Prescott, J.R.V. (1965) *The Geography of Frontiers and Boundaries*. London: Hutchinson.

Priore, M. (1975) 'The Illegals: Restrictions Aren't the Answer', *The New Republic*, 172 (February).

Priore, M. (1979) *Birds of Passage: Migrant Labour and Industrial Societies*. Cambridge: Cambridge University Press.

Riekert Commission (1978) *Commission of Inquiry into Legislation affecting the Utilization of Manpower (Excluding the Legislation administered by the Departments of Labour and Mines)* (Chairman P.J. Riekert). Pretoria: Government Printer.

Rosberg, G. (1978) 'Legal Regulation of the Migration Process: The "Crises" of Illegal Immigration', in W.H. McNeill and R.S. Adams (eds.), *Human Migration: Patterns and Policies*. Bloomington: Indiana University Press.

Short, J.R. (1982) *An Introduction to Political Geography*. London: Routledge and Kegan Paul.

*South African Newsletter*. Periodic handouts from the South African Embassy in London.

Turner, F.J. (1962) *The Frontier in American History*. New York: Holt, Rinehart and Winston.

Verbunt, G. (1985) 'France', in T. Hammer (ed.), *European Immigration Policy*. Cambridge: Cambridge University Press.

Wachter, M.L. (1978) 'Second Thoughts about Illegal Immigrants', *Fortune*, 22(May): 78 – 86.

Wages Commission (n.d.) *Riekert: Don't Worry, Everything's Okay*. Mimeographed pamphlet. Cape Town: Students Representative Council, University of Cape Town.

# 6
# Women Electronics Workers in Southeast Asia: the Emergence of a Working Class
## Vivian Lin

The structure of the world capitalist system has taken on new dimensions in recent times. Whereas the early period of colonization was characterized by plunder and the more recent phase of neo-colonialism by the production of raw materials in less developed countries (LDCs), manufacturing processes of commodities have now become increasingly divided and production facilities are increasingly located in LDCs which are promoting themselves as 'export platforms'. This phenomenon has been labelled by theorists as a 'new international division of labour' (Frobel et al., 1980). The electronics industry has been seen as an example par excellence of the new international division of labour, where transnational corporations (TNCs) gear their production more profitably towards existing markets at home by taking advantage of international wage differentials.

The changes in the structure of production, especially in the electronics industry, has meant a shift of world attention to Asia. Since the mid-1960s, Asian countries have vied successfully for foreign manufacturing investments. The electronics industry, a dynamic and diverse industry with an international assembly line, has a substantial presence in Asia, as regards both the number of firms and the number of workers employed. The industry has been considered to be central to the 'economic miracle' that has occurred in many Asian countries.

In its operations in Asia, the electronics industry has brought large numbers of women into the manufacturing workforce. While women have always worked — in agriculture and in the urban informal sector — in Asian and other LDCs, women dominating the workforce in world market factories is an historically unprecedented event. The impact of these developments has been of interest worldwide. Journalistic accounts and social research in the late 1970s pointed mostly to the negative impact of the industry on the lives of women electronics workers. On the job, they were said to be paid low wages for long hours; they worked rotating shifts and frequent overtime; they were exposed to a variety of health hazards; their femininity was the basis of supervisory control and manipulation; they learned few skills on the job and had little or no prospects for job advancement. Outside the factory, it was said that they lived in crowded conditions, could not afford to eat well, had little time for recreation or family visits, were not accepted by the local community, and had little opportunity to meet men. It is argued that their backgrounds — young, unmarried, with little education, coming from rural areas — made them ideal employees from the management's viewpoint. These reports pointed to the ruthless exploitation, in the pejorative sense, of workers by TNCs. Such documentation of 'exploitation' further pointed to the injustices of this newest phase of world capitalist development.

This chapter describes some changes in the workforce profile and in the lives of the workers in the 1980s. The data are based on a survey of 903 workers (with 11 percent subsample interview) in five semiconductor factories in Singapore and Penang, Malaysia. Interviews with management personnel and participant observation within the factories supplement the survey and interview data. While the results apply specifically to the Singaporean and Malaysian social formations, they may also suggest general trends in other East and Southeast Asian countries.

The study results suggest that, rather than a temporary workforce whose lives are manipulated at the whim of management (or dictated purely by the economic imperatives of the industry), a new working class is emerging. Work is no longer a short-term, pre-marriage phenomenon. The experience of industrial work has brought changes to workers' lives, their identity, and their motivation and expectations. While the emergence of this new working class occurs within the context of the internationalization of capital, the dynamics and development processes internal to the social formation may be more important than the new international division of labour in shaping the development of the new working class. The chapter will first briefly describe relevant background on the development of the semiconductor industry in Asia and in Singapore and Malaysia in particular. Characteristics of the labour force, working conditions, and workers' lives are then presented, contrasting the findings of the existing literature with the results of this study. The implications of these changes are raised in the final section.

## The Semiconductor Industry in Asia

The semiconductor industry is a most important and dynamic segment of the electronics industry. Coming into being in the 1950s with the development of the transistor, the industry mushroomed in the 1960s, when the integrated circuit (IC) was developed and the demand for computers grew. By the early 1970s, there were 96 US companies producing semiconductors.

Although the types of ICs are numerous, the production processes fall into the same basic flow: mask-making, wafer fabrication, assembly and testing (Oldham, 1977). The workforce that is required for the production of semiconductors consists of a large number of talented scientists and engineers and a large number of semi-skilled and unskilled production workers (US Department of Commerce, 1979). Because the production process can be segmented easily into the four steps, because the products are small and lightweight, and because manufacturers need to hold labour costs down, American semiconductor firms began to set up an international assembly line in the 1960s. European and Japanese competitors followed quickly thereafter.

The semiconductor industry's search for off-shore locations coincided with the adoption of export-oriented industrialization strategies by many Asian countries. To attract foreign investments, Asian governments set up free trade zones and offered a variety of incentives — tax holidays, waiver of import duties, unlimited repatriation of profits, control of labour-organizing activities, etc. Although these governments were interested in all types of direct foreign investments, what they got were electronics (of all types), garment, footwear, toys and other labour-intensive factories.

The first semiconductor assembly plant in Asia was set up in Hong Kong in 1962. The gate was opened to Taiwan in 1964, Korea in 1966, Singapore in 1968, Malaysia in 1973, and Thailand, the Philippines and Indonesia in 1974. The Caribbean area and Mexico also have assembly plants although Asia has been the preferred region for off-shore sourcing. In all these countries, the semiconductor firms were involved in the most labour-intensive process of production — assembly. By the late 1970s nearly every established US semiconductor firm was engaged in some off-shore assembly. Economic imperatives were important in the move to develop a global assembly line. In surveys of industry leaders (Saxenian, 1981; Lim, 1978), the most important reason cited for locating overseas is low wages. Other issues identified as important locational factors for the corporations were: cost, reliability and accessibility of transportation and communications; tax holidays and other investment incentives; proximity to local markets; local infrastructure; and political stability (including ability to control labour unrest).

All of the off-shore operations employ large numbers of women. While fewer than 50 percent of the workers employed by manufacturing industries in Asia are women, the proportion of women among electronics workers in these same countries ranges from 75 to 90 percent (Eisold, 1982; International Labour Office, 1982). Thus, women's concentration in the electronics industry is disproportionately high.

A variety of reasons have been given by company management and researchers for the preference for female labour (Grossman, 1979; UNIDO, 1980; Frobel et al., 1980; Lim, 1978; Elson and Pearson, 1980; Eisold, 1982). These are: physical characteristics (that women have nimble fingers, agile hands and keen eyesight and so are more efficient and careful then men); social and cultural attitudes and behaviour (that women are more patient, more co-operative, easier to control and so more respectful of authority, more passive and obedient, and more malleable than men); and position in the labour market (wages that women earn in LDCs are even lower than prevailing wages for men, as women are seen to be without financial obligations and without career aspirations).

For these reasons, the electronics companies have sought out women workers in Asia for labour-intensive, monotonous, repetitive and low-wage jobs with no career prospects. Today, in most Asian countries, the electronics industry accounts for a large proportion of the female labour force. Within the electronics industry, semiconductor firms have been the largest employers.

**Developments in Singapore and Malaysia**
Formed in 1957, the Federation of Malaysia is made up of 11 states on the peninsular mainland and the territories of Sabah and Sarawak in north Borneo. The total population is 13.8 million, with 55 percent Bumiputra (Malay and other indigenous peoples), 35 percent Chinese, and 10 percent Indian. The island of Singapore, located at the tip of the Malayan peninsula, was originally part of the Federation but became an independent city-state in 1965. Its population today is 2.4 million, with 76 percent Chinese, 15 percent Malay, and 9 percent Indian. Because of their geographical positions, trade and migration have been important historical themes for both countries. It was during the period of British rule, beginning in the 1800s, that the bases for present-day political and economic developments were laid. British rule established the framework of a dependent export economy, hardened the lines of racial division, and developed the infrastructure necessary for surplus extraction and industrialization. By the time of independence, there already existed a pool of wage labour (one highly segmented along racial lines), an education system (also racially segregated), a communications and transportation system, as well as the legal and administrative apparatus serving the requirements of a market economy dependent on price fluctuations in the world market. The rationale given for export-oriented industrialization by Singapore and

Penang is similar, if not simple or logical. Both are islands with few resources besides their people, and unemployment rates were high in the 1960s. Both are experienced free ports, have good infrastructure and service facilities, and have low-cost land. TNCs provide instant jobs, access to world markets, and bring in new technology and managerial know-how. The adoption of such an industrialization policy coincided with the time of rapid expansion of TNCs and the competition among TNCs for off-shore manufacturing locations. By maintaining low-wage costs and labour stability and offering other investment incentives, the governments were successful in attracting world market factories, particularly the electronics industry, in the 1970s.

In 1981, there were 185 establishments of 'Electronic Products and Components' in Singapore, employing 69,358 workers (Singapore Department of Statistics, 1982). Compared with other industries in Singapore, the electronics industry comes first in numbers employed and second in direct exports, value added, and output. The semiconductor devices industry employed 17,100 workers, with women accounting for 81.5 percent of the total semiconductor workforce (although they make up 91 percent of the production workers). While developments were a little slower in Malaysia, in 1982 there were 172 firms involved in the manufacturing of household radios, electrical appliances, and miscellaneous electrical apparatus, employing 73,673 workers (Malaysia Ministry of Labour and Manpower, 1982). Because the electronics industry employs large numbers of women, the female labour force participation rate in the manufacturing sector is higher than the overall rate, 38.8 percent compared with 27.8 percent. As the industry employs large numbers of young women, the female labour force participation rate for those aged 15−24 is a high 46.9 percent.

Despite these increased job opportunities, the female labour force remains marginal and secondary. Statistics from Singapore show that women have greater preparation, that is, English-medium education, than men. They are concentrated in certain industries — garments, textiles, electronics, domestic services, education, health care and social welfare (Lim, L.Y.C., 1982). Income statistics indicate occupational segregation by sex. The jobs in which women are concentrated tend to be those that are poorly paid, impart few skills, and provide few promotional opportunities (Singapore Department of Statistics, 1982). In Malaysia, the wages for women factory workers are also lower than for men. A wage survey found that, in 1974, while 72.9 percent of male factory workers in Penang earned between M$200-M$400 per month, 94.8 percent of women earned less than M$200 per month (Penang Development Corporation, 1982).

While the overall industrialization strategies have been similar for Singapore and Malaysia, there have been some important differences as well. The major difference has been in social policy. When Singapore embarked upon its export-oriented industrialization strategy, a range of social programmes was developed to complement business incentives and to consolidate political power. The government undertook a massive programme of public housing, which led to a deliberate mixing of racial groups. An efficient and reliable public transport service was set up. The government has maintained expenditure at 5 percent for health and 6 percent for community, environment and social welfare.

In contrast, the Malaysian government has provided little by way of infrastructural support and social welfare services. Public housing has been slow to develop and public transport barely exists. In the national capital, Kuala Lumpur, squatter areas surround the city and the free trade zones. Although government expenditure on health has increased, its proportion of total government expenditure was 3.7 percent in 1980. The major policy objective of increasing Bumiputra participation in the market economy has led to extensive migration of Malays, many of them young and single women, into the urban areas, adding to the existing demand for social services.

Singapore and Malaysia are both recent examples of successful economic development, and the electronics industry has played a key role in both countries. At the same time, there have been differences in Singaporean and Malaysian approaches to government intervention, both in supporting economic development and in the social reproduction of labour. In Malaysia, the division of economic and political power along racial lines has dominated all aspects of policy development. Singapore has concentrated on investments in social and economic infrastructure as the basis for the consolidation of political power. These differences filter through to the lives of the electronics workers.

## Profile of the Workers
### Socio-demographics

The socio-demographic profile of Asian electronics workers has been well documented in the earlier literature (Arrigo, 1980; Snow, 1978; Frobel et al., 1980; Blake and Moonstan, 1982; Chia, 1981; Woon, 1982; Universiti Sains Malaysia, 1982; Maex, 1982). The workers' backgrounds appear to be fairly similar throughout the continent. They have been characterized as: young, female, mainly rural migrants, with little education or skills, unmarried, and coming from the lower socio-economic strata.

The youth of electronics workers has always been the first noticeable feature. Snow (1978) found that 50 percent of his sample in the Philippines were aged between 18 and 22; the average age among Chia's (1981) respondents in Penang was 19; Arrigo (1980) found that 40 percent of women workers in Taiwan were aged between 16 and 19; Datta-Chaudhuri (1982) reported the average age of women working in Malaysia's free trade zones to be 21.7; Blake and Moonstan (1982) found the average age to be 19 in Thailand's largest electronics company. It has been suggested that the upper age limit is tied to marriage in many places. Blake and Moonstan (1982) found that 85 percent of production workers in a Thai electronics plant were unmarried; Castro (1982) reported that 83 percent of the workers in the free trade zones in the Philippines were single; among the same group of workers in Malaysia, 70 percent was the estimate by Datta-Chaudhuri (1982). The literature suggests that the young age reflects not only marital status but also previous work experience and educational backgrounds. The majority of workers have been recent entrants to the labour market. The estimates range from 72 percent in Malaysia (Woon, 1982) to 64 percent in the Philippines (Castro, 1982). While the educational level varies according to national laws, most workers are primary school graduates or secondary school leavers.

The places of origin of the workers vary. Rural–urban migrants and international migrants both form important segments of the electronics workforce. Castro (1982) reports that 62 percent of workers in the Bataan Export Processing Zone in the Philippines were recent migrants, while studies in Malaysia (Chia, 1981; Universiti Sains Malaysia, 1982) suggest 41–45 percent for Penang. Heyzer (1980) estimates the proportion of 'foreign guest workers' in Singapore's labour force to be 15 percent.

The 903 survey respondents and the 101 interviewees participating in the present study indicate a changing profile for the electronics workforce. The average age of workers in Penang was 24 years while it was 27.5 in Singapore. There was no age difference by job category, although the Chinese workers were slightly older (28.5 in Singapore and 24.5 in Penang) and the Malay workers were slightly younger (26.5 in Singapore and 23.5 in Penang).

Along with age, the proportion of married workers has also increased. In Singapore, 46.5 percent of the workers were married or had become separated, widowed or divorced. In Penang, that group constituted 24.5 percent of the workers. Marital status did not differ significantly by job category, but there were differences according to race. In Singapore, fewer Indians were married (38 percent compared to 47 percent for the other two groups); in Penang, more Chinese were married (29 percent compared to 19 percent for Malays and 21 percent for Indians). In both countries, there was a difference in the average length of time in electronics according to marital status, as shown in Table 1. Contrary to earlier reports, more women are now staying in the industry and the workforce upon marriage.

TABLE 1
Time in electronics employment by marital status (in years)

| | Singapore | Malaysia |
|---|---|---|
| Single | 6.8 | 4.2 |
| Married | 8.9 | 7.2 |

*Source:* Survey Data.

Maternity leave records of one firm show that over 100 people (about 3 percent of the workers but a much higher proportion of married workers) give birth every year. Many stay working after childbirth. In Singapore, 79 percent of the married workers have children, as do 78 percent in Penang. There is also no difference in family size, as the average number of children is 1.8 and 1.7, respectively.

Education levels have also risen over the years. In Singapore where compulsory education covers only primary school, the average length of education among workers was 8.3 years; in Malaysia it was 9.7 years. In Malaysia there was a substantial difference in level of education according to job category — the clerical workers averaged 11.4 years, compared to 9.5 for production workers. In both countries, the newer workers are the ones with more education; many are secondary school graduates. Thus, the level of education can no longer be considered low among recent entrants to the industry.

The proportion of workers without previous job experience remains high: 74.2 percent in Singapore and 86.7 percent in Malaysia. The average length of employment, however, is no longer short, as Table 2 indicates. In both Singapore and Malaysia the workers are spending the bulk of their working lives so far in electronics, and indeed, mostly with the same firm.

TABLE 2
Length of employment of electronics workers (in years)

| | Singapore | Malaysia |
|---|---|---|
| Average total years worked | 8.3 | 4.2 |
| Average in electronics | 7.8 | 4.8 |

*Source:* Survey Data.

As might be expected, the proportion of migrant workers is higher in Malaysia than in Singapore. In Singapore 13.5 percent of the workers were from Malaysia or another foreign country. In Malaysia the proportion of migrants from outside Penang was 38.5 percent. The Chinese make up nearly half of the migrant workers in Singapore. Many of them leave Malaysia because of anti-Chinese sentiments there and seek employment in higher-waged Singapore. In Penang, Malays form the majority of migrant workers, an expected outcome of the government's policy of increasing Bumiputra participation. The overall racial differences are worthy of additional comment. That the Chinese tend to be older may reflect the fact that the entrance of the other groups is a more recent phenomenon; in other words, the Chinese, as a group, have been working longer in the industry. The lower proportion of Indians in Singapore and of Indians and Malays in Malaysia among married workers may be related to the preservation of the traditional ideology in rural households. More Indian interviewees reported marriage at a younger age and by family arrangement, often with unknown men. More Indian and rural Malay interviewees also reported discontinuing school early (because the family believed girls did not need education) and seeking work later (because the family did not believe girls should work).

The overall differences observed between Singapore and Malaysia also deserve some comment. That the workers are older in Singapore and have worked longer reflects the longer presence of electronics production in the Singaporean economy. That workers in Singapore have had more job experience suggests greater job opportunities for women as well as less stable employment. That there are more married women among respondents in Singapore than Malaysia suggests differences emerging in both the female labour force and how women perceive work.

*Working Conditions*
Previous literature suggests that workers in the electronics industry are paid low wages even taking into account the standard of living in Asian countries (Grossman, 1979; Frobel et al., 1980; Lim, L.L., 1982). Basic expenses (rent, food, transportation) can take up a considerable portion of a worker's monthly pay, as seen in Table 3.

TABLE 3
Monthly wages in the electronics industry and expenses, 1978 (in US$)

| Country | Starting wage | After 2 years | Expenses |
|---------|---------------|---------------|----------|
| Hong Kong | 136 | 187 | 123 |
| Indonesia | 19 | 29 | 26 |
| Malaysia | 57 | 100 | 45 |
| Philippines | 40 | 75 | 37 |

*Source:* Grossman, 1979.

Previous literature also suggests that the jobs are insecure and the work is demanding and hazardous. Fluctuations in product demand mean frequent overtime as well as retrenchments. During the 1974 recession, an estimated 15,000 electronics workers in Singapore (about half of the industry) were retrenched (Lim, 1978). Long hours are otherwise the norm. According to Datta-Chaudhuri (1982), 23 percent of free trade zone workers in Malaysia work more than 48 hours per week; Castro (1982) reports that one-quarter of the workers in the Bataan Export Processing zone put in more than 60 hours per week. Productivity is maintained through production quotas. Competition among workers is used by management to maintain the pressure on productivity (Grossman, 1979; Lim, 1978), and the quotas are continuously increased to points just beyond worker capability (Woon, 1982).

On the job, a variety of other problems is encountered. Eyesight deterioration is the result of working with microscopes (Grossman, 1979; Woon, 1982; Blake and Moonstan, 1982; UNIDO, 1980). Rotating shiftwork disrupts eating and sleeping patterns as well as social and family life (Lim, 1978; Universiti Sains Malaysia, 1982). Gas and radiation leakages pose hazards to reproductive health (*Global Electronics Newsletter*, various issues). Because of these problems, young women reportedly leave work by age 25, when their eyesight and general health are no longer able to cope with the demands of the job (Grossman, 1979; Frobel et al., 1980; Elson and Pearson, 1980). Mass hysteria — women running amok — occurs because of the lack of channels for grievance resolution (Ackerman, 1980).

The literature reports that management control is exerted through other means as well. Most important of these is the inculcation of Western images and ideals of femininity through sewing classes, beauty contests and other social activities (Grossman, 1979; Eisold, 1982). Social control on the production floor is based on Western feminine imagery and company welfare services are provided as paternalistic reinforcements.

The present study found some aspects of working life unchanged and others significantly changed from those reported elsewhere. Rotating shiftwork continues to disrupt workers' lives, as do production quotas, and overtime and cut-backs continue to characterize the rhythm of industrial work. However, both the nature of the production process and workers' perceptions have changed. Most workers characterize the work as fast, repetitive, and closely supervised. Over 70 percent of workers work to production quotas. As mechanization and automation are introduced, however, the achievement of the daily target shifts from being dependent on manual dexterity to the smooth functioning of the machines. Interviewees further suggest that the possibility of worker sabotage has also increased by greater use of machinery.

The amount of overtime is highly variable. At the time of the study, the average amount of overtime was one hour per week in Singapore and 3.4 hours per week in Penang. Some interviewees were anxious that these hours be increased; many depended on the extra income to supplement their low basic wages. Few respondents feared retrenchments. Many of the older interviewees (in fact, 20 percent of the total sample in Singapore) even expressed desire to be retrenched. They had been working in the same industry and same firm for a long time, and the retrenchment benefits can provide the excuse and the capital for a new life, possibly by starting a small shop.

Although the literature suggests that workers most often leave for reasons of ill health, a review of 'exit conference' records over a 14-month period in one firm shows that most resignations occur within the first year of employment, rather than on account of general exhaustion after years of work. The major reasons for resignation, in rank order, were: dislike of shiftwork; no childcare; better paying job elsewhere; family pressure; and household move. There appears to be a self-selection process among the workers. Those who can cope and adapt, and who have no other alternatives, tend to stay.

The survey confirmed a number of occupation-related health problems. Eyesight deterioration, skin complaints, muscular strains from repetitive work and menstrual irregularities were found to be associated with specific production processes. The incidence of injury and accidents, however, was found to be declining. This is a direct result of new capital investments; most new machinery has better safety guards, and mechanization and automation insulate the workers from direct exposure to hazards. Increased awareness of occupational health and safety on the part of corporate headquarters as well as governments and workers has further led to improved monitoring of hazardous work areas.

Interviewee responses call into question the effectiveness of management programmes aimed to introduce and reinforce Western feminine ideals, if indeed those are the intentions of management. Some workers say they have no time to participate in company-sponsored activities because of family responsibilities. Others say the hours are inconvenient, for they would have no means of transport back to their places of residence. Still others see activities as designed for male staff. Many prefer to socialize with fellow workers without management staff present. Many prefer to enrol in courses where they can learn typing, English, or other technical skills that can open up possibilities for other jobs. If workers were once receptive to management manipulation, they have now become more sophisticated, if not cynical.

Just as workers are not receptive to company welfare services aimed at morale-boosting and socialization, neither are they keen about union activities where, as in Singapore, unions are allowed to exist, though are highly controlled by the government. They find the after-hours meetings and activities to be insensitive to the workers' dual role as factory and household worker. They also find the union to be uninterested in the concerns of working mothers, such as childcare. It appears to be the nature of unions, not their presence per se, that is an important factor in improving the living conditions that go with industrial work.

For electronics workers in Asia the work continues to be tedious and demanding. Many of the changes in the working conditions noted in the present study are related to changes in the production process. That production technology is changing suggests not only changes in the industry in general but also changes in the nature of the industry in Asia. Although initial operations in Singapore and Malaysia involved only assembly work, forward linkages have occurred for most companies so that testing operations are now done at the same plants. Such a development at a time of general automation in the entire production process suggests that regional markets are becoming increasingly important to the industry, relative to the low wage differential which was previously the most significant locational factor. As the industry loses its 'footlooseness', the permanency of the workforce also becomes more established.

It is significant that reasons for labour turnover do not include marriage and childbirth as leading causes of resignation. This finding complements the finding of the changing socio-demographic profile of the labour force. The changing identity of the workers may also be the reason that workers are not receptive to the social activities offered by the companies.

*Changing Lives*

The need for family support, either in terms of additional income or decreased burden on the family, is an important reason that these workers engage in factory labour (Kung, 1978; UNIDO, 1980; Salaff, 1981; Wolfe, 1984). The desire to achieve individual freedom and especially economic independence is another important motivation for entrance into the labour force (Jamilah, 1981). In the course of industrial employment workers do develop new perspectives and new identities.

Interview data suggest that the family background of workers is poor. A large majority of the workers (80 percent in Singapore and 60 percent in Malaysia) have four or more brothers and sisters, with six to eight siblings being quite common. Seventy-six percent in Singapore have fathers with blue-collar jobs while 85 percent of the workers in Malaysia come from socio-economically disadvantaged backgrounds. While the majority of the interviewees regret leaving school early, thus forgoing job advancement opportunities, most suggest that they did not have a family environment which lent support, financial or otherwise, to school work.

Most interviewees took whatever jobs were available. As electronics factories provided air conditioning and higher wages, jobs there were viewed as preferable to other non-skilled employment. While the older workers came into the factory in response to advertisements, a majority of the younger workers entered electronics as the result of an introduction by a friend or a relative. Working at a new factory job is, therefore, increasingly an extension of an existing social network. Few workers, however, had high hopes of their jobs. They needed money and electronics seemed to be the best field given their educational backgrounds.

An overwhelming proportion of the survey respondents (85 percent) felt that various aspects of their lives had improved since they had been working. Besides obvious improvements in income, workers pointed to better housing, more friends, and improved diet. The hours and the physical and mental demands of work, however, dominate workers' lives. With limited spare time, a majority of workers report that they spend their spare time doing housework, including childcare. The double burden appears to be quite heavy for most women.

At the same time, however, there are substantial differences in how workers spend their spare time, according to marital status and race, as seen in Tables 4 and 5. In both Singapore and Malaysia, married workers have more household responsibilities and less time for rest and recreation. In both countries, it is the Chinese workers who have fewer household responsibilities and hence more time for rest and recreation. Cultural differences resulting from historically distinct material conditions affect lifestyle in important ways.

Reasons for leaving the job reveal the workers' assessment of their jobs in relation to their personal situation and structural position. Money was the main reason that pushed people to work, and better money was the main reason for survey respondents to consider leaving

TABLE 4
Spare time activities by marital status (in percent)

|  | Singapore | | | Malaysia | | |
|  | Single | Married | Total | Single | Married | Total |
| --- | --- | --- | --- | --- | --- | --- |
| Housework | 48.3 | 70.1 | 60.2 | 52.2 | 59.6 | 54.0 |
| Rest and recreation | 22.4 | 7.1 | 15.5 | 18.7 | 17.0 | 18.3 |
| Solo activities | 29.3 | 22.8 | 24.3 | 29.1 | 23.4 | 27.7 |
| Total | 100.0 | 100.0 | 100.0 | 100.0 | 100.0 | 100.0 |

*Source:* Survey Data.

TABLE 5
Spare time activities by race (in percent)

| | Singapore | | | | Malaysia | | |
| | Chinese | Malay | Indian | Total | Chinese | Malay | Indian | Total |
|---|---|---|---|---|---|---|---|---|
| Housework | 51.6 | 64.9 | 71.3 | 59.8 | 42.1 | 56.4 | 64.8 | 52.4 |
| Rest and recreation | 21.5 | 10.1 | 9.2 | 13.2 | 38.1 | 8.5 | 12.2 | 20.7 |
| Solo activities | 26.9 | 25.0 | 19.5 | 27.0 | 19.8 | 35.1 | 23.0 | 26.9 |
| Total | 100.0 | 100.0 | 100.0 | 100.0 | 100.0 | 100.0 | 100.0 | 100.0 |

*Source*: Survey Data.

their current jobs. Better working conditions — in terms of physical environment, work hours, and job security — was the second most important reason for quitting. There were, however, some interesting differences among workers by marital status, job category, race and work experience, as well as between Singapore and Malaysia.

In both Singapore and Malaysia, single workers were more likely to leave for better pay and better working conditions while married workers were more inclined to work until retirement. This reflects the fact that fewer single workers have economic burdens and that many married workers stay working out of economic necessity. 'Graveyard' shift workers in Singapore, most of whom work these unsocial hours out of necessity, are also more inclined to stay working until retirement. As the interviewees indicated, many feared their age and lack of education would render them unemployable if they quit. In fact, if they had taken the same job in another company, they would have started at the bottom of the pay scale once again.

Clerical workers, compared with production workers, are more inclined to leave for better wages. They are aware of their skills and they do not want to do factory work. Workers who have not had previous employment experience or who have not been transferred between work areas in the same firm are much less willing to leave, even for better wages. Interview evidence suggests that those without varied work experiences lack the confidence to change jobs. By the same token, those who have moved around will gladly take on new changes and challenges. Thus, experience brings both desire for change as well as the confidence to bring about change.

While respondents in Singapore nominated 'children' as a reason for quitting work, those in Malaysia nominated 'marriage'. There being more married workers in Singapore and more single in Malaysia only partly explains the difference. The married interviewees indicated that additional children would make the cost of babysitting too high, thus making it uneconomic to continue working. The calculation appears to be pragmatic rather than emotional or ideological. In addition, there do seem to be some real differences in how workers in the two countries perceive the importance of their jobs and their reasons for work.

Table 6 summarizes the responses provided by interviewees when they were asked 'Would you work if you did not need the money? If yes, why?'. While the majority of Malaysians would stay at home and not work, the majority of Singaporeans would work for the sake of work, by which they mean experience, knowledge, interest in the outside world, etc.

When the respondents were asked what is important to them about their jobs, however, independence and experience were as important to the Malaysians as to the Singaporeans, as Table 7 shows. Yet somehow,

TABLE 6
Reasons for work by job category

| | Singapore | | Malaysia | |
| | Production | Clerk | Production | Clerk |
| --- | --- | --- | --- | --- |
| Stay home | 7 | — | 15 | 1 |
| To pass time | 11 | 7 | 13 | 1 |
| To work for work's sake | 14 | 4 | 10 | 1 |
| For friends at work | 5 | — | — | — |

*Source:* Survey Data.

TABLE 7
Job importance

| | Singapore | | Malaysia | |
| | Production | Clerk | Production | Clerk |
| --- | --- | --- | --- | --- |
| Not important | 10 | 3 | 12 | 2 |
| Money | 8 | — | — | — |
| Friends/social life | 8 | — | 5 | — |
| Pass time | 3 | — | 2 | — |
| Independence and experience | 6 | 6 | 9 | 2 |

*Source:* Survey Data.

the abstract notion of work for work's sake has not been internalized by the Malaysians. The more traditional notion of a woman's place being in the home is still much more prevalent in Malaysia. Interviewees in both countries indicated that the fact of working has changed their role in their own families. For instance they now make their own choice of partner rather than giving in to family preferences, are listened to for their advice on family finances, etc., but more of the Malaysians saw the main benefit of work as 'being able to buy anything I want', that is, being an independent consumer. It appears, then, that the fact that more Singaporean workers expect to work after marriage and childbirth reflects not only economic necessity but also the growing abstract importance of working. By the same token, the abstract institution of marriage is still important in Malaysia. Singapore appears to have more successfully adopted 'industrialism as a way of life' (Kumbhat, 1978).

Additional differences in outlook can be found among the three racial groups. Previous data already illustrated that, in both countries, more Indians spend time doing housework than the other groups, while the Chinese do the least. At the same time, there are more Chinese who find time to shop, visit friends and go out. As for reasons for leaving work, more Indians in both countries quit under family pressure, while the Chinese in both countries most readily leave for better paying jobs. More Indians in Singapore and Malays in Malaysia leave for marriage. These results bear out the impressions gained from the interviewees that Indian families are more traditional and Chinese workers more economistic in orientation. The Chinese would also appear to have successfully adopted 'industrialism as a way of life'.

When asked what they liked about their jobs, over 60 percent of the interviewees from both countries were quick to reply 'money and friends'. It appears that although the original motivation for employment is economic, the social aspects of work are an unanticipated benefit that keep workers interested. As for their dislikes, while the majority of Malaysian interviewees nominated factory discipline, especially the strict supervisorial system, the Singaporeans were more concerned about work hours and the physical work environment. The difference in Malaysia can be attributed to a more traditional agrarian emphasis on social relations.

It is evident that, in becoming part of the urban–industrial workforce, the outlook and aspirations of many young women are changing. They have evolved new ways of adapting and coping. Increasingly, young women with few skills seek jobs in electronics factories as a means to gain economic and social independence as well as to find new friends from different places and backgrounds. These friends are the first source of advice in times of personal crisis. They are also an antidote to boredom on the job. They provide support whether a worker faces difficulties in private life or in factory work. Some workers have even refused promotion opportunities in the interests of solidarity with fellow workers. Peer group identification begins to displace the centrality of the family in workers' lives, especially for migrant workers. The new pattern of interaction with workmates is the basis for learning about and coping with different social situations. It also forms the basis for job actions. While concerted protests and protracted labour struggles are still rare, job actions have not been absent. Slow-downs, long breaks, and visits en masse to the toilet are some of the protest measures.

The work experience not only has led to new-found friendships and solidarity but also has meant personal growth. Although the skills acquired on the job remain limited, the job experience has given many workers the desire to hope for better opportunities. Most interviewees indicated they would not want to work in another electronics company, or even a factory. While some are pursuing further vocational studies, others are thinking about opening their own shops. Women workers are thinking about their futures in ways unprecedented for them.

These new working experiences have also taught workers social skills. Many interviewees suggested that they are now capable of solving a variety of human relations problems which they would not have been able to do before. Several even suggested that their ability to articulate their thoughts and feelings, especially to a stranger (such as the interviewer), is the direct result of the work experience.

In Singapore and Malaysia, women still constitute a marginal labour force with their concentrated presence in certain industries. They continue, as well, to occupy a secondary position in the labour market in that they are low wage earners. Their work experience does intervene in positive ways. Previous racial barriers are being broken down as new social support networks are formed on the assembly line. The experience at work also transforms the worldviews of the workers. The new coping mechanisms adopted by the workers to mediate between the demands of traditional society and new urban–industrial ways of life signify the emergence of a new working class. Their new determination to remain working is also a sign of this new class position.

**Discussion and Conclusions**
The establishment of labour-intensive, export-oriented industries in LDCs, especially in Asia, has brought large numbers of women into the formal sector labour force for the first time ever in those societies. While women have always worked (Boserup, 1970), it is as a result of the incorporation of peripheral societies into the world capitalist system today that women are entering into wage labour in the manufacturing workforce in large numbers. This is a process of fundamental social and economic transformation, vital to the development of capitalism in those LDCs. A working class is being created in the LDCs, and women workers are central to the proletarianization process.

The changes in women's role in Asian societies in the twentieth century are remarkably similar to those of nineteenth century Europe and America. In Europe then and Asia now, as women were 'free' labour, unattached to other trades, they were identified as a trainable, docile, and cheap labour force for early industrialization, whether in nineteenth-century textile mills or twentieth-century electronics factories. In both times and places, more and more women were brought into the factory workforce. Employers demanded longer hours of work per day, and the level of labour discipline and work intensity were also increased. Between the rapidly changing technology and the ever increasing competition among manufacturers, the textile and electronics industries experienced crises of over-production and excess capacity. The instability of the industry was passed on to the lives of the women workers.

Early textile corporations in America adopted a unified set of policies from the outset (Dublin, 1979). The organization of production and the labour policies were virtually identical, and the various establishments minimized competition in wages or working conditions. The electronics industry in Asia operates in a similar manner today.

With the introduction of the factory system, and the development of the textiles industry in particular, women's employment outside the home, as wage labour, increased sharply (Tilly and Scott, 1978). The same phenomenon is now occurring in Asia. In both nineteenth-century Europe and twentieth-century Asia, the concentration of industrial jobs in certain cities and regions drew young rural women away from their homes. Women's work was no longer being defined by household labour needs, but by the household's need for money. Daughters dominated the labour force in mill towns and free trade zone areas and made important and expected contributions to the family fund. In Europe then and Asia now, young girls sent away — as migrants to the cities — were in the most vulnerable position, for they were outside the context of family and the community. While expecting to earn enough money to enable them to get married and have a family, some found their wages were barely sufficient for their own support. Employers justified the low wages on the basis that women were only supplementary wage earners in the family.

The phenomenon of women working in factories was socially controversial in nineteenth-century Europe (Engels, 1973; Berch, 1976). While some commentators welcomed jobs for women, others were alarmed at the sight of women operating machines and disturbed about the social consequences of women working away from home. Eventually there were waves of concern over the deterioration of the health and morals of women, of their ability and desire to bear children and of the stability of the family as a social institution. Such concerns are regularly expressed in Asia today.

In the course of industrial work, however, women developed new attitudes. Historical research suggests that a close-knit community developed among women workers at the workplace and in the boarding houses (Dublin, 1979; Tilly and Scott, 1978). There is emerging evidence from Asia of the same trends.

Although the nature of the capitalist system and the political and cultural conditions are different, the history of women's work in the early phase of capitalist development is being repeated in Asia today. The similarities between conditions of women workers in twentieth-century Asia and those facing women workers in nineteenth-century Europe and America are not surprising. The proletarianization of women is integral to capitalist development. The position of women in the labour force fluctuates in consonance with the requirement of capital accumulation and expansion (Mackintosh, 1981; Fernandez-Kelly, 1983). Their labour is required in periods of early industrialization, when the male labour supply is diminished, in situations of fierce competition, and when there is a reduction of costs in the reproduction of labour power. Women's marginal role and secondary status in the labour force is not unique to the 'new international division of labour'.

In Singapore and Malaysia, while the structural position of women electronics workers is slow to change, the nature of the labour force is changing, along with the outlook of the workers. To be sure, workers are still trapped in a cycle of working-class life. Coming from a background of poverty, the young woman with few skills finds a job in a factory. The wages, although low, are a real asset to her and her family. With shiftwork, she has few opportunities to increase her education. She does not acquire sufficient skills on the job to obtain another job. Most likely, she has been educated in her own language medium which is another barrier to job opportunities. Her income increases with her seniority, but her career is trapped in the factory.

While the electronics workforce in Singapore and Malaysia is still made up largely of young, single women who lack educational and work experience, they are growing older, getting married and becoming more educated. Many have been working for as long as the industry has been there. They have become wives and mothers in that time and stayed in the workforce. They have experienced retrenchments and consequently changes in employers. As forward linkages occur in the production process, many have acquired experience working in a variety of work areas. In this time, they have gained more confidence in themselves — in their ability to find employment, to get along with people of different backgrounds, to understand politics at the workplace. They have also come to realize that while their family and economic burdens have grown, their job opportunities have not. They have acquired few transferable skills. More of them are enrolling in courses, to the extent allowed by shiftwork, so as to acquire alternative career paths.

Increasingly, work is no longer a temporary, pre-marriage phenomenon. While the economic need to work is still the central motivation, women are increasingly realizing that working also means being valued as productive beings. Values central to capitalist development are becoming internalized. Working on the assembly line with members of different racial groups has begun to break down the colonial legacy of segregation and is helping to build a new multi-cultural working class. The interpersonal relationships found at work consitute a new form of social relations for women.

The cultural differences shape workers' outlooks in ways distinct from the working class of other periods of early capitalist development. The Chinese came to Malaya as traders and wage labourers; they have been enmeshed in capitalist relations for much longer. These perspectives are embodied within the family. Whereas Indian and Malay families tend to restrict daughters' attendance in schools and entrance into the workforce, Chinese families tend to push daughters into being economically contributing members of the household. While Indians and Malays speak at length about new friendships established on the assembly line, the Chinese are more concerned with income. Their status within the family also rises as their income-earning ability increases. The Indians and Malays spend most of their precious spare time in unpaid household work; the Chinese have more opportunities for rest and recreation. For the Chinese daughter the contradiction between tradition and modernity is much less.

As capitalist relations have also penetrated further in Singapore than Malaysia, there are also differences in the outlook of workers in the two countries. Singaporean workers appear to have self-confidence and value work as a learning experience in ways not expressed by workers in Malaysia. While money and friends were important aspects of work for workers in both countries, Singaporeans were more inclined to identify a broadening of horizons as an important facet of the work experience. Indeed, more Singaporeans indicated a desire to continue working regardless of financial need, suggesting that work has meaning at an intrinsic and not merely instrumental level.

Although working conditions and management practices are relatively similar across companies and countries, they, too, are changing. With each economic downturn, labour is being replaced by machines. As machines increase, the proportion of women workers begins to decrease. Increases in the use of machines also leads to higher production targets, with the targets no longer tied to a person's dexterity but to the machines. While supervisors still remain central authority figures, the machines now provide a buffer against management demands for productivity.

These changes in the workforce and in workers' outlook reflect developments in the industry as well as in the two countries of concern. In the years since the industry first located in Asia, there have been tremendous growth and changes in the industry and in the region. Automation possibilities coupled with a growing regional market have led to forward linkages in the production process making factory work a more diverse experience. With increased capital investment and more production of sophisticated products, the companies have become less 'footloose'. Though their initial tax holidays have come to an end, companies are increasing their investments rather than pulling out. More locals are also being hired to take over positions formerly occupied by expatriates. With growing industrial development and economic diversification in these countries, the electronics industry is beginning to shed its enclave character (Lim and Pang, 1982).

There is no doubt that the electronics industry has contributed to capitalist development in these countries. A new working class is being constituted in large measure by women. While their occupational mobility may be as restricted as their social class position, work can change their standing within the family, and the intrinsic rewards of work can change their own outlook. Thus, the participation in industrial work can change not only the economic standing of workers but also their ideologies (Saffiotti, 1983). Out of the new understanding of the working world comes new consciousness, however rudimentary, of being a woman and a worker. The experiences of women electronics workers in Singapore and Malaysia may foreshadow what is to come for women in many other LDCs.

## References

Ackerman, S. (1980) *Cultural Process in Malaysian Industrialization: A Study of Malay Women Factory Workers*. Ph.D. dissertation. San Diego: University of California.

Arrigo, L.G. (1980) 'The Industrial Workforce of Young Women in Taiwan', *Bulletin of Concerned Asian Scholars*, 12(2): 25–37.

Berch, B.E. (1976) *Industrialization and Working Women in the 19th Century: England, France, and the US*. Ph.D. dissertation. Madison: University of Wisconsin.

Blake, M. and C. Moonstan (1982) *Women and Transnational Corporations: The Electronics Industry in Thailand*. Honolulu: East–West Center, University of Hawaii.

Boserup, E. (1970) *Women's Role in Economic Development*. London: Allen and Unwin.

Castro, J. (1982) *The Bataan Export Processing Zone*. Bangkok: ARTEP, International Labour Office.

Chia, K.C. (1981) *The Housing Crisis of the Female Migrant Workers: A Case Study of the Bayan Lepas Free Trade Zone, Penang, Malaysia*. M.S. thesis. Bangkok: Asian Institute of Technology.

Datta-Chaudhuri, M. (1982) *The Role of Free Trade Zones in the Creation of Employment and Industrial Growth in Malaysia*. Bangkok: ARTEP, International Labour Office.

Dublin, T. (1979) *Women at Work: The Transformation of Work and Community in Lowell, MA, 1828–60*. New York: Columbia University Press.

Eisold, E. (1982) 'Young Women Workers in Export Industries: The Case of the Semiconductor Industry in Southeast Asia'. Unpublished manuscript. Geneva: International Labour Office.

Elson, D. and R. Pearson (1980) 'Nimble Fingers Make Cheap Workers: An Analysis of Women's Employment in Third World Export Manufacturing', *Feminist Review*, Spring: 87–107.

Engels, F. (1973) *The Condition of the Working Class in England in 1844*. Moscow: Progress Publishers.

Fernandez-Kelly, M. (1983) *For We are Sold, I and My People: Women in Industry in Mexico's Frontier*. Albany: State University of New York Press.

Frobel, F., J. Heinrichs and O. Kreye (1980) *The New International Division of Labour*. Cambridge: Cambridge University Press.

Grossman, R. (1979) 'Women's Place in the Integrated Circuit', *Pacific Research*, 9(5–6): 2–17.

Heyzer, N. (1980) *The Peripheral Workforce: Young Women and Migrant Workers in*

*Singapore*. Townsville: Southeast Asian Studies Centre, James Cook University.

International Labour Office (1982) *Yearbook of Statistics*. Geneva: ILO.

Jamilah, M.A. (1981) 'The Adaptation Process and Adaptive Strategies of Female Rural-Urban Migrants. The Case of Malay Factory Girls in Malaysia'. Paper presented at Workshop on the Social Development of Factory Workers, Universiti Sains Malaysia, Penang.

Kumbhat, M.C. (1978) 'Job Satisfaction Among Assembly-line Workers in a Developing Country', *Southeast Asian Journal of Social Sciences*, 6(1–2).

Kung, L. (1978) *Factory Work, Women, and the Family in Taiwan*. Ph.D. dissertation. New Haven: Yale University.

Lim, L.L. (1982) 'Towards Meeting the Needs of Urban Female Factory Workers in Peninsular Malaysia'. Paper presented at Conference on Women in the Urban and Industrial Labour Force in Asia, Manila.

Lim, L.Y.C. (1978) *Women Workers in Multinational Corporations: The Case of the Electronics Industry in Singapore and Malaysia*. Occasional Papers in Women's Studies. Ann Arbor: University of Michigan.

Lim, L.Y.C. (1982) *Women in Singapore's Economy*. Economic Research Centre Occasional Paper. Singapore: National University of Singapore.

Lim, L.Y.C. and Pang E.F. (1982) *Technology Choice and Employment Creation: A Case Study of Three Multinational Enterprises in Singapore*. Economic Research Center Occasional Paper. Singapore: National University of Singapore.

Mackintosh, M. (1981) 'Gender and Economics. The Sexual Division of Labour and the Subordination of Women', in K. Young, C. Wolkowitz and R. McCullagh (eds.), *Of Marriage and the Market*. London: CSE Books.

Maex, R. (1982) *Employment and Multinationals in Asian Export Processing Zones*. Bangkok: ARTEP, International Labour Office.

Malaysia, Ministry of Labour and Manpower (1980) *Labour and Manpower Report*. Kuala Lumpur: Ministry of Labour and Manpower.

Oldham, W. (1977) 'The Fabrication of Microelectronic Circuit', in Scientific American Book, *Microelectronics*. San Francisco: W.H. Freeman and Co.

Penang Development Corporation (1982) *Investment Guide to Penang*. Penang: PDC.

Saffiotti, H. (1983) *The Impact of Industrialization on the Structure of Female Employment*. Working Paper on Women in International Development. East Lansing: Michigan State University.

Salaff, J. (1981) *Working Daughters of Hong Kong*. Cambridge: Cambridge University Press.

Saxenian, A. (1981) *Silicon Chips and Spatial Structure: The Industrial Basis of Urbanization in Santa Clara County, California*. IURD Working Paper. Berkeley: University of California.

Singapore Department of Statistics (1982) *Yearbook of Statistics*. Singapore: Department of Statistics.

Snow, R. (1978) 'Export-oriented Industrialization and its Impact on Women Workers: The Case of the Bataan Export Processing Zone in the Philippines', *Philippines Sociological Review*, 26(3, 4): 189–199.

Tilly, L. and J. Scott (1978) *Women, Work and Family*. New York: Holt, Rinehart and Winston.

UNIDO (1980) *Women in the Redeployment of Manufacturing Industry to Developing Countries*. Working Paper on Structural Change. Geneva: United Nations Industrial Development Organization.

Universiti Sains Malaysia (1982), *Urban Services for Young Workers in Penang: Progress*

*Report for IDRC Participatory Urban Services Meeting*, Penang: School of Social Sciences, Universiti Sains Malaysia.

US Department of Commerce, Industry and Trade Administration (1979) *A Report on the US Semiconductor Industry*. Washington, DC: US Government Printing Office.

Wolfe, D. (1984) 'Industrialization, Women Workers and the Family in Indonesia'. Paper presented at World Congress of the International Institute of Sociology, Seattle.

Woon, L. (1982) *Workers' Needs and Employer-organized Labour Welfare Programs: A Case Study*. Unpublished thesis. Penang: Universiti Sains Malaysia.

# III
# Regional Consequences of Global Restructuring

## 7
## Exploring the Spatial Effects of the Internationalization of the Mexican Economy
### Manuel Perlo Cohen

Recent Mexican development clearly shows the profound impact that the internationalization of the economy can exert on a peripheral capitalist country. It is difficult to find a city or region in Mexico that is not in some way linked to the international system: whole regions produce agricultural products mainly for export; many cities and regions depend entirely upon the influx of foreign tourists; various states send hundreds of thousands of migrants abroad, and free production zones manufacture exclusively for the foreign market.

More specifically, the transformation of the world economy since the 1970s, coupled with Mexico's internal dynamic, has strongly influenced the spatial changes the country has undergone in recent years. The explosive urbanization during the 1970s in the states of Veracruz and Tabasco is intrinsically associated with Mexico's oil export boom; the huge investments by several transnational corporations in tourism, transportation and other services have been crucial in explaining the sudden growth of tourist towns such as Cancun, Ixtapa and Acapulco. Finally, the expansion of assembly operations and the growing importance of export platforms in the northern states and along the entire US–Mexico border link these regions more strongly to the international economy than to that of the nation (see Figure 1).

The main goal of this chapter is to discover what type of urban and regional impact the internationalization of the Mexican economy has had in certain regions of Mexico. Among the questions I wish to answer are the following. Have the different regions followed a similar pattern, or can significant variations in their urban and regional effects be identified? Have these regions developed stronger links with the international economy than with the rest of the country? Has their rapid urban growth been concentrated in a few large cities, thereby

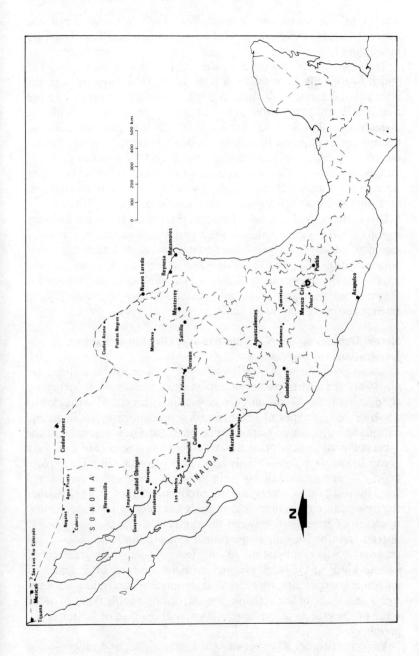

FIGURE 1
Mexico: Sonora–Sinaloa and the border region

weakening the small and medium-size cities? Are they attracting migrants from other regions of the country, or expelling their own inhabitants?

To answer these and other questions, I have selected two regions which historically have shown a high degree of integration with the international economy.[1] These regions are Sinaloa–Sonora and the northern border municipalities. The aim is to identify significant differences and explore their causes. In my view the differences in these regions are a result, on the one hand, of various types of articulation between the circuits of international capital and the national economy and, on the other, of local conditions which prevailed either before or during the establishment of the external links with the national market, local entrepreneurship, and local patterns of capital accumulation.

Due to the limited scope and length of this paper, I have not included regions or cities weakly linked to the international economy, nor have I included Mexico's largest metropolitan areas (Mexico City and Guadalajara). My analysis does not assess the impact of the international economy on the country as a whole, and the conclusions drawn from the cases under analysis should not be automatically extended to other regions and cities.

### Recent Debates on the New International Division of Labour: Implications for our Analysis

According to some of the better known authors on this issue (Frobel et al., 1980), the clearest and most important expression of the structural changes in the world economy can be succinctly presented as the closing down of certain types of manufacturing operations in the industrial nations and their subsequent installation in foreign subsidiaries of the same company in developing nations where a vast reserve of extremely cheap labour is available. This relocation of production takes place mainly — but not exclusively — in industrial areas which are isolated from the rest of the country: the free production zones. It is argued that the new pattern of industrial location is not altering the fundamental structure of inequality between the centre and the periphery but is instead reinforcing their dependent integration into the world economy. Superexploitation of the labour force, the granting of various kinds of tax incentives and subsidies, and the enforcement of measures guaranteeing capital accumulation and controlling workers' rights and trade union activities are, according to this point of view, some of the effects of the new international division of labour in the periphery.

Various critiques have been levelled against this and other similar approaches (e.g. Wallerstein, 1974, 1979). For example, Portes and Walton (1981) claimed that such an approach has generally been conducted at a high level of abstraction with the world economy as a whole as the only viable unit of analysis and has tended to produce sweeping conclusions applicable to the entire system. Brenner (1977) identified the fundamental weakness in Wallerstein's theory as his failure to analyse the tendency of capitalism to expand by increasing relative surplus value through increased labour productivity. Jenkins (1984) maintained that the world system approach has based its analysis of the new international division of labour on an exchange- oriented theory of circulation emphasizing the sphere of exchange and distribution, and disregarding the sphere of production, innovation, and technological development in the accumulation process.

In his well-aimed critique, Jenkins confronted the notion that the relocation of production to Third World countries is the most important expression of the structural changes in the world economy. On the one hand, the relocation of production seems to involve primarily industries such as electronics and clothing and might also be temporally limited since other forms of capitalist restructuring (particularly technological innovation) may lead to the reimportation of these labour processes to the advanced capitalist countries. On the other hand, there are other important aspects of the internationalization of capital that are essential to the new international division of labour. One is the growing export of means of production (particularly fixed capital) from the advanced capitalist countries to the Third World; the second is the massive growth of international financial markets, especially the Euro-currency market, and the substantial increase in bank lending to the Third World, particularly to the newly industrializing countries.

The approach I will use in this paper breaks away from the highly one-dimensional picture of the new international division of labour identified with certain labour-intensive sectors which have relocated to free production zones. I will build on the approach proposed by Jenkins which relies on Marx's analysis of the circuits of capital, stressing the unity of production, distribution and exchange as aspects of the expansion of capital. This approach makes it possible to identify different aspects of the internationalization of capital in terms of the three circuits of capital: the circuits of commodity capital, money capital, and productive capital. In the context of the internationalization of capital the three circuits have been identified respectively with the growth of world trade, the growth of international capital movements, and the growth of the operations of transnational corporations and the international circulation of products within such firms.

This approach has some relevant implications for the analysis of Mexico's economic internationalization. The first is that there is no single emergent pattern characterizing the integration of the Third World into the international division of labour. Different countries or areas have been affected by different models of capital accumulation, making it impossible to generalize about the effects of the internationalization of capital on the Third World as a whole. Mexico's economic internationalization is based neither on free production zones nor on export platforms. It relied, since the 1940s and until Mexico's recent entry to the GATT in 1985, on a strategy of import-substitution industrialization that encourages production for the internal market through various incentives and subsidies, and through highly restrictive tariff and non-tariff barriers.

In Mexico different patterns of integration with the world economy coexist and conflict. In order to grasp the complex picture of Mexico's economic internationalization, we must focus not only on the three circuits of capital but also on the economic actors involved. These include not only large transnational corporations with monopolist control, but also a wide array of economic agents of different sizes, ranging from US banks of regional importance, medium and even small firms, large and medium-size private investors, regional import–export firms, and so forth.

A second debate concerns the role that the internal social conditions of the Third World countries have played in the process of internationalization. Jenkins (1984) has criticized the world system approach on this point, asserting that by locating the dynamic which leads to the new international division of labour in trends of accumulation at the centre, such an approach denies the Third World any independent dynamic, and policies to promote exports or attract foreign capital are therefore considered to result from the 'needs' of the core countries rather than those of the local economy. Mexico is, beyond any doubt, dependent upon the United States; however, from this we cannot conclude that it lacks its own internal dynamic and that its accumulation model is simply an answer to the needs of the United States or that it is an appendage of the US economy. One of the most amazing things about the Mexican economy is not its high degree of integration into the US economy, but rather, that the integration is not complete.

Mexico has one of the most protected domestic industrial sectors of any capitalist country. It applies very restrictive laws to foreign investment, and has perhaps the largest state- owned sector of any non-socialist country. Nationalist and protectionist policies have been more than the result of a powerful state seeking legitimacy behind the banners of independence and sovereignty. They are instead the outcome of a broad economic, social and political coalition that includes large national capitalists, transnational firms producing for the internal market, small and medium-size firms which survive against foreign competition only with the aid of protectionist measures, subsidized farmers who can export only with the support of the state, and so forth. All these interests underpin some of the most relevant policies of the Mexican state.

The complex, heterogeneous, and contradictory nature of Mexico's economic internationalization referred to above has many implications for urban and regional phenomena. First, we find in most regions and cities the coexistence of firms originating in different circuits of capital, with different competitive structures competing in different markets and from different regions. In the same city or region a group of transnational corporations may produce for the internal market, national firms may produce for export, giant supermarket chains may finance local exporters, and so forth.

Each activity linked to the international market generates certain urban and regional effects such as demographic and economic concentration, urban growth, migration and changes in interregional relations. Usually it is assumed that the economic sector linked to the international economy will induce demographic and economic concentration in a few urban places, create a limited number of jobs, and develop stronger links to other countries rather than within the country. However, I contend that this is a very simplistic view. Actually the urban and regional effects of economic internationalization will depend on the kind of capital circuit in operation, whether the company is a transnational or a US firm whose regional sphere of influence includes parts of Mexico, and whether it is competitive or monopolistic, producing for export or for the internal market. It will also depend significantly on some of the social, economic and even political features of the region or city where the link with the international economy takes place.

### The Sonora–Sinaloa Region

The links connecting Sinaloa and Sonora to the US economy were created around the turn of the century. In 1882 trains began to operate between Guaymas and Nogales. In 1890 Guggenheim's ASARCO began to invest in Sonora (Florescano and Moreno, 1976), and from New York firms began to install the large sugar refineries (Almada Sugar Refining Co., Sinaloa Land Co.) that led to the formation of towns such as Los Mochis (Baird and McCaughan, 1982). The government of Porfirio Diaz granted US 'colonizing companies' permission to subdivide tracts of land in Sonora's Yaqui Valley (Hewitt, 1976) and to sell them to American investors.

The Revolution of 1910 brought drastic economic, social and political changes. The revolutionary agenda proclaimed by different governments and by the 1917 Constitution included the distribution of large landholdings to landless peasants, state control of natural resources and the nationalization of certain foreign investments. The core of the revolutionary programme, however, was not fully enforced until the administration of Lazaro Cardenas (1934–40) when the largest landholdings were subdivided and distributed in the form of communal properties known as *ejidos*, and foreign-owned companies in such sectors as railroads, sugar refining, mining, etc. were nationalized. The dramatic effects of these changes were also felt in Sonora and Sinaloa: the most productive tracts of land in the Yaqui Valley (in northern Sonora) and in Los Mochis were subdivided and made into collective *ejidos*, and the United Sugar Company, founded in 1886 and based in Los Mochis, was nationalized (Baird and McCaughan, 1982). As a result, many foreign investors withdrew from Mexico and the flow of foreign capital into the country stopped. Bilateral relations were strained during those years and US investments plummeted from more than US$900 million in 1919 to US$300 million in 1940 (Vazquez and Meyer, 1981).

But despite all the problems and constraints, businesses in some sectors maintained their pace or even expanded. This was true of winter vegetable exports, particularly tomatoes. During World War I tomatoes, sugar and raw ore were shipped to US markets (Schramm, 1984). In the 1920s the cultivation of tomatoes expanded in Sonora and Sinaloa. US companies (American Fruit) and individuals began to grow and pack tomatoes for export, while providing Mexican growers with credit to produce more vegetables, fruits and cotton for the US market (Baird and McCaughan, 1982).

Thus although economic relations between the two nations were at a low point in the period 1920 to 1940, those areas which maintained close ties to the US economy on a bilateral basis, as in the case of Sonora and Sinaloa, were less affected.

Focusing on the spatial changes in the Sinaloa–Sonora region, we find that from the outbreak of the revolution in 1910 until 1940, the population remained predominantly rural. In 1940, while 80 percent of the nation's inhabitants lived in rural areas, in Sinaloa the proportion was 89 percent and in Sonora 95 percent. Urban growth was slow overall. Traditional urban centres experienced very modest growth. In 1900 Hermosillo had 10,613 inhabitants; by 1940 it had reached only 18,601. During the same period, the population of Culiacan increased from 10,380 to 22,025, and that of Mazatlan went from 17,852 to 32,117. Other northern cities such as Monterrey, Torreon, Ciudad Juarez, and Nuevo Laredo increased in population by 205 percent, 632 percent, 495 percent, and 340 percent respectively.

But while traditional urban centres experienced rather slow growth,

TABLE 1

Population, by decade, 1900–80, Sonora and Sinaloa; and annual rates or growth for Sonora and Sinaloa; and cities with populations greater than 15,000 at the start of the decade

| | Population 1900 | Pop. 1910 | Growth rate (%) | Pop. 1921 | Growth rate (%) | Pop. 1930 | Growth rate (%) | Pop. 1940 | Growth rate (%) | Pop. 1950 | Growth rate (%) | Pop. 1960 | Growth rate (%) | Pop. 1970 | Growth rate (%) | Pop. 1980 | Growth rate (%) |
|---|---|---|---|---|---|---|---|---|---|---|---|---|---|---|---|---|---|
| Sinaloa | 296,701 | 323,642 | 0.8 | 341,265 | 0.5 | 395,618 | 1.4 | 492,821 | 2.1 | 635,681 | 2.5 | 838,404 | 2.7 | 1,266,528 | 4.0 | 1,849,879 | 3.7 |
| Culiacan | 10,380 | 13,527 | — | 16,034 | 1.6 | 18,202 | 1.4 | 22,025 | 1.9 | 48,936 | 7.6 | 85,024 | 5.4 | 172,004 | 6.8 | 304,826 | 5.5 |
| Mazatlan | 17,852 | 21,219 | 1.7 | 25,254 | 1.6 | 29,380 | 1.6 | 32,117 | 0.9 | 41,754 | 2.6 | 76,874 | 5.8 | 126,325 | 5.0 | 199,830 | 4.5 |
| Los Mochis | 517 | 1,188 | — | 6,649 | — | 10,004 | — | 12,937 | — | 21,552 | 5.0 | 38,307 | 5.6 | 69,251 | 5.8 | 122,531 | 5.6 |
| Guasave | 800 | 936 | — | 971 | — | 2,004 | — | 4,997 | — | 8,506 | 5.2 | 17,510 | 6.9 | 26,422 | 4.1 | 55,535 | 7.1 |
| Guamuchil | 522 | 427 | — | 2,185 | — | 3,042 | — | 4,526 | — | 5,865 | — | 7,878 | — | 17,514 | 5.1 | 36,308 | 7.0 |
| Escuinapa | 3,136 | 4,364 | — | 5,032 | — | 3,909 | — | 5,864 | — | 9,015 | — | 9,920 | — | 16,785 | 7.6 | 20,247 | 1.9 |
| Sonora | 221,682 | 265,383 | 1.7 | 275,127 | 0.3 | 316,271 | 1.3 | 364,174 | 1.4 | 510,607 | 3.3 | 783,378 | 4.2 | 1,098,720 | 3.3 | 1,513,731 | 3.1 |
| Hermosillo | 10,613 | 14,578 | — | 14,745 | — | 19,959 | 3.3 | 18,601 | -0.7 | 43,519 | 8.0 | 96,019 | 7.5 | 180,237 | 6.1 | 297,175 | 4.9 |
| Ciudad Obregon | — | 38 | — | 1237 | — | 8,469 | — | 12,497 | — | 30,991 | 8.5 | 67,956 | 7.5 | 117,183 | 5.3 | 165,572 | 3.4 |
| Nogales | 2,738 | 3,177 | — | 13,475 | — | 14,061 | — | 13,866 | — | 24,478 | 5.5 | 37,657 | 4.2 | 53,119 | 3.4 | 65,603 | 2.1 |
| Guaymas | 8,648 | 12,333 | — | 8,558 | — | 8,534 | — | 8,796 | — | 18,890 | 7.3 | 34,865 | 5.9 | 58,434 | 5.1 | 54,826 | -0.6 |
| Navajoa | 2,955 | 2,430 | — | 5,473 | — | 9,154 | — | 11,009 | — | 17,345 | 4.5 | 30,560 | 5.5 | 44,373 | 3.7 | 62,901 | 3.5 |
| San Luis Rio Colorado | — | — | — | 175 | — | 910 | — | 558 | — | 4,079 | 15.2 | 28,545 | 15.0 | 51,118 | 5.7 | 76,684 | 4.0 |
| Cananea | 891 | 8,909 | — | 6,974 | — | 12,932 | — | 11,006 | — | 17,892 | 4.8 | 19,683 | 1.0 | 17,085 | 1.4 | 19,551 | 1.3 |
| Empalme | — | 1,534 | — | 2,309 | — | 3,985 | — | 4,703 | — | 10,379 | 7.5 | 18,964 | 5.8 | 24,994 | 2.7 | 31,555 | 1.3 |
| Agua Prieta | — | 656 | — | 3,236 | — | 4,674 | — | 4,106 | — | 10,471 | 8.7 | 15,339 | 3.8 | 21,017 | 3.1 | 28,862 | 3.1 |
| Caborca | 915 | 1,190 | — | 1,404 | — | 1,880 | — | 2,321 | — | 3,997 | — | 9,338 | — | 21,308 | 7.8 | 33,696 | 4.5 |
| Huatabampo | 1,458 | 2,592 | — | 3,511 | — | 4,508 | — | 5,643 | — | 7,701 | — | 10,228 | — | 18,842 | 5.9 | 22,635 | 1.8 |

Growth rate in each case refers to the average annual rate over the previous decade.

For the calculation of the annual rate of growth, see Table 3, note 1.

*Sources:* 1900–70: Unikel (1976) Table I-A2; 1970–80: X Censo General de Poblacion y Vivienda, Mexico City, 1980.

the situation of small and new towns was quite different. As we can see in Table 1, localities such as Los Mochis, Guamuchil, and Guasave grew at a hectic pace. Ciudad Obregon, Nogales and Navojoa in Sonora also experienced impressive population increases. As a result, urban growth in the region was fairly balanced and provided a solid basis for the formation of the regional urban network which emerged after 1940.

After the outbreak of World War II, economic and political relations between Mexico and the United States improved considerably. The US boycott of Mexican oil was lifted when the Mexican government and the American oil companies whose Mexican operations were nationalized in 1938 reached an agreement on compensation (Vazquez and Meyer, 1981), and in 1942 Mexico joined the United States in the war against the Axis countries. Both countries signed a commercial agreement by which trade barriers were lowered considerably and Mexico was soon exporting oil, cattle, beer, ore and agricultural products to the United States.

In addition to expanding foreign trade, investment and credit, the two governments initiated the Bracero programme, which provided for shared control over the hiring, transportation and protection of Mexican workers in jobs in US agriculture and railroads. During the next three years, 300,000 workers were hired through the programme. Many others entered the United States illegally.

Under the new conditions created during the war, Sonora and Sinaloa began again to export sugar, cotton, tomatoes, fruits and other products to the US, and soon surpassed their previous levels of output. As a result of this economic spurt large groups of migrants from less dynamic states moved to work in the fields and cities of Sonora and Sinaloa. At that time, migration to the US from Sinaloa–Sonora was minimal. Actually, most migrants to the US — about 60 percent — came in those years from the 'sending states' (Cross and Sandos, 1981), a group of six states located in north central Mexico (Durango, Quanajuato, Michoacan, Jalisco, San Luis Potosi and Zacatecas).

The economic upswing initiated in the region was to outlive the war. In the two decades following the war, the region maintained an impressive rate of growth, becoming the most productive and modern agricultural region in the country. The causes and implications of this transformation are worth examining. In the 1940s Mexico instituted an industrial policy based on the import-substitution model. To pursue its industrialization goals, a whole set of fiscal, monetary, price and social policies was implemented. Under this strategy the role of the agricultural sector was to provide the basic food products needed by the increasing urban population, to make food imports unnecessary and to generate exports that would earn the foreign exchange needed to import machinery, technology and industrial inputs.

Concurrent with this shift towards an industrially focused economy, an important change took place in Mexican agrarian policy. After 1940, agrarian reform was drastically curtailed; large private landholdings as yet untouched were protected by legislation, and support for the existing collective system was reduced. Thus, the production of basic foodstuffs (wheat and corn) necessary for self-sufficiency was placed in the hands of a small number of private landowners who received all the available support to modernize the agricultural production. To modernize the production of basic foodstuffs the government used an array of measures including the construction of expensive hydraulic systems, support for public and private research aimed at improving the productivity of seeds for wheat and hybridization for corn, the provision of credit and the improvement of communications. They also guaranteed a very profitable price for basic foodstuffs (Barkin, 1983).

In a matter of years these investments bore fruit. By 1950 the northwest (Sonora, Sinaloa and Baja California) was producing 38 percent of all the wheat in Mexico. By 1960 Sonora itself was producing 46.5 percent of the total, and by 1964 it had increased this figure to 71 percent (Hewitt, 1976). Sonora had become the 'breadbasket' of the country.

While Sonora specialized in producing basic grains (wheat, sorghum, soy and beans) for the national market, Sinaloa added the production of fresh vegetables for export to the list. Production of vegetables for export intensified during the 1960s. Following the US trade embargo on Cuban goods, there was a large demand for Mexican fresh vegetables in the United States, and exports rose. In 1965 the US imported tomatoes, cucumbers, and melons worth $33 million; the next year's imports grew to $95 million (Baird and McCaughan, 1982). These products came mainly from Sinaloa.

Despite its undeniable successes, the agricultural policy followed for almost three decades had many negative consequences and limitations and proved highly costly in the long term. As Cross and Sandos (1981) point out, the modernization of Mexican agriculture was a highly stratified process. The benefits of the Green Revolution accrued only to those with the land, capital and initiative to take advantage of the new methods, leading to a higher concentration of income by class and region. The great majority of Mexican farmers were bypassed by modernization.

**The Spatial Effects of Government Policy in Sinaloa and Sonora during the Period 1940 to 1970**
During the period 1940 to 1970 the country underwent its most rapid phase of urbanization in the century (Unikel, 1976) and perhaps in its entire history. In 1900, only 10.5 percent of Mexico's total population

lived in cities of more than 15,000 inhabitants. By 1940 this proportion was 19.9 percent and by 1970 it had reached 44.5 percent. Both Sinaloa and Sonora were among the least urban in the country in 1900: the former had an urban population of 5.1 percent and the latter did not have a single city with a population above 15,000. By 1940, their urban populations were still only 10.9 percent and 5.1 percent respectively. However, by 1970, 33 percent of Sinaloa's total population was urban and Sonora was well above the national average with 54.3 percent (Unikel, 1976).

Rapid urban growth was due in part to the higher rates of natural growth experienced by the country as a whole since the 1940s. However, the main cause, especially during the period 1940 to 1960, was social growth, that is, migration. Migrants came mainly from rural areas, whether in the same state or from others. With its economic boom, better living standards and abundant government resources, the Sinaloa–Sonora region lured people from neighbouring states who lacked the same economic and social opportunities.

But despite their rapid urban growth rates, neither of these states followed the pattern of metropolization seen in other rapid urban growth states such as Baja California Norte, Jalisco, Nuevo Leon, Puebla and Morelos between 1940 and 1970. Each state developed an urban system, dominated by two major cities (Culiacan–Mazatlan in Sinaloa, and Hermosillo–Cuidad Obregon in Sonora), followed by various medium-size cities such as Los Mochis, Guasave, Nogales, Guaymas and Novojoa. From 1940 to 1970 the small and medium-size cities gained a larger share of the total urban population. The level of urban concentration was higher in Sinaloa than in Sonora, and in 1970 Culiacan and Mazatlan held 69.5 percent of its total urban population (see Table 2). Although in the 1970s a shift towards concentration in the major cities was seen in both states, the Sinaloa–Sonora region has developed a fairly balanced urban system.

Another factor with important spatial implications in the Sinaloa–Sonora region is its inner and interregional economic links. Interpreting data on railroad freight movements, air traffic and telephone traffic,[2] Scott (1982) has pointed out that the region shows both strong internal links and fairly developed ones with the rest of the country, especially when compared with the Tijuana–Mexicali region whose main links are with southern California. The region has more extensive links with the northeast (Monterrey and Monclova) and the southwest (Guadalajara and Salamanca) than with Mexico City.

However, Scott has observed that the two main cities in the region have developed different patterns of links. While Culiacan had stronger links within the region (with Hermosillo, Mazatlan, Nogales and Ciudad Obregon), Hermosillo had strong links with Mexico City and

TABLE 2

Population distribution in cities of more than 15,000 inhabitants in the states of Sonora and Sinaloa, by decade, 1940–80

|  | 1940 | 1950 | 1960 | 1970 | 1980 |
|---|---|---|---|---|---|
| (1) Sinaloa | | | | | |
| Total urban population | 54,142 | 112,242 | 217,715 | 428,301 | 739,277 |
| (2) Culiacan | | | | | |
| Total population | 22,025 | 48,936 | 85,024 | 172,004 | 304,826 |
| Share of state urban | | | | | |
| population in Culiacan (2/1) | 40.6% | 43.5% | 39.0% | 40.1% | 41.2% |
| (3) Mazatlan | | | | | |
| Total population | 32,117 | 41,754 | 76,874 | 126,325 | 199,830 |
| Share of state urban | | | | | |
| population in Mazatlan (3/1) | 59.3% | 37.1% | 35.3% | 29.4% | 27.0% |
| Other cities | — | 19.4% | 25.7% | 30.6% | 31.8% |
| (4) Sonora | | | | | |
| Total urban population | 18,601 | 153,115 | 349,588 | 607,710 | 859,060 |
| (5) Hermosillo | | | | | |
| Total population | 18,601 | 43,519 | 96,019 | 180,327 | 297,175 |
| Share of state urban | | | | | |
| population in Hermosillo (5/4) | 100% | 28.4% | 27.4% | 29.6% | 34.5% |
| (6) Cuidad Obregon | | | | | |
| Total population | — | 30,991 | 67,956 | 117,183 | 165,572 |
| Share of state urban population | | | | | |
| in Ciudad Obregon (6/4) | — | 20.2% | 19.4% | 19.2% | 19.2% |
| Other cities | — | 51.4% | 53.2% | 51.2% | 46.3% |

*Sources:* 1940–70: Unikel (1976) Table I-A1; 1980: X Censo General de Poblacion y Vivienda, Mexico City, 1980.

many other regions in the country. Moreover, when analysing the origin and destination of railroad cargo traffic in the year 1970, Hermosillo and Ciudad Obregon show strong links not only with Mexico City, Guadalajara and Monclova, but also with cities in central Mexico such as Puebla, Queretaro and Toluca. In contrast, Culiacan and Mazatlan show a narrower range of links with other cities in the country.

Why did the Sinaloa–Sonora region develop a relatively balanced urban system with strong internal links? And why have the two major cities in each state developed different patterns of links with the rest of the country? Once again we must look to the role played by the international economy and by the local pattern of capital accumulation in regional development to answer these questions.

One can explain, in part, the existence of a wide web of urban centres in both states by analysing the way in which agricultural resources have been created and by whom they are owned. Certainly the key element is land. Land ownership in Mexico is difficult to verify since large tracts operated as single agricultural enterprises often appear under different names — names 'borrowed' from relatives and friends of the real owners — as a way of bypassing the legal limit of 100 hectares of irrigated land per person. Various authors (Hewitt, 1976; Aguilar, 1971; Baird and McCaughan, 1982) have gathered enough evidence to prove that land ownership is highly concentrated in both states.

At the same time, however, an historical view of the changes in land tenure yields a different picture, to wit, that during the last 50 years the pattern of land tenure has gone through a cycle of concentration and deconcentration.

Before President Cardenas undertook his programme of agrarian reform in the mid- 1930s, the vast majority of the arable land was in the hands of the Porfirista landowners of pre-revolutionary Mexico, plus a group of revolutionary military officers and politicians. Cardenas' policies spurred profound changes in the pattern of land tenure, to the detriment of the old landowners and the benefit of the peasants and landless workers in both states. Between 1930 and 1940 the share of land worked by *ejidatarios* in the state of Sonora increased from 13 percent to 40 percent (Aguilar, 1971), a clear indication that redistribution of property took place.

On the other hand, the process of concentration of land ownership continued as more arable land was made available by the irrigation works of the 1940s. This land was held entirely by the private sector which included the pre-reform elite, a group of men who sold (or lost through expropriation) properties in other commercial farming areas of the country and used the new land to re-establish themselves in agriculture. Thousands of hectares were purchased by government officials, bureaucrats and businessmen (Hewitt, 1976).

Government-financed irrigation works were carried out in the 1940s in Hermosillo, Guaymas, Caborca, the Yaqui and Culiacan valleys, and in other parts of the region. Those cities or towns located near the water districts — Caborca, Guaymas, Guasave and others — received not only thousands of migrants seeking jobs in public works projects or in agriculture but also new opportunities to do business in the areas of trade, services and agriculture.

Thus, water districts in these areas generated multiplier effects whose internal economic and social dynamics have kept urban growth rates above those of the main cities for decades. Regarding the question of interregional links, Sinaloa and Sonora developed different patterns of links to other regions in Mexico according to the degree that both states were linked to the international economy.

While Sonora became the nation's most important wheat producer and wheat also dominated its economy, Sinaloa became the largest national producer of tomatoes and other winter vegetables (approximately 30 percent), and tomatoes became one of its most important products. But unlike wheat, approximately two-thirds of the tomatoes produced were exported (Schramm, 1984). By 1979 the export of tomatoes and other winter vegetables amounted to almost US$260 million (Weintraub, 1983). Sales to domestic markets were insignificant until the mid-1970s.

I do not intend to portray Sonora as completely nationally oriented and Sinaloa as totally export oriented. However, I do contend that the importance of wheat and winter vegetables in their economies and the different markets each had, help to explain Sonora's stronger links to various wheat-consuming and processing regions in Mexico and Sinaloa's stronger links to the United States (Baird and McCaughan, 1982).

## Recent Trends in the Economic Internationalization of Sonora and Sinaloa

Until the mid-1960s, Sinaloa's and Sonora's ties to the international economy were mainly the result of the relationship between Mexico and the United States. They produced products — such as cotton and sugar — which were geared to the world market and which also played an important role in the economy of each. But in general, trade relations, investment, the flow of capital, etc., stemmed mainly from this bilateral relationship. For example, US winter vegetable distributors who played a key role in providing credit to tomato growers in Mexico were regional, as opposed to international, economic agents. However, from the mid-1960s on, the Sinaloa–Sonora region entered into a new phase in its relations with the international economy, in which the emphasis was on its ties to the world economy rather than the bilateral relationship.

Unlike the previous period (1940s to mid-1960s), when international relations were linked to agricultural trade, later economic ties were spread across new economic sectors such as services (tourism), industry (assembly firms and the automobile industry) and agribusiness, and were linked through direct investments. International tourism has played a crucial role in Sinaloa. In the mid-1960s international consortia such as Western International, Holiday Inn, Hilton Hotels and Sheraton Hotels began to operate on a large scale in Mexico, buying many national chains and building many new hotels. In the Sinaloa–Sonora region, Mazatlan was the centre of the tourist boom which triggered the rise of new services, and escalated real estate values. In 1978, Mazatlan received 5.6 percent of foreign tourists in Mexico (Schramm, 1984).

As for assembly firms (see next section), in less than a decade Mexico became the United States' most important partner in assembly activities (Grunwald and Flamm, 1985). Sonora has been most strongly affected.

Although the overall economic impact of these plants has been less in Sonora than in the states of Baja California Norte or Chihauhua, plants have been established in Sonora's most important border cities: Nogales, San Luis Rio Colorado and Agua Prieta, with a few also in Hermosillo. Although assembly firms have had a significant impact on employment in Sonora's borderlands, I will argue in the next section that their links to the state and national economies have not been strengthened as a result.

The latest manifestation of the internationalization of the regional economy is Ford's investment in a plant in Hermosillo producing automobiles for export. Other similar investments have been made in various northern cities in Mexico by General Motors and Chrysler (Saltillo), Renault (Gomez Palacio) and Nissan (Aguascalientes). There has also been a major shift in agricultural relations between Mexico and the United States. The US now exports basic foodstuffs to Mexico while Mexico has substantially increased the production of winter vegetables, fruit and cattle for export (Sanderson, 1981). In 1980, Mexico imported almost half of its total consumption of basic products — 10 million tons of basic grains, a large part of a total $3 billion in agricultural trade.

As pointed out by Barkin (1983), the fundamental causes of these changes in the relations of production in Mexico's agricultural sector were the growing influence of international economic forces on farm-level activity in Mexico combined with Mexican economic policies which have facilitated transmission of international prices and the growth of direct investment, industry and foreign agricultural distributors in the primary producing sector. In sum, both states became more export-oriented and dependent on transnational corporations for inputs such as finance, technology, organizational models and markets for a large proportion of their domestically oriented production (Barkin, 1983).

What kind of spatial effects has this new stage of internationalization in the Sinaloa–Sonora region brought? This question is not easy to answer since we are in the midst of the new stage and lack the information and previous analytical background necessary to proceed with an assessment. However I will suggest some possibilities.

It is clear that both states experienced a slower rate of urban growth than in previous decades. Between 1960 and 1970 Sonora and Sinaloa grew at annual rates of 5.2 percent and 6.3 percent respectively. Between 1970 and 1980 these rates rose 3.6 percent and 5.5 percent. Sonora grew at a considerably slower rate than Sinaloa. Looking at cities individually we also find some interesting differences. Hermosillo and Caborca in Sonora and all cities except Escuinapa in Sinaloa grew at an annual rate of over 4 percent while Nogales, Huatabamp, Empalme and Guyamas have much lower rates. Overall the big cities grew faster than the smaller ones, especially in Sonora. Moreover, the share of the state's population concentrated in Hermosillo increased from 29.6 percent in 1970 to 34.5 percent in 1980 (see Table 2).

These changes seem to be associated with changes in employment. In both states the population employed in agriculture has decreased. In 1970, in Sonora, 109,377 people were employed in agriculture. By 1980 this figure had fallen to 100,765, a decrease of 7.8 percent. In Sinaloa the decline was even greater: from 177,691 in 1970 to 156,542 in 1980, which is a decline of 11.9 percent. Yet while fewer people were directly employed in agriculture, the number of those employed in manufacturing increased, rising in the state of Sonora by 63.7 percent — from 28,393 in 1970 to 46,493 in 1980. The highest rates of employment growth in manufacturing were found not in the two largest cities but in Nogales (146 percent), Agua Prieta (184.5 percent), and San Luis Rio Colorado (84.6 percent). In Sinaloa, employment in manufacturing grew from 30,803 to 40,197 (30.4 percent) and was concentrated basically in the largest urban centres such as Culiacan, Mazatlan and Los Mochis.

The decline in agricultural jobs may have been associated with the displacement caused by the mounting modernization of the increasingly export-oriented sector and the expansion in the manufacturing sector which, in Sonora, has been linked to the mushrooming of assembly plants along its international border. It is not surprising that 40.9 percent of all manufacturing jobs created between 1970 and 1980 in Sonora were located in the border cities of Nogales, San Luis Rio Colorado and Agua Prieta.

It is clear that industrial growth has not been able to offset the losses in agriculture or to provide enough jobs to employ all those who recently entered the labour market. Where have all these people gone? Trade grew considerably in both states. In 1970 Sonora employed 32,838 people in trade. By 1980 the number had increased to 51,286, that is, by 56.1 percent. In Sinaloa the number rose from 29,478 to 51,912 in the same period, an increase of 76.1 percent. Unfortunately, information in the 1980 census for employment in services is not comparable to that of 1970. Nevertheless, I do not think growth in service employment provides the answer. The answer is that under-employment has grown at amazing rates. As different authors have stated (Urquidi and Mendez, 1978), the population census does not permit accurate quantification of open unemployment and underemployment; however, the latter can be gauged by focusing on 'time worked', 'income', and through a very broad, vague concept labelled 'insufficiently specified' (those receiving little or no income, working only a few months a year under very unstable conditions). The increase in people who are labelled 'insufficiently specified' is truly surprising. In Sinaloa there were 22,540 in 1970 and 101,632 in 1980, an increase of 350 percent. In Sonora the figure rose from 16,121 to 74,664, or 363.1 percent. Interestingly, both states are below the national average increase of 776 percent, from 747,525 in 1970 to 6,552,037 in 1980.

Regarding the economic links within the region and with other regions in Mexico, I can only speculate that they have grown weaker, while links with the international economy have grown stronger. Export-oriented agricultural activities have traditonally developed stronger links with the international economy — as was the case of Sinaloa when compared with Sonora during the period 1940–65 — while assembly firms have developed no ties whatsoever to the national economy (see next section). I have little information on the Ford plant in Hermosillo, so an assessment of its ties to the national economy cannot yet be made. However, if the Ford plant operates as the assembly firms do, exempt from local content requirements and producing only for export, its links to the national economy will be rather weak.

**The Spatial Effects of Assembly Operations on the Border Region**
Over the last decade Mexico's northern border has drawn the attention of a wide audience of scholars, planners and public officials. Their interests and approaches are numerous and diverse, including topics such as international migration, urban and regional development, binational relations, environmental issues and many others (Bustamante, 1980). One area of special interest has been the assembly firms.

Unfortunately, much of the mounting attention focused on the phenomenon has simplified the complex and multi-dimensional reality of the border. One finds in numerous works a tendency to equate the border with the assembly plant phenomenon or to assign to the latter a major role in the region's economy, employment and urban and regional growth. There is no doubt that assembly operations have had a strong impact on the border; however, it is mistaken to conceive of them as playing a major role in the formation and current functioning of the region. In this final section of the chapter I will assess the urban and regional impact of assembly plants on the border region.

*The Maquiladora Boom along the Border*[3]
In 1965, the Mexican government, emulating the examples of Hong Kong, Taiwan and Puerto Rico (Fernandez, 1977) established the Border Industrialization Program (BIP), which was fully operational by 1967. The BIP granted assembly firms a legal status different from that granted other foreign-owned companies in Mexico. The government waived all duties and regulations on the importation of raw

materials and capital equipment. They also exempted assembly firms located within a 12.5-mile deep strip of land along the US–Mexico border, who exported 100 percent of their finished products, from the 'Mexicanization' requirement of Mexican majority ownership in any foreign-owned firm. If the company imported 100 percent of raw materials and components and exported 100 percent of the output, they paid no corporate income tax, nor any other tax associated with profits, sales or dividends. They were allowed to negotiate waivers of municipal and state taxes with local governments. The BIP ceased to be a 'border' programme in 1971 when it was extended to a 12.5-mile wide coastal strip and in 1972 when it was extended to the whole country (Fernandez, 1977). According to Fernandez- Kelly (1983), the latter change laid the legal foundation necessary to transform the whole country into an export processing zone. That has not occurred. By 1983 only 11 percent of the total assembly plants in the country were located outside the border region (Grunwald and Flamm, 1985).

One of the primary goals of the BIP was the alleviation of the widespread unemployment along the 2,000-mile border caused largely by the end of the Bracero Programme (1965) and the sharp decline in cotton production in the border municipalities (Fernandez, 1977). According to some sources unemployment fluctuated from 40 per cent to 50 per cent in the borderlands in 1966. Assembly operations were thought to be a solution and some people went so far as to predict that by 1980 the Mexican border cities could employ 500,000 *maquiladora* workers (cited by Martinez, 1978). Other goals included the introduction of new methods of manufacturing that would industrialize the border, increased consumption of Mexican raw materials, the promotion of industrial decentralization, and the amelioration of the trade balance (Fernandez, 1977).

To what extent has the BIP met its original goals? It has been widely criticized on both sides of the border (Bustamante, 1975; Tamayo and Fernandez, 1983). Its critics contend that due to their very nature, assembly operations constitute an enclave in the Mexican economy and that the jobs they generate tend not to absorb the mainstream of unemployed and under-employed workers. In addition, most of the jobs created require unskilled workers and this trend will continue. It is also argued that although many of the assembly plants use sophisticated equipment and technologies, little technology is transferred to the rest of the Mexican economy. The consumption of Mexican inputs has been negligible. In 1976 Mexican goods amounted to a modest 3 percent of all inputs used by assembly plants (Fernandez-Kelly, 1983); by 1977 this figure had decreased to 1.6 percent, and in 1979, 1.5 percent (Christopherson, 1982). In addition, only part of the wages paid to assembly workers are spent on Mexican goods and services; the assembly workers are spent on Mexican goods and services; the population near the border purchases a significant portion of its goods across the frontier (Grunwald and Flamm, 1985).

Bustamante (1975) even suggests that assembly firms have actually increased unemployment. He points out that unemployment along the border increased by 83 percent from the start of the programme until 1975. At the same time, the assembly firms have served as a magnet, attracting migrants to border cities but unable to absorb most of those it attracts. Instead, most migrants are employed in the service sector or are not employed at all.

In the next section I will present a general picture of the border region in both spatial and economic terms, while focusing on the areas where the assembly plants are located. Often, the border region is presented as homogeneous and little attention is given to the individual cities where assembly firms function. Yet if we want to understand the spatial effects of assembly operations, we must take into consideration the traits and particular conditions of each site, such as size, economic structure, geographic location, and so forth.

*Urbanization in the Border: from Fast to Moderate Growth*
Along the border everything seems to happen at a hectic pace. The assembly plants sprang up very rapidly along the 2,000-mile border and between 1940 and 1960 it had the highest rate of urban growth in the country. During the 1950s the rate of growth of the largest cities on the border surpassed that of Mexico City (Fernandez, 1977). From a political-administrative point of view, Mexico's northern border region encompasses 35 municipalities located in the states of Baja California Norte, Chihauhua, Coahuila, Nuevo Leon and Tamulipas. According to the 1980 census, almost 3 million people lived in the region, of which 75.5 percent were concentrated in the 12 largest cities (see Table 3). Of the total population, 57.9 percent is concentrated in the five largest cities. The population of the border municipalities represents 27.6 percent of the total population of the border states and 4.4 percent of the national population. The 12 largest cities contain 20.8 percent of the total population of the border states, and 3.3 percent of the national population.

To grasp the meaning of these numbers it is important to remember that in 1940 those same cities contained only 6.8 percent of the population of the border states and 0.9 percent of the national population. At the turn of the century, none of the cities in the border region had more than 10,000 inhabitants; Tijuana was a hamlet and Mexicali was not even recorded in the 1900 census. However, cities such as Nuevo Laredo, Matamoros, Piedras Negras and Ciudad Juarez had experienced some growth during the last decades of the nineteenth

TABLE 3
Population of the border states and the most important cities along the northern border (1900–80)

| | Population | | | | | | | | | Annual rate of growth[1] | |
|---|---|---|---|---|---|---|---|---|---|---|---|
| | 1900 | 1910 | 1921 | 1930 | 1940 | 1950 | 1960 | 1970 | 1980 | 1960–70 | 1970–80 |
| Nation | 13,607,259 | 15,160,369 | 14,334,096 | 16,552,644 | 19,649,162 | 25,779,254 | 34,923,129 | 48,381,547 | 66,846,833 | | |
| Border states | 1,400,872 | 1,657,733 | 1,717,082 | 2,054,345 | 2,617,721 | 3,762,963 | 5,541,100 | 7,848,169 | 10,691,887 | | |
| Tijuana | 242 | 733 | 1,028 | 8,384 | 16,486 | 59,952 | 152,473 | 341,067 | 429,500 | 7.6 | 2.2 |
| Mexicali | — | 462 | 6,782 | 14,842 | 18,775 | 65,749 | 179,539 | 276,167 | 341,559 | 4.2 | 2.1 |
| San Luis Rio Colorado | — | — | 175 | 910 | 558 | 4,079 | 28,545 | 51,118 | 76,684 | 5.7 | 4.0 |
| Nogales | 2,738 | 3,177 | 13,475 | 14,061 | 13,866 | 24,478 | 37,657 | 53,119 | 65,603 | 3.4 | 2.1 |
| Agua Prieta | — | 656 | 3,236 | 4,674 | 4,106 | 10,471 | 15,339 | 21,017 | 28,862 | 3.1 | 3.1 |
| Ciudad Juarez | 8,218 | 10,621 | 19,457 | 39,669 | 48,881 | 122,566 | 262,119 | 414,908 | 544,496 | 4.5 | 2.7 |
| Villa Acuna | 667 | 933 | 2,423 | 5,350 | 5,607 | 11,372 | 20,048 | 30,838 | 38,898 | 4.2 | 2.3 |
| Piedras Negras | 7,888 | 8,518 | 14,233 | 15,878 | 15,663 | 27,581 | 44,992 | 40,885[2] | 67,455 | −1.0 | 4.9 |
| Nuevo Laredo | 6,548 | 8,143 | 14,998 | 21,636 | 28,872 | 57,668 | 92,627 | 152,325 | 201,371 | 4.9 | 2.7 |
| Reynosa | 1,915 | 1,475 | 2,107 | 4,840 | 9,412 | 34,087 | 74,140 | 140,480 | 194,693 | 6.2 | 3.2 |
| Rio Bravo | — | — | 515 | 746 | 936 | 4,610 | 17,500 | 39,933 | 55,236 | 7.8 | 3.2 |
| Matamoros | 8,347 | 7,390 | 9,215 | 9,733 | 15,699 | 45,846 | 92,327 | 140,660 | 188,745 | 4.2 | 2.9 |
| Total main border cities | 36,563 | 42,108 | 87,654 | 140,723 | 178,861 | 468,459 | 1,017,306 | 1,702,517 | 2,233,462 | 5.0 | 2.6 |

[1] Annual rate of growth was calculated using the following expression: $(2P_1 − P_0)/(P_1 + P_0) \cdot 1/n \cdot 100$, where $P_0$ and $P_1$ are the population of the city at the beginning and the end of the period considered, respectively, and $n$ is the number of years.
[2] A data mistake.
*Sources:* 1900–1970: Unikel (1976) Tables I-A1 and 1-A2; 1970–1980: X Censo General de Poblacion y Vivienda, Mexico City, 1980.

century and had already developed ties to the national economy. Actually, the regions of Nuevo Laredo and Reynosa can be traced back to the eighteenth century and their foundation was not determined by the border (Margulis, 1981). Ciudad Juarez has experienced considerable economic and demographic growth since the last half of the nineteenth century (Martinez, 1978).

Tijuana and Mexicali, on the other hand, experienced their greatest periods of urban growth more recently. In 1910, Mexicali with a population of 462 inhabitants began to grow rapidly as a result of Colorado River irrigation projects, largely financed by US capital. By 1921 its population had increased to 6,782. Tijuana also grew dramatically in the 1920s but for other reasons. With the prohibition of horse racing in California in 1915 and of prostitution and dance halls in 1917, as well as the 1920 constitutional prohibition of alcoholic beverages, Tijuana and Ciudad Juarez began to thrive on the 'tourism of vice' (Hansen, 1981).

The real boom did not take place, however, until World War II. The war triggered a huge demand for Mexican raw materials and labour in the United States so that the border cities not only regained but improved their position as commercial centres in this new movement of goods and workers (Martinez, 1978). Between 1940 and 1950, Matamoros, Ciudad Juarez, Mexicali and Tijuana tripled in size and Reynosa quadrupled. Between 1950 and 1960 the average annual increase in population across the border municipalities was 6.3 percent. Particularly high growth rates were found in Tijuana (9.8 percent), Mexicali (8.5 percent), and Ciudad Juarez (7.8 percent). Between 1960 and 1970 the average annual increase in population for the border municipalities fell to 4.1 percent (Urquidi and Mendez, 1978), but Tijuana, San Luis Rio Colorado and Reynosa doubled in size.

During the 1970s the border cities experienced a drastic fall in their rate of growth. The average annual rate of growth for the 12 largest cities (see Table 3) was 2.6 percent, almost half the rate between 1960 and 1970. It was the decade with the lowest rate of growth since 1940. The rate of urban growth in the border region decreased between 1960 and 1980. This was due to a fall in migration to the region, particularly between 1970 and 1980. It is important to note that during the period 1940 to 1960 the border's urban growth was mainly social, that is, due to the inflow of migrants (Unikel, 1976). With the exception of Mexico City, the border area has drawn more domestic migration than any other part of the country (Urquidi and Mendez, 1978). The vast majority of the migrant population came from rural areas in the states of Jalisco, Durango, Zacatecas and Nuevo Leon.

However, the economic changes the border region has undergone since the 1960s have eroded the economic opportunities that spurred

TABLE 4
Economically active population (EAP) by field of activity, 1980

| | Mexico Number | % | Border states Number | % | Border municipalities Number | % |
|---|---|---|---|---|---|---|
| Total EAP | 22,066,084 | | 3,464,422 | | 1,010,804 | |
| Agriculture, livestock, hunting, fishing, forestry | 5,699,971 | 25.8 | 532,867 | 15.3 | 102,417 | 10.1 |
| Mining | 477,017 | 2.1 | 24,850 | 0.7 | 4,811 | 0.4 |
| Manufacturing | 2,575,124 | 11.6 | 525,590 | 15.1 | 156,490 | 15.4 |
| Electricity, water, gas | 115,932 | 0.5 | 11,704 | 0.3 | 3,351 | 0.3 |
| Construction | 1,296,337 | 5.8 | 231,145 | 6.6 | 66,283 | 6.5 |
| Trade | 1,729,296 | 7.8 | 383,963 | 11.0 | 132,447 | 13.1 |
| Transportation, communications | 672,111 | 3.0 | 159,153 | 4.5 | 45,906 | 4.5 |
| Financial services | 405,754 | 1.8 | 72,431 | 2.0 | 19,913 | 1.9 |
| Communal services | 2,418,114 | 10.9 | 516,522 | 14.9 | 157,346 | 15.5 |
| Insufficiently specified | 6,552,037 | 29.6 | 980,226 | 28.2 | 313,766 | 31.0 |
| Unemployed | 124,391 | 0.5 | 25,971 | 0.7 | 8,074 | 0.7 |

*Source:* X Censo General de Poblacion y Vivienda, Mexico City, 1980.

migration to the region. The largest cities along the border, with the exception of Tijuana, were all closely tied to very productive hydraulic districts and an important proportion of their employment and profits was dependent upon agriculture. However, from the 1960s onward the fall in the international price of cotton and the loss of Mexicali's fertile soil due to the increased salinity of the Colorado River (Unikel, 1976) dealt a strong blow to border agricultural activities. The subsequent shift to crops other than cotton — soya, sorghum, cartamus, etc. — was based on highly mechanized systems that further displaced agricultural workers. As a result, the number and proportion of people employed in agriculture in the border region has fallen steadily since the 1960s. In 1969, the proportion of the economically active population employed in agriculture was 39.4 percent for the nation as a whole, 29.2 percent for the border states and 23.2 percent for the border municipalities. In 1980 these proportions had fallen to 25.8 percent, 15.3 percent and 10.1 percent respectively (see Table 4).

While agricultural employment went into a steep decline, trade and services kept growing rapidly. The increase between 1950 and 1970 in the economically active population engaged in trade and services in the border municipalities (from 25 percent to 46 percent) was significantly larger than that at the national level (from 25 percent to 32 percent). We may conclude, therefore, that wage-earning in services and trade is remarkably high in the border municipalities and accounts for a large share of the regional economy (Urquidi and Mendez, 1978).

Despite the rapid growth of services and trade, employment

opportunities have been shrinking since the 1960s, while unemployment and under-employment have risen steadily. As mentioned earlier, the population census does not permit an accurate quantification of open unemployment; nevertheless, it does show that the number of unemployed workers in the border municipalities increased from 2.4 percent in 1960 to 4.1 percent in 1970. According to Urquidi and Mendez (1978), these figures are lower than they should be, since they do not include those seeking work for the first time. Thus unemployment in the border municipalities in 1970 was probably no less than 7 percent of the economically active population (EAP).

More sobering than the level of unemployment is the level of under-employment. Although accurate data on under-employment is not available, research done in 1970 by the National Tripartite Commission concluded that under-employment was 16.1 percent of EAP in the border municipalities. Additional research carried out by the former Secretary of Industry and Commerce determined that if all workers receiving incomes below the minimum wage are considered under-employed, then manufacturing under-employment in the border region in 1970 would amount to 34.2 percent of the regional EAP, and under-employment in construction would reach 38.5 percent.

However, according to the census, in 1980 only 25,971 people or 0.7 percent of the EAP were unemployed, which is an obvious under-estimate. However, if the category of 'insufficiently specified' is used as an indicator of under-employment, the number falling into that category is dramatic: 313,766 people or 31 percent of the EAP of the border municipalities (see Table 4). The proportion exceeds both the national figure (29.6 percent) and that for the border states (28.2 percent).

Shrinking employment opportunities and mounting under-employment may help to explain the decline in migration to the border since the period 1940 to 1960. However, the fact that permanent migration to the border has slowed down in comparative terms, thus slowing the rate of urban growth, does not mean that the flow of migrants to the border has been reduced. It is important to keep in mind that many migrants are still lured to the border with the hope of crossing to the other side. Therefore, migration to the border on a temporary basis (floating population) might still swell the border towns. Unfortunately, we do not have the information necessary to estimate the floating population in the border cities.

What economic impact have assembly operations exerted on the border? In 1970 manufacturing industry (which includes workers hired by assembly plants) provided employment for 94,052 individuals or 15.6 percent of the region's EAP and 4.3 percent of the nation's. In the same year assembly firms employed 20,327 workers (Grunwald and

Flamm, 1985) or 21.6 percent of the border municipalities' manufacturing EAP and 3.3 percent of the national EAP in manufacturing. In 1980, the proportion of the border municipalities' EAP employed in manufacturing (Urquidi and Mendez, 1978) decreased slightly to 15.4 percent; however, the number of people employed in manufacturing went up considerably to 156,490, a 66.3 percent increase above the 1970 level. In national terms, manufacturing at the border did quite well. Manufacturing as a share of the national EAP fell from 16.7 percent in 1970 to 11.6 percent in 1980 (see Table 4), while the number employed in manufacturing rose by only 18.7 percent — a small increase when compared with manufacturing in the border municipalities.

The most interesting change during the years between 1970 and 1980 was the considerable importance workers employed by assembly firms achieved within the border municipalities' manufacturing EAP, increasing its proportion from 21.6 percent in 1970 to 65.7 percent in 1980 (see Table 5). In other words, growth in manufactures was due mainly to the expansion of assembly plants. Workers employed in assembly plants also increased their share of the border municipalities' total EAP from 3.3 percent in 1970 to 10.4 percent in 1980 — that is, one in ten economically active individuals was engaged in assembly work. Assembly operations were highly concentrated in the main border cities in 1980. Of all people employed in them, 88.6 percent were concentrated in 11 cities along the border (see Table 5). Ciudad Juarez, Matamoros, Tijuana, Mexicali and Nogales alone contained 72.8 percent of the national total, and 82.2 percent of that for the border municipalities.

While the number of workers employed in assembly plants is certainly a good indicator of the economic significance of assembly operations in the border economy, it is also important to examine other variables such as capital invested and income received. In 1970, machinery and other equipment in assembly plants was valued at 149 million pesos, representing 5.3 percent of gross capital in all manufacturing. Income received from this particular type of industry accounted for 27 percent of the total reached in border manufacturing (Urquidi and Mendez, 1978). As noted by Grunwald and Flamm (1985), assembly wages appear to have risen steeply during the mid-1970s, outpacing the consumer price index. The payroll per employee — for both blue-collar and white-collar workers — increased about 16 percent in real terms from 1973 to 1974 and about 7 percent from 1975 to 1976. Since 1977, remunerations per worker, however, have declined so that by 1983 they were (in real prices) 13 percent below the 1973 level.

Minimum wages in the border areas have tended to be considerably

TABLE 5
Economically active population, manufacturing EAP and workers
employed in assembly plants in border cities, 1980[a]

| Location | Total EAP (1) | EAP in manufacturing (2) | Assembly workers employed (3) | 3/1 % | 3/2 % |
|---|---|---|---|---|---|
| Nation | 22,066,084 | 2,575,124 | 119,546 | 0.5 | 4.6 |
| Border states | 3,464,422 | 525,590 | 106,032[b] | 3.0 | 20.1 |
| Border municipalities | 1,010,804 | 156,490 | 105,775[d] | 10.4 | 67.5 |
| Mexicali | 170,675 | 19,283 | 7,146 | 4.1 | 37.0 |
| Tecate | 10,168 | 2,066 | 672 | 6.6 | 32.5 |
| Tijuana | 162,064 | 27,075 | 12,343 | 7.6 | 45.5 |
| Ciudad Acuña | 14,599 | 2,669 | 2,931[c] | 20.0 | 100.0 |
| Piedras Negras | 26,345 | 4,061 | 2,592 | 9.8 | 63.8 |
| Ciudad Juárez | 206,868 | 44,586 | 39,402 | 19.0 | 88.3 |
| Agua Prieta | 13,124 | 3,682 | 4,625[c] | 35.2 | 100.0 |
| Nogales | 26,060 | 6,527 | 12,921[c] | 49.5 | 100.0 |
| Matamoros | 86,470 | 15,317 | 15,231 | 17.6 | 99.4 |
| Neuvo Laredo | 64,892 | 8,582 | 2,462 | 3.7 | 28.6 |
| Raynosa | 68,069 | 10,617 | 5,450 | 8.0 | 51.3 |

[a]The information on EAP (1), EAP in manufacturing (2) and assembly workers (3) for each city actually corresponds to the Municipal level; however, since the municipal population is highly concentrated in each of the cities, it provides a close estimate.

[b]Besides the 11 municipalities presented in Table 5, it includes Ensenada. However, the exact number was not estimated because no information on geographical location outside the border was found. The actual number must be slightly higher and would include assembly plants located in Hermosillo and other non-border locations in the border states.

[c]The result is either a data mistake or is due to the fact that the 1980 Census and the Estadistica de la Industria Maquiladora were gathered for different periods.

[d]The Estadistica de la Industria Maquiladora de Exportacion, 1974–1982, omits the municipality of San Luis Rio Colorado, where two assembly plants were in operation in 1978. Information was not available for 1980.

*Sources:* columns (1) and (2): X Censo General de Poblacion y Vivienda, Mexico City, 1980; column (3): Estadistica de la Industria Maquiladora de Exportacion, 1974–1982, Secretaria de Programacion y Pre-supuesto, Mexico City, 1983.

higher than the national average, exceeding the latter by more than half at the beginning of the BIP. Since then the border average has fallen behind so that by the early 1980s the difference between border wages and those in the rest of the country was reduced to less than 20 percent. In those plants located in the interior, assembly wages averaged more than 20 percent higher than the national average minimum wage during the period 1975 to 1983 (Grunwald and Flamm, 1985).

One conclusion to be drawn from an analysis of Table 5 is that the economic significance of assembly plants has varied among cities along the border. Towns such as Nogales, Agua Prieta and Ciudad Acuna are obviously highly dependent on assembly operations, with more than 20 per cent of their total EAP engaged in assembly. Their dependence coincides with their size; they are the smallest of all cities where assembly operations function. Matamoros and Ciudad Juarez both have a considerable economic stake in assembly operations due to the overall importance of assembly in their economies. Most of their manufacturing activities are assembly oriented. A third group of cities — Nuevo Laredo, Piedras Negras, Tijuana and Mexicali — are less dependent on assembly operations, though they represent a fairly large share of manufacturing employment. In Tijuana, Reynosa and Piedras Negras, the share of assembly jobs in the manufacturing EAP reached 45.5 percent, 51.3 percent and 63.8 percent, respectively, in 1980.

To sum up, there can be no doubt about the economic significance of assembly operations for the border economy since the 1970s. However, as the analysis presented above shows, the border should not be seen as an homogeneous region but rather as a varied group of cities unevenly influenced by assembly operations. The smaller cities seem to fall into the category of highly dependent. Ciudad Juarez, the largest city along the border, is the exception to this rule. Along with size, economic diversification seems to be an important determinant of the degree of importance assembly operations hold. Cities with a variety and strong tradition of services and trade activities (Tijuana, Nuevo Laredo) or with agricultural or industrial backgrounds other than assembly (Mexicali, Reynosa) are less dependent upon assembly operations. If assembly plants were to close down their operations, the economies of Nogales, Agua Prieta, Ciudad Acuna and Nogales would be hard hit, but for the rest of the border the situation would not be unbearable. In these places the economic relationship between Mexico and the United States has been and still is the base of their economies. The world economy — assembly operations in this case — is far from dominant in the border economy.

*The Urban and Regional Impact of Assembly Operations*
As we saw in previous pages, the inflow of migrants to the border slowed significantly between 1970 and 1980. However, this was precisely the decade when assembly firms expanded their operations. How can this be explained?

Different surveys of people employed in assembly plants (Konig, 1981; Seligson and Williams, 1981) — albeit limited by their exclusion of the rest of the general population — have led to the conclusion that assembly plants contribute only marginally to internal migration to northern Mexico and international migration to the United States. As pointed out by Grunwald and Flamm (1985) and by Fernandez-Kelly

(1983), women comprise more than three-quarters of the labour force employed by assembly firms. It is beyond the scope of this chapter to tackle the issue, but it is important to mention that this contingent was not drawn from the traditional pool of unemployed or under-employed, but from a sector of the population that has not traditionally worked or looked for work, members of the so-called 'inactive' population. Thus, by creating a new labour pool and incorporating a new working contingent, the assembly firms have bypassed the majority of male workers, who are mostly rural migrants. Most women employed by assembly firms are not recent migrants. About 80 percent of interstate migrant assembly workers had lived for more than three years in the cities in which Seligson and Williams conducted their 1981 survey and only 5 percent had lived there less than one year.

In sum, assembly expansion has not played a significant role in migration and hence on the border's urban growth. But what about the role of assembly operations on intraregional links and links with the rest of the country?

As mentioned before, assembly operations in Mexico use a minor percentage of Mexican inputs. The explanation lies in a set of conditions prevailing in both countries. In Mexico these conditions include low productive capacity, failure to meet rigorous specifications and lack of interest in doing business with the assembly firms on the part of Mexican businessmen. On the US side, the use of Mexican components would compel firms to pay high duties which would increase the cost of assembly goods in the US market. Since the Mexican assembly plants are so close to the US, it is cheaper to use US inputs. The important fact that until 1985 assembly firms were not permitted to sell in the Mexican market also discouraged the use of Mexican components.

The lack of any significant linkage with other sectors of the national economy — both in the border or the interior — has accentuated the traditional position of isolation which the border has maintained vis-a-vis the rest of the country and within itself, while strengthening its ties to the world economy. Nevertheless, it is important to note that the border subregions vary significantly in their relationships with the rest of the country and the United States, depending on their economic structure, history and distance from the country's main economic centres. As pointed out by Tamayo and Fernandez (1983), Tijuana, Mexicali, Tecate and San Luis Rio Colorado constitute a subregion within the border. Highly urbanized, this zone's main links are to the economy of southern California (Scott, 1982), and it is weakly linked to the rest of the country. At the east end of the border, Nuevo Laredo, Matamoros and Reynosa are also strongly linked to the US economy and enjoy important connections with the rest of the country, especially Monterrey.

To sum up, assembly operations have reinforced the border's historical isolation from the rest of the country and further weakened its intraregional links. In most countries where assembly plants operate, they have an enclave status. However, the degree of linkage with the national economy varies significantly, depending on the country's policies towards assembly operations (Grunwald and Flamm, 1985). It seems that the more developed and economically diversified the country, the more it has to separate and maintain assembly operations within a free enterprise enclave. It has been argued that by allowing assembly firms access to the national market, and strengthening their links to the national economy, new investments would be spurred and the existing border economy would be revitalized. However, to achieve this, the country would have to change the industrial strategy of import-substitution it has followed for more than 40 years and shift to an export processing zone model. Mexico has recently made significant changes in this regard by joining the GATT at the end of 1985 and particularly by allowing assembly firms to sell 20 percent of their finished products in the Mexican market if they buy raw materials or components locally (*New York Times*, 19 January 1986).

Under these conditions, assembly firms might find it profitable to expand their activities and to include more input produced in Mexico in order to seize a share of the country's large internal market. That would undoubtedly lessen the isolationist effect they have had on the border towns and would strengthen their links with the national economy.

However, the situation is more complicated. On the one hand, producers operating in Mexico — either national or foreign — have proved incapable of meeting the rigorous specifications required by assembly firms or have lacked the interest in producing for them. On the other hand, protectionism has been very difficult to dismantle. Assembly firms interested in the Mexican market would have to face the competition and certainly the opposition of producers with economic importance and political clout who could make a case against the varied and diverse fiscal, labour and legal privileges that assembly firms enjoy. Thus the battle has just started.

## Conclusions

Those who advocate the world systems approach have contended that the new international division of labour is characterized primarily by the relocation of various types of traditional industries from core to peripheral countries. I have shown in this paper that the links between the Sonora–Sinaloa and border regions and the international economy were also shaped by economic activities geared to the expansion of commodity and money capital (such as trade, tourism, banking, transportation), as well as by industrial investments linked to the internal markets. The findings imply that regional economies with diverse and extensive links to the world economy may produce a more dynamic and well balanced style of capitalist growth than those linked through a few large firms concentrated in a few branches of the economy. A greater number of firms linked to the international economy (either national or foreign) in various sectors (industry, mining, agriculture, trade, etc.) might help to articulate the economy as a whole, raise overall productivity and allow capital and managerial skills to spread into new sectors of the economy.

The stronger the economic power and level of development of the national business class, the stronger its participation will be in the world economy. However, international capital formed by an array of firms from varied sectors of the economy and composed of firms of different sizes will tend to associate with local partners, establish relations with national or regional producers and consumers, and thus may enhance opportunities for national or regional firms and individuals to participate in the economic expansion often associated with the operations of international capital.

The process of economic internationalization in peripheral countries does not always lead to economic and demographic concentration in one or more urban centres and does not necessarily result in the isolation of entire regions from the rest of the country. A multi-dimensional pattern of internationalization, reflecting the need of capital to have access to both internal and international markets as well as varied natural and human resources, coupled with the strong participation of the national business community, might instead spread operations throughout the region or the nation, thus developing and strengthening urban networks and links within and between regions.

When analysing the economic and spatial consequences of the internationalization of the economy on peripheral countries, one should keep in mind not only the form and structure of international capital and the different degrees of development and peculiarities of peripheral countries. One should also focus on the differences between regions and even localities. The regional economic, social and political differences found in these countries influence the way in which each region establishes and defines its link to the world economy. Moreover, the economic and spatial implications of internationalization may vary significantly between regions within a country and trends in one region may differ from those measured at a national level. Some regions have been better articulated to the world economy, further widening the huge regional disparities found in most peripheral countries. A better understanding of the causes and factors determining the pattern of articulation between regions and the world economy would help to correct these disparities.

## Notes

I would like to thank Richard Corwin, Jose Luis Curbelo and especially Manuel Castells for their useful critiques and pertinent ideas. I also want to acknowledge Elizabeth Mueller and Electra Long for their help in editing the paper.

1. The Mexican case contrasts with that of other capitalist countries because the internationalization of its economy has taken place not only as part of a worldwide trend but also as a result of what various authors have called the 'silent' or 'de facto' integration of the Mexican economy into the economy of the United States (Reynolds, 1981; Rico, 1983). At first glance, it would appear difficult to distinguish between the two, but we believe that it is of paramount importance to distinguish between the causes of the internationalization of the economy originating at a world level and those stemming specifically from the relationship between Mexico and the United States. Each process has its own historic point of departure, very often involving different social, economic and institutional agents and different patterns of urban and regional location. Therefore, in this paper I will keep an analytical distinction between the world economy and the bilateral relationship between Mexico and the United States. The term 'international economy' refers to the two of them together.

2. The lack of an interregional input–output table in Mexico leaves scholars no choice other than to use these available indicators, despite their limitations.

3. *Maquiladora* is a term used in Mexico for assembly plants.

## References

Aguilar, A. (1971) 'Un Grave Problema Socioeconomico la Concentration de la Tierra en el Noroeste', *Problemas Estructurales del Subdesarrollo Mexico*, pp. 226–269. UNAM.

Baird, P. and E. McCaughan (1982) *Mexico – Estados Unidos: Relaciones Economicas y Lucha de Classes*. Mexico City: ERA.

Barkin, D. (1983) 'The Internationalization of Capital and the Spatial Organization of Agriculture in Mexico', in F. Moulaert and P.W. Salinas (eds.), *Regional Analysis and the New International Division of Labor*. New York: Kluwer and Nijhoff.

Brenner, R. (1977) 'The Origins of Capitalist Development: A Critique of Neo-Smithian Marxism', *New Left Review*, 104: 25–92.

Bustamante, J.A. (1975) 'El Programa Fronterizo de Maquiladoras: Observaciones Para una Evaluacion', *Foro Internacional*, 16: 183–204. Mexico City: El Colegio de Mexico.

Bustamante, J.A. (1980) *Mexico – Estados Unidos: Bibliografia General sobre Estudios Fronterizos*. Mexico City: El Colegio de Mexico.

Bustamante, J.A. (1981) 'La Interaccion Social en la Frontera Mexico-Estados Unidos: Un Marco Conceptual para la Investigacion', in S.R. Gonalez (ed.), *La Frontera del Norte*. Mexico City: El Colegio de Mexico.

Christopherson, S.M. (1982) 'The Evolution of Ciudad Juarez, Mexico, as an Industrial City'. Mimeogaphed. Berkeley: Department of Geography, University of California, Berkeley.

Cross, H.E. and J.A. Sandos (1981) *Across the Border*. Berkeley: Institute of Governmental Studies, University of California, Berkeley.

Fernandez, A.R. (1977) *The United States – Mexico Border*. Notre Dame: University of Notre Dame Press.

Fernandez-Kelly, M.P. (1983) *For We are Sold: Women and Industry in Mexico's Frontier*. Albany: State University of New York Press.

Florescano, E. and A. Moreno Toscano (1976) 'El Sector Externo y la Organizacion

166 *Global Restructuring and Territorial Development*

Espacial y Regional en Mexico (1521 – 1910)', in W.J. Wilkie, C.M. Meyer and W.E. de Monzon (eds.), *Contemporary Mexico: Papers of the IVth International Congress of Mexican History*. Berkeley: University of California Press.

Frobel, F., J. Heinrichs and O. Kreye (1980) *The New International Division of Labour*. Cambridge: Cambridge University Press.

Green, R. (1984) 'Mexico y los Bancos Norteamericanos', in R.A. Coronoa and L.J. Gibson (eds.), *Impactos Regionales de las Relaciones Economicas Mexico – Estados Unidos*. Mexico City: El Colegio de Mexico.

Grunwald, J. and K. Flamm (1985) *The Global Factory*. Washington, DC: The Brookings Institution.

Hansen, N. (1981) *The Border Economy*. Austin: University of Texas Press.

de Hewitt, A.C. (1976) *Modernizing Mexican Agriculture*. Geneva: UNRISD.

Jenkins, R. (1984) 'Divisions over the International Division of Labour', *Capital and Class*, 22: 28 – 57.

Konig, W. (1981) 'Efectos de la Actividad Maquiladora Fronteriza en la Sociedad Mexicana', in S.R. Gonzalez (ed.), *La Frontera del Norte*. Mexico City: El Colegio de Mexico.

Margulis, M. (1981) 'Crecimiento y Migracion en una Ciudad de la Frontera: Estudio Preliminar de Reynosa', in S.R. Gonzalez (ed.), *La Frontera del Norte*. Mexico City: El Colegio de Mexico.

Martinez, O.J. (1978) *Border Boom Town: Ciudad Juarez since 1848*. Austin: University of Texas Press.

Portes, A. and J. Walton (1981) *Labor, Class and the International System*. New York: Academic Press.

Reynolds, W.C. (1981) 'Las Perspectivas Economicas y Sociales de Mexico y sus Implicaciones para las Relaciones con los Estados Unidos', in C. Tello and C. Reynolds (eds.), *Las Relaciones Mexico – Estados Unidos*. Mexico City: Fondo de Cultura Economica.

Rico, C. (1983) 'The Future of Mexican – US Relations and Limits of the Rhetoric of 'Interdependence'', in C. Vazquez and G.M. Garcia (eds.), *Mexican – US Relations: Conflict and Convergence*. Los Angeles: University of California, Los Angeles.

Sanderson, S.E. (1981) *The Receding Frontier: Aspects of the Internationalization of US – Mexican Agriculture and their Implications for Bilateral Relations in the 1980s*. Working Papers in US – Mexican Studies, 15. La Jolla: University of California, San Diego.

Schramm, G. (1984) 'Regional Effects of US – Mexican Current Account Transactions', in R.A. Coronoa and L.J. Gibson (eds.), *Impactos Regionales de las Relaciones Economicas Mexico – Estados Unidos*. Mexico City: El Colegio de Mexico.

Scott, I. (1982) *Urban and Spatial Development in Mexico*. Baltimore: The Johns Hopkins University Press.

Seligson, A.M. and J.E. Williams (1981) *Maquiladoras and Migration Workers in the Mexico – United States Border Industrialization Program*. Mexico – United States Border Research Program. Austin: University of Texas.

Tamayo, J. and Fernandez, J.L. (1983) *Zonas Fronterizas (Mexico – Estados Unidos)*. Mexico City: Centro de Investigacion y Docencia Economica.

Unikel, L. (1976) *El Desarrollo Urbano de Mexico*. Mexico City: El Colegio de Mexico.

Urquidi, V.L. and S. Mendez (1978) 'Economic Importance of Mexico's Northern Border', in S. Ross (ed.), *Views Across the Border: The United States and Mexico*. Albuquerque: University of New Mexico Press.

Vazquez, J.Z. and L. Meyer (1981) *Mexico Frente a Estados Undios: Un Ensayo Historico, 1776 – 1980*. Mexico City: El Colegio de Mexico.

Wallerstein, I. (1974) *The Modern World-System I: Capitalist Agriculture and the Origins of the European World-Economy in the Sixteenth Century.* New York: Academic Press.

Wallerstein, I. (1979) *The Capitalist World Economy.* Cambridge: Cambridge University Press.

Weintraub, S. (1983) *Free Trade Between Mexico and the United States?* Washington, DC: The Brookings Institution.

# 8
# Social Forces, the State and the International Division of Labour: the Case of Malaysia

*Kamal Salih and Mei Ling Young*

The specific character of Malaysia in the international division of labour in the 1980s is the product of an evolution of society reflecting the contradictions in the history of Malaysia's incorporation in the modern world system. The resultant uneven development reveals features that are common to all peripheral capitalist countries as well as those that are unique to this particular society. The incorporation of the Malay peninsula into the world economy, and its specialization in primary commodity export under the sponsorship of the British colonial state was completed by the second decade of the present century (see Salih, 1981, for an elaboration). For the next 50 years the economy expanded according to the conjunctural cycles of the capitalist world economy, through the period of stagnation between the two wars, and the years of expansion after World War II until the 1970s. The establishment of the post-colonial state in 1957, while a political moment of some consequence, did not represent any significant break in Malaysia's status within the metropolitan-dominated world economy. Indeed, it became more entrenched.

The domination of foreign capital in the economic life of the country, not only in the capitalist plantation and mining sector but also in the commercial and trading sector, reached its highest point in the 1960s. Under the aegis of the colonial state, capitalist production in the primary sector was organized through the recruitment of cheap contract labour from India and China. These waves of immigration produced the basic multi-racial character of Malaysian society today (Salih and Young, 1981). The incorporation of female labour in the 'modern' sector took place during this period. Further capitalist penetration led to a differentiation of the peasantry into a 'traditional' sector and a semi-feudal smallholder sector producing for the world market. The traditional role of women in peasant households as manifested in productive and reproductive activity became transformed

We wish to thank IDRC for its support for the project 'Household Responses to Industrial and Urban Change in Malaysia'. This chapter draws on our work for that project.

with the expansion of schooling and the successful entry of some women, particularly in the urban areas, into the government and service sectors. This transformation was not an emancipation but merely a reconstitution of women's role in the sexual division of labour (Salih et al., 1985: 66–92).

The rise of the post-colonial state saw an alliance between the non-indigenous merchant class and an indigenous administrative–aristocratic class which was conducive to the continued role of foreign capital in the Malaysian economy. This alliance of dominant forces had historically undermined the position of labour and produced marked inequalities between regions, racial groups and social classes (Muzaffar, 1979; Lim, 1980; Jomo, 1986). Towards the end of the 1960s these imbalances became politically untenable, and the rupture of the political alliance, marked by the racial riots of 1969, produced a crisis in the Malaysian state which paved the way for its reconstitution through the introduction of the New Economic Policy (NEP) in 1970.

The specificity of the Malaysian social formation within the new international division of labour in the 1970s reflected not only the changing conditions of production and accumulation on a world scale into which it had been moulded, but the changing social forces which determine the resolution of internal economic and political problems. This chapter discusses the interplay of internal social forces, particularly the state, as well as external forces, in determining the role of Malaysia in the international division of labour. It is divided into three parts. The first part describes the social forces created by the historical division of labour. The second examines the role of the state in articulating with both external and internal co-determining economic and social structures. In the final part, through a case study of the semiconductor industry in Penang, we examine how the local economy is articulated with the international division of labour and the consequences of this articulation.

## Social Forces in the Malaysian Formation

The structure of the Malaysian social formation at the end of the 1960s was the product of the historical incorporation of the Malay peninsula under the impetus of colonial capitalism, which created, in the process of an extension of British capital, a multi-racial social structure differentiated in rather rigid terms along sectoral and political lines. It also created a post-colonial state which, given the conjunctural politics during the period of crisis in the metropolitan centres, had to mediate an emerging indigenous (Malay) consciousness regarding economic deprivation, and the dominant coalition of foreign capital and local non-indigenous commercial capital. The structure of Malaysian society as a peripheral capitalist economy, evidenced by its specialization as a principal primary commodity producer within the colonial division of labour, created internal structural inequalities in the organization of production and the distribution of surplus between capital and labour, and between racial groups. These social forces and groups must be examined in their distinct complementary and contradictory relationships with each other, taking into account these relations as they are expressed in the political process and the role of the state within it.

*Foreign Capital*

The role of foreign capital in the development of Malaysia in the 'modern' period (post-1875), beginning with the penetration of British capital into the Malay States, is well documented (see for example, Lim 1967; Hoffman and Tan, 1980; Saham, 1980; Li, 1982). Through its policies towards land and labour, the British colonial administration effectively organized the Malayan economy at the turn of the century as a producer of rubber and tin. The revenues went towards the salaries of the British civil service in Malaya, the support of the Malay sultanates and local chiefs, initially into public works such as rail and road, but the larger part went to the British Treasury and towards military expenses. Expenditure on infrastructure was aimed at assisting accumulation by British estate and mining interests. Insignificant proportions were spent on education and medical services (Li, 1982: 24–39).

While there was partial divestment leading to the sale and fragmentation of estates and a transfer of mining interests to indigenous non-Malay merchant capital with the approach of independence, the dominance of foreign capital continued after 1957 under the policies of a state committed to the free enterprise system. The nascent Malay administration which was recruited mainly from the aristocratic class was carefully nurtured to ensure that the transition in the transfer of power was not to the detriment of the foreign sector (Roff, 1976). The initial years of the new administration were given over to the usual functions of a facilitory state, although part of the surplus revenue, which came within its control through its fiscal powers, was used to finance social expenditures in rural areas.

Even after independence, portfolio investment continued, operating out of London and other metropolitan centres. The local operations were taken over by financial capital and agency houses (which earlier had operated in the form of commodity extraction and later, import-substitution), which after independence had transformed themselves into large and multifarious holding companies (Saham, 1980; Lim, 1981). Originally engaged mainly in trading, these agency houses became managing agents of foreign capital investing in plantations and mines. To these were added other commercial activities such as shipping, insurance and finance. According to Saham (1980: 110), in the 1950s these agency houses controlled 65–75 percent of imports. Between 1960 and 1970 they handled an estimated 40–50 percent of all manufacturers supplying the Malaysian market. Besides their handling activities, most agency houses later participated also in the equity of large foreign companies in which they were frequently regarded as the 'local' partners.

State promotion of export-oriented industrialization in order to solve the problems of rising youth unemployment coincided with increased searches by multinational corporations for cheap labour, which by the late 1960s and early 1970s had led to a resurgence of direct foreign investment. The discovery of new oilfields off the east coast of peninsular Malaysia, and in Sarawak, also helped to buttress the stagnation of the mining sector (mainly tin) during the 1970s.

The 'boom' of the early 1970s was somewhat short-lived, although it contributed to an increasing share of industrial production: 16.4 percent of GDP in 1975 and 20.5 percent in 1980 (Malaysia, Ministry of Finance, 1981: 11). There was a decrease in the flow of foreign capital into Malaysia, in spite of state promotional efforts (Salih, 1981: 13). This stagnation of foreign investment was a function of the present recession in the advanced capitalist countries, uncertainty over the Industrial Coordination Act introduced as part of the implementation of the NEP, and political instability.

The encouragement of foreign investment in the development of the Malaysian economy is a state policy, and investment is sought especially from among the 'new' industrial branches. At the same time the NEP poses as one of its targets, the reduction in the share of foreign capital in national wealth and assets. In addition, there are moves to achieve greater local control of national resources, for example the Petroleum Development Act, the creation of the National Oil Corporation (PETRONAS), and the security market operations of the National Trading Corporation (PERNAS). Meanwhile, there are also attempts to 'bring home' some of those agency-house holding companies where Malaysian shares of equity have reached majority control (for example the case of Sime Darby and Malaysian Tin). These efforts, on the one hand, may be seen as the promotion of foreign capital in the export processing zones and, on the other, may represent an attempt to realign the role of foreign capital in national development. But what is critical for the internal political economy of Malaysia is the effect of these readjustments. While they are a function of the structure of capital accumulation on a world scale, they also have implications for the division of wealth and assets among internal fractions of capital, and for income distribution and poverty in general. The problem, then, becomes the ability and efficacy of the state in mediating the competition between different 'national' capitals, and the alliances it will have to form in the pursuit of its restructuring goals.

## Non-indigenous Local Merchant Capital

Chinese and Indian merchant capital had their origins during the colonial period, finding their first foothold in the Straits Settlements. These had been ceded to the British much earlier to form networks of entrepots in the Malay peninsula. With British intervention in the Malay States this merchant capital created a niche for itself in the Malayan economy by performing an intermediary role between foreign capital and the peasantry. It first dominated the sphere of circulation, concentrating on the wholesale and retail sale of imports, as well as collection and transfer of local export products to the agency houses.

During the 1952–62 period, this comprador merchant capital ventured into rubber estates and tin mining, building on initial footholds established during the earlier days of British rule. After Independence, this non-Malay bourgeois class prospered under the laissez-faire policy of the post-colonial state, making their largest impact in the transport, construction and the initial import-substitution industries. This capitalist fraction controlled about 34 percent of the economy in GDP terms in 1970, increasing to 37 percent in 1975 (Young et al., 1980: 69). Its control of the retail and wholesale trade is now formidable, and it has ventured into the manufacturing sector in the production of light consumer goods and automobile assembly.

The interests of this local non-Malay commercial bourgeoisie found its political expression in the Malaysian Chinese Association (MCA), a party which was a partner in the pre-1969 Alliance Party (with the United Malay National Organization — UMNO — and the Malaysian Indian Congress — MIC) and later, with other non-Malay partners, of the (currently) ruling National Front in the post-1969 situation. While intercommunal co-operation was achievable at party leadership level, at times and increasingly (as in the 1969 elections), this association appeared to be somewhat fragile. This happened when the Chinese no longer saw the MCA, which earlier derived its legitimacy from its role in the independence negotiations, as representing their interests. A similar situation has arisen when members of the lower and middle classes, and petty bourgeoisie (the small-scale shopkeepers, hawkers and artisans), begun to feel threatened by the aggressive implementation of the NEP.

Like foreign capital, the capital-owning segment of the Chinese community will be affected also by the restructuring strategies of the state, if the accumulation and expansion of capital is insufficient. Already the fear of the aggressive nature of the state's equity participation through its public corporations, manifested in the recent creation of the National Investment Corporation as a repository of all government shares in successful private companies, has further added to this apprehension. The MCA, a political party, has responded by establishing its own Multi-Purpose Holdings Ltd. which is aimed at mobilizing smaller fractions of local Chinese capital.

## The Middle Class

There was no substantial middle class in the early modern history of Malaysian society; the middle class is a relatively recent creation. Without attempting an exact definition of this social group, it may be said to consist of people in the professional–technical class, together with the higher and middle-level, managerial–administrative workers. This group increased greatly after independence especially with Malayanization in the public sector, and with increasing industrialization and urbanization. The impact of a near-universal schooling system, and expansion at the tertiary level, has contributed to the growth of this group.

The Malays in this group are found mostly in the public sector, whereas the non-Malays are in the professional–technical group (Tham, 1977). The attempt under the NEP to restructure society in terms of employment and ownership of wealth (Malaysia, Government of, 1971: 1–6) has had two effects on the middle class as presently constituted. First, the objective of restructuring employment has increased Malay representation in the professions and in the managerial–administrative group. The major instruments for this are access to tertiary educational opportunities and recruitment policy. The introduction of a quota system to achieve this restructuring through state sponsorship and subsidies and through administrative fiat, is one of the most politically and socially contentious policies of the state. This 'contest for the middle' has caused other issues, such as the role of vernacular languages and the proposal for a private university (Merdeka University), to be seen as a danger to the promotion of national unity, and to the preservation of the present political compromise between the races.

The second effect has been the creation of a Malay bourgeoisie recruited from the upper echelons of the bureaucracy, from bureaucrat – managers of the public corporations and subsidiaries, and from the aristocracy itself. This has given rise to criticisms that the NEP has managed to benefit only a small minority of Malay bureaucrat – capitalists, further increasing inequality within the Malay community. The absence of a traditional indigenous merchant class (a result of combined and uneven development under colonial capitalism), made this policy decision of the Malay-dominated post-colonial state highly controversial. As has been suggested elsewhere, this policy reflects the class content of the state itself (Muzaffar, 1979; Jomo, 1986).

## The Working Class

The original class of wage-workers was created by the penetration of capital during the colonial period. It was an immigrant labour force which grew with the expansion of the plantation and mining sectors according to the cycles and rhythms of world capitalist development. As for the indigenous Malay population, a small fraction was incorporated as salaried workers in the lower rungs of the colonial administration and in the security services. The bulk of the Malay labour force, however, remained in the peasant sector.

Independence, and the continued penetration of capitalist social relations into the peasant sector (through the formal schooling system), released more labour from petty commodity production in rural areas into the public sector. The second and later generations of non-Malay labour found their way into services, construction and the commercial sector. The result was an expanding tertiary sector which absorbed a large proportion of the labour force.

The increased incidence of youth unemployment in the 1970s created the opportunity for the expansion of foreign capital into the export processing sector which was promoted by the state. This required the proper management of labour in relation to the interests of capital. The labour movement in Malaysia is relatively underdeveloped, although trade unions have existed since the end of World War II. The state maintains a very tight control over industrial relations because of the fear of infiltration by communists. Organized labour is not able to find an adequate political channel to express its collective interests. That the working class is fragmented by sector and race may account for its lack of political mobilization. It is here that the emergence of a large Malay workforce organized in trade unions, particularly in the public sector (utilities and the public corporations) as well as in the new industrial sector (the free trade zones — FTZs), becomes politically significant. However, there is still a tendency towards an over-riding racial identification rather than class consciousness among Malaysian workers, which may prevent the realization of greater class-based mobilization.

In the balance of forces between labour and capital, the emergence of workers as a social force may be constrained in the present conjuncture by the persistence of a semi-proletarianized sector. Only in recent years, as industrial capital expanded, has this group appeared to threaten the 'contract' between capital and the state.

## The Peasantry

The bulk of the peasantry was comprised of indigenous Malays who were engaged in traditional padi-farming and fishing under a feudal mode of production. As a result of the imposition of the colonial state and capitalist penetration into the rural economy, the peasantry became increasingly differentiated. A part of the peasantry became commercialized, creating a semi-feudal class of smallholders (producing rubber); a smaller part was absorbed into the lower echelons of colonial administration; and the rest were confined to native agriculture contributing to the reproduction of labour power for the capitalist spheres of production. Colonial efforts to improve food production in the latter sector were inadequate, while subsidies, such as those for rubber replanting, were biased towards the estates and the larger smallholders (Lim, 1977). In spite of this, the tax on peasant production contributed as much as 45 percent of government revenues, and as such was the largest contributor to total receipts by the time of independence (Salih, 1981: 16–17).

The importance of the rural sector for the post-colonial state can be seen from the nature of the electoral system. The distribution of parliamentary seats, a concession extracted by the Malay ruling group at the time of negotiations for formal independence, gave considerable electoral power to the Malay peasantry. This factor predetermined the political disposition of the state towards the rural sector.

Expenditure in the rural sector reflected the relative autonomy of the state in mediating the relationship between capital and the peasantry. Access to state-created assets was unequal, and with the use of political patronage as an instrument of influence, both contributed to further differentiation among the peasantry. A new 'middle' peasantry emerged in the semi-feudal sector through new land development projects.

These developments resulted in increasing income inequality among the peasantry. They created a new class of agricultural workers in the state-sponsored plantations (palm oil and rubber) which were part of the new regional land development schemes. The reluctance of the 'traditional' peasantry to participate as share-holders in the public estates, and the low remuneration for work as estate workers, has given rise to the utilization of illegal immigrant labour from Indonesia.

## The Relations between Social Groups: a Summary

There are three unfolding processes which are at the core of the interrelationships between social groups in the Malaysian formation. The contradictions and tensions that are created by these questions as they are crystallized in the political and social sphere vis-a-vis each other will determine the future development of Malaysian society.

The first is the creation of a *Bumiputera* (literally, sons of the soil — Malays) capitalist class under the sponsorship of the state, in competition with non-indigenous local capital, and with foreign capital. The second is the emergence of a Malay middle class which is in

competition with its racial counterparts for the patronage of the state
and the sale of its labour-power to capital. The third is the 'social
question', ie. of poverty in both the rural and urban sectors, and overall
income inequality. All three phenomena, and their consequences,
depend on the role of the state. The position of the state, in turn,
depends on the alliances it forms with one or the other of these social
fractions. In the Malaysian context, this is dependent on the direction
of racial politics. To the extent that the state is at this juncture Malay-
dominated, the disposition of favours by the state and its programmes
will be determined mainly by the ideology of the NEP.

A codetermining element here is the world economic situation. This
will have a great influence on the mode of accumulation of the
Malaysian economy, and thus on the 'room for manoeuvre' available
to the state in mediating the social forces in Malaysian society, and the
tensions and conflicts generated.

## The State and the Political Economy of
## the New Economic Policy, 1970–90

*Formation of the Malaysian State*
The Malaysian state was constituted in 1957. It was a smooth transfer of
power from Britain. A Parliament based on the Westminster model was
created. The main instrument of the state was the Federal Constitution
which, after the defeat of the Malayan Union proposals in 1946, besides
reinstating the position of the Malay sultans, provided for the
protection of the Malays through the provision of special privileges
until such time as it was considered no longer necessary. The
Constitution also made Islam, the religion of Malays, the state religion,
and made Malay the official language. As part of the political
compromise, the immigrant races were granted citizenship, freedom of
worship and pursuit of their vernacular language and culture.

The political dominance of the Malays derived from their status as
the indigenous population, their greater numerical strength, and their
higher level of organization and mobilization. From the beginning, the
role of UMNO in this mobilization of Malay politics gave it the mantle
of 'protector' for the majority of the Malay population. According to
Muzaffar (1979: 115), the manipulation of the feudal notion of loyalty
to the rulers, and of the fear Malays have regarding a threat to their
indigenous position from the other races, enabled UMNO, as the
dominant partner in the ruling coalition since independence, to create a
convergence of interests between the ruling class and the Malay
community. This protector–loyalty nexus has repeatedly been
demonstrated in Malaysia's political history, as well as in internal
UMNO politics itself. When in 1959 for instance, the MCA demanded a

higher allocation of seats (from 31 to 40) to contest as part of the Alliance in that year's general elections, the UMNO leadership was able firmly to refuse this, thus enhancing its image as protector of the special position of the Malays. Similarly, in 1965, the Prime Minister of Singapore (then part of Malaysia) raised fears among Malays regarding their political position and questioned their indigenous status as provided for in the Constitution, with his call for a 'Malaysian Malaysia'. UMNO again was able to reinforce its role in safeguarding the political position of the Malay community by securing the separation of Singapore (which has a predominantly Chinese population) from the Federation.

The dominance of UMNO in the ruling coalition is expressed mainly through the larger number of electoral seats given to it compared to those allocated to the other coalition partners like the MCA and MIC. Greater weight is assigned to rural, predominantly Malay areas, in the drawing of electoral boundaries. Following the successful performance of the Alliance in the elections of 1959 and 1964, UMNO was able to dominate both the federal government and state governments, except for the state of Kelantan. This Malay dominance in government, and the nature of the bureaucracy and armed services, define the content and predisposition of the Malaysian state.

From Independence and up to 1969, the political compromise struck between the three racial parties in the Alliance created an atmosphere of political stability which was necessary for the steady expansion of the economy under essentially similar conditions vis-a-vis the world economy and capital, as prevailed during the colonial period. The only shift appeared in the form of heavy public expenditure in rural development and a more determined Malayanization programme.

The internal contradictions of Malaysian society were brought to the forefront of the political arena with the post- election riots of 1969. Such explosions of racial violence had occurred before, but these had not been on the same scale, nor more importantly, had such an impact on the stability of Malaysian society. These events pointed to the relatively fragile foundations of the political compromise that had been erected 12 years previously.

The '13 May Incident' represented a conjunctural crisis which required a reformulation of the political contract between the three races. In the 1969 general elections, for the first time, the ruling Alliance Party suffered several setbacks in both the federal Parliament, and the state assemblies. What was evident was an 'erosion of both Malay and non-Malay support from the Alliance' (Muzaffar, 1979: 82). Opposition jubilance, and hints towards a non-Malay Chief Minister in Selangor state, once again raised racial sentiments and resulted in a leadership crisis in UMNO. The then Prime Minister, Tunku Abdul

Rahman, was considered too accommodative to the non-Malays. His administration was replaced by a new group in UMNO under the leadership of Tun Razak when Parliament (and therefore democratic processes) was suspended. When parliamentary democracy was reinstated after the National Operations Council interregnum in 1971, a constitutional amendment was introduced which made it illegal for anyone to question the following: the special position of the Malays and other indigenous peoples (mainly in Sabah and Sarawak); the status of Malay as the official and national language; and the sovereignty of the Malay monarchs. The National Education Policy, which makes Malay the main medium of instruction, was reaffirmed and the New Economic Policy was introduced. These actions, as well as the reconstitution of the Alliance into a larger coalition of political parties besides the old partners MCA and MIC, under the leadership of UMNO, consolidated further the structure of the Malaysian state. However, by the beginning of the 1970s the economic and social conditions had changed.

## The Economy and Society in the 1970s

The post-colonial state faced a basic dilemma: to maintain a pattern of accumulation successfully imposed by colonial capitalism and cope as best it could with the resulting contradictions of distribution in a multi-racial society, or to restructure the pattern of distribution and face a crisis of accumulation which could eventually undermine its efforts at political compromise and economic stabilization. Given how the state was formed in the process of transfer of power from Whitehall to a ruling group committed to maintaining a free enterprise system with strong links with the West, and the economy's dependent position within the world economy, the manner in which the post-colonial government resolved the dilemma in its first 10 years of power was almost pre-determined. It opted for continuity.

The success of the neo-colonial policies was due as much to the stability of the political compromise achieved between the three major racial groups as to the fortuitous conjunctural situation during the first two post-war decades which allowed the state to undertake expansionary policies. However, it was constrained to implement programmes and direct resources to the peasant sector on which it depended for its power. Its role vis-a-vis capital was to facilitate its development directly. The state expanded public capital formation in order to create conditions for accumulation in the private sector. Expenditures on physical infrastructure, public utilities, transport and social services were therefore large, as seen in the first two Malaya Plans (Malaya, Government of, 1956; Malaysia, Government of, 1961) and the First Malaysia Plan (Malaysia, Government of, 1966).

We have discussed the consequences of this strategy in the 1957–70 period. There had been little change in the racial profile of the economic sectors; productivity and income levels remained low in the agricultural sector, particularly among the Malay peasantry. Income distribution deteriorated, the bottom 40 percent only managed a 5 percent share of the total increase between 1957/58 and 1970 (Snodgrass, 1980: 80–81). But, as Muzaffar suggests, it has been the inability of the Malaysian state 'to come to grips with the underlying causes of Malay poverty, of the disparity between urban and rural areas, of the poverty of Malays in commerce, industry and the professions' which is the crucial factor in the Malaysian social formation. The irony and therefore the error was that 'the UMNO Leadership from 1957 to 1969 saw itself as the protector of a community that lacked capital while encouraging the growth of an economy based upon capital' (Muzaffar, 1979: 82).

The introduction of the NEP in 1970 had both an economic and racial basis. The objectives of the NEP are easily stated: the restructuring of society so as to eliminate the identification of race with occupation, and the eradication of poverty regardless of race (Malaysia, Government of, 1971: 1–6). This socio-economic goal required that the economy expand sufficiently so that the restructuring of society could be achieved without creating new racial tensions.

There are several crucial questions in the state management of the economy implied by the NEP. First, could the economy expand sufficiently so as to enable this redistribution of wealth at the same time as solving the poverty problem? What changes were occurring in the national model of accumulation in response to the changing world economic situation? What new imbalances were created as a result?

The model of accumulation was committed to primary export expansion in which new public capital formation and investment was brought about in the primary sectors. At the same time, public trading corporations and investment trusts were actively pursuing equity participation, acting in trust for the Malay commercial and industrial bourgeoisie. With the establishment of a National Investment Corporation in 1980 the state encouraged Malay investors and ordinary people from all walks of life to buy up government shares in successful companies in which the state had invested earlier. This public 'divestment' strategy aimed to bolster and speed up the participation of Malays in the holding of stocks and shares.

In attempting to restructure the wealth ownership patterns between the foreign, non-indigenous local capital, and this new emerging *Bumiputera* capitalist class, the state faces a dilemma in its attempts to manage the conflict between these capitals. On the one hand, the state wants to reduce foreign wealth ownership from 60 percent to 30 percent of GDP, and transfer it, within the context of expanded accumulation, to the new indigenous class. On the other hand the state needs to continue to attract foreign capital in order to promote industrialization, especially of the export-processing or free trade zone (FTZ) type. If capital formation and accumulation is not expanded in other sectors through increased public sector participation, then the asset redistribution between the three types of capital will be possible only by encroachment on domestic non-indigenous bourgeois interests. The competition between these two sectors, the non-*Bumiputera* capital and the public sector is already evident. Any slowing down of the rate of accumulation will pose critical problems.

On the industrial side, the 1970s represented a shift in industrialization policy towards export-oriented manufacturing. This shift seemed reasonable since by the late 1960s obvious areas for import-substitution industrialization appeared to have been exhausted, and unemployment, particuarly among the urban youth, was rising. This industrialization had necessitated a change in the Industrial Incentives Act, as well as the creation of numerous FTZs, and careful monitoring of the labour situation.

At the local level, the major beneficiary of developments in the 1970s had been the middle class. The emergence of a new Malay middle class and a rise in income of Malays as a whole has contributed to an expansion of the domestic market. Salary revisions, a lower relative tax incidence compared to the other income groups, and generally better access to opportunities created by the state, have led to a high liquidity in the hands of this group and an explosion of commodity consumption. The number of registered motor vehicles jumped 100 percent in the five years from 1971 to 1975 (Salih, 1981: 23). Pressure on the housing market and land led to prices far beyond their scarcity value, whilst involvement in stocks and shares increased. Although increased oil prices in the 1970s partially caused the boom, inflation had been rising to over 4 percent per annum by 1984 (Bank Negara, 1984: 29–30). A second round of import-substitution to counteract the middle-class proclivity for spending has been instituted in an attempt to reduce imports.

In the expansion of the middle class, two contradictory consequences emerge: one, a rise in the conflict between Malay and non-Malay segments of the middle class; and two, aggravation of the situation of the poor. One is a question of race, the other a question of class. These contradictions can only be resolved by larger structural changes and a more direct confrontation of the social question by the state. Structural change will mean a transformation of the model of accumulation within the capitalist world system while the issue of poverty necessitates the introduction of more direct programmes for its eradication.

Given the structure of the Malaysian formation in the present historical period, both these questions imply an increased role of the state in economy and society, and continued supremacy of politics in resolving the contradictions between race and class. Both at the level of economic practice, and at the level of mediating social conflict, these contradictions of accumulation and distribution within an essentially capitalist mode of production may imply an increasingly repressive state, as it finds its room for manoeuvre increasingly restricted, and as it seeks to perpetuate itself in its present form. A prolonged economic crisis at the world level would constitute one of the forces which would restrict its room for manoeuvre, as that crisis translates into internal economic deformations and racial and class instability.

## Malaysia in the International Division of Labour: the Case of the Semiconductor Industry in Penang[1]

In this final section, we turn our attention to the state which in many ways has become the part of Malaysia most thoroughly incorporated into the current global economy. Penang, one of the 13 states of the Federation, is the epitome of the changing articulation of the Malaysian economy with the emerging international division of labour. The free-port status which it enjoyed for 180 years since the British obtained Penang from the Sultan of Kedah was lost when the central government decided in 1969 to integrate it into a common custom union with the rest of the peninsula. Within the colonial and post-colonial division of labour, Penang's port was the outlet for the export of primary products from its rich hinterland, and the distribution point for imported goods and machinery. The erosion of its entrepot trade began with the rise of competing ports further south as the centre of gravity of industrial production and political power shifted towards Kuala Lumpur, the federal capital. As a result, by the mid-1960s its economy, lacking an alternative base, stagnated; unemployment rose and net outmigration occurred. It was, therefore, inevitable that Penang, a Chinese-dominated peripheral state, was won by the Opposition in the 1969 general elections.

The incorporation of the Gerakan Party into the National Coalition after parliamentary government was restored in 1971, the introduction of the NEP which represents the new social contract between the races and the formulation of a new industrialization strategy emphasizing employment creation and export-orientation, were a conjuncture of events which effectively over the next 10 years repositioned the local economy within the international division of labour. Through the establishment of FTZs Penang was rearticulated with the world economy.

The late 1960s and early 1970s marked at the same time a turning point in the development of the world economy. The current economic crisis and associated structural adjustments are associated with several distinguishing features (Frobel, 1982; Kreye, 1980). These features are: a fall in rates of overall economic growth in the market economies as a whole, and especially in the industrial countries, to well below the average of 4 percent per annum achieved in the previous decades; a stagnation in new capital investment, especially in plant and machinery, with slow expansion of capacity as well as increasing under-utilization of existing capacity; structural crisis in the traditional industries such as steel and shipbuilding, increasing competition from lower-cost producers in the developing as well as the centrally-planned countries; growing synchronization of business cycles, thus precluding the possibility of implementing effective national counter-cyclical measures by taking advantage of internationally unsynchronized cycles; increasing inflation and unemployment in the industrialized countries themselves; the breakdown of the Bretton Woods Agreement and increasing instability in the international monetary system, especially after the adoption of floating exchange rates; increasing debt burdens of the developing countries; industrial rationalization and deskilling due to the introduction of new technologies; and roll-back of state-supported social services and increasing popularity of privatization schemes as a measure to reduce government deficits. But most importantly, changes in the structure of the international division of labour itself enabled not only shifts in manufacturing facilities from one core region to another (e.g. the United States to Western Europe), but increasingly, too, to the developing countries themselves. With promotional incentives offered by these latter countries, and their better infrastructure and lower labour costs, some of these developing countries (the so-called newly industrializing countries) have been able to increase their export of manufactures to the advanced countries, and move higher up the 'industrialization learning curve'.

Malaysia, and particularly Penang, has taken advantage of this redeployment of industries, by active promotion and provision of generous incentives. This has had an impact on manufacturing exports and employment. However, in contrast to the situation in the 1970s, the Malaysian economy has finally been caught by the recession which had engulfed many other countries on a similar path of development. Although there are signs of recovery in the United States economy, and Japan continues to show economic resilience, there are pressures which threaten any upswing in economic activity. Some of these factors are cyclical in nature, such as the present recession in the electronics industry. However, other pressures reflect important underlying structural processes. It is the longer term structural adjustments which should be monitored, especially in indicating directions for the reformulation of industrialization strategy.

*Penang's Industrial Performance, 1972–84*

*Investment and employment.* The impact of the industrialization strategy on the growth of Penang's economy has been tremendous (Salih and Tan, 1985). The most immediate effect was the establishment of the industrial estates. A direct consequence of this was the growth in the number of factories, from 36 in 1971 to 243 in 1983, and in employment from 4,500 to 57,600 over the same period (Table 1).

TABLE 1

Penang: number of factories and employment in Penang Development
Corporation industrial areas, 1971–83

| Year | Number of factories in operation | Percent increase | Number employed | Percent increase |
|------|------|------|------|------|
| 1971 | 36 | | 4,500 | |
| 1972 | 50 | 28.0 | 9,877 | 54.4 |
| 1973 | 74 | 32.4 | 23,359 | 57.7 |
| 1974 | 91 | 18.7 | 27,278 | 14.4 |
| 1975 | 108 | 15.7 | 31.887 | 14.5 |
| 1976 | 181 | 40.3 | 39,269 | 18.8 |
| 1977 | 167 | 8.4 | 40,775 | 3.7 |
| 1978 | 183 | 8.7 | 45,605 | 10.6 |
| 1979 | 190 | 3.7 | 51,261 | 11.0 |
| 1980 | 216 | 8.7 | 56,021 | 6.9 |
| 1981 | 230 | 4.6 | 55,679 | 1.1 |
| 1982 | 228 | 0.9 | 56,718 | 1.8 |
| 1983 | 243 | 6.2 | 57,600 | 1.5 |

*Source:* Penang Development Corporation (1974, 1983).

The impact of the world economy in the form of the recession in 1975 and since 1980 (which Penang only felt a year later, on both occasions) is reflected in the sluggish increase during those periods in the number of factories, and especially in employment, which was drastically affected between 1980 and 1983. Nonetheless, the growth in investment is evident, both in terms of the number of factories and in terms of paid-up capital, which increased from M$678.9 million in 1980 to M$961.6 million in 1983. An additional 58 factories are under construction; these promise the creation of 4,114 jobs and an additional M$98.8 in paid-up capital. Moreover, in 1983, 143 further factories were approved, which are expected to provide 8,861 jobs and M$127.6 million in paid-up capital (Penang Development Corporation, 1983).

Table 2 shows employment characteristics by industry in the Penang FTZs in 1982. Several highlights may be drawn from the data shown. First, in terms of paid-up capital, 31.1 percent of the investments are in the textiles/garments industry, 8.5 percent are in electronics, 8.4

TABLE 2

Penang: employment characteristics by industry in Free Trade Zones, 1982

| Type of industry | Number of factories | Paid-up capital ($ m) | Ethnicity | | | Sex | | Category of employment of factory workers | | | Total |
|---|---|---|---|---|---|---|---|---|---|---|---|
| | | | Expatriate | Bumiputera | Non-Bumiputera | Male | Female | Skilled labour | Semi-skilled labour | Unskilled labour | |
| Electronics/electrical | 27 | 64.69 | 34 | 10,894 | 13,518 | 5,359 | 19,087 | 12,653 | 250 | 4,918 | 24,446 |
| Textiles/garments | 14 | 239.04 | 92 | 5,739 | 6,407 | 4,272 | 7,966 | 6,831 | 748 | 1,937 | 12,230 |
| Food processing/ canning | 13 | 53.83 | 1 | 615 | 662 | 695 | 583 | 547 | 5 | 316 | 1,278 |
| Chemicals/fertiliser | 10 | 28.30 | 6 | 503 | 457 | 652 | 314 | 196 | 41 | 419 | 966 |
| Metal products | 17 | 63.79 | 13 | 1,319 | 1,253 | 2,001 | 584 | 133 | 101 | 196 | 685 |
| Rubber-based industries | 6 | 32.64 | 7 | 1,100 | 931 | 1,084 | 954 | 409 | 91 | 1,103 | 2,038 |
| Machinery/motor and bicycle parts | 9 | 14.07 | 6 | 217 | 411 | 535 | 99 | 834 | 247 | 720 | 2,585 |
| Timber-based industries | 5 | 6.43 | 4 | 309 | 372 | 396 | 289 | 64 | 18 | 130 | 362 |
| Feedmeals industry | 4 | 27.39 | 2 | 159 | 201 | 295 | 67 | 308 | 92 | 351 | 1,005 |
| Paper products/printing works | 10 | 42.10 | 1 | 429 | 575 | 604 | 401 | 75 | 89 | 253 | 634 |
| Industrial gases | 3 | 64.44 | — | 17 | 51 | 66 | 2 | 17 | 9 | 3 | 68 |
| Processing of agricultural products | 6 | 50.50 | 5 | 448 | 756 | 1,036 | 173 | 37 | 3 | 169 | 348 |
| Plastic products | 6 | 11.80 | 5 | 145 | 198 | 238 | 110 | 400 | — | 220 | 1,209 |
| Others | 24 | 64.92 | 50 | 1,927 | 2,234 | 2,167 | 2,044 | 772 | 39 | 1,799 | 4,211 |
| Total | 154 | 763.74 | 226 | 23,821 | 28,026 | 19,400 | 32,673 | 23,276 | 1,733 | 12,542 | 52,073 |

Source: Penang Development Corporation, unpublished data, 1983.

percent in metal products and another 8.4 percent in industrial gases. Second, in terms of employment, the electronics/electrical industry was responsible for nearly half (47 percent) of the jobs created, the other big employer being the textiles/garments industry. Third, there is a distinct bias towards female workers, particularly in the electronics and textiles/garments industries. These features are similar to those observed at the national level.

With regard to the aims of the NEP, the racial breakdown of the workers suggest that Penang's industrial estates have been a major source of employment for Malays who are more easily absorbed in large, formal companies than in informal small-scale industries which tend to be family-labour oriented (see Goh, 1976; Salih et al., 1985).[2] This is of particular importance because of the overwhelming predominance of Chinese in Penang's urban population. The major source of the Malay workforce in Penang's industrial estates is rural–urban migration, mainly of young female school-leavers. These are from the neighbouring states of Kedah and Perak which made up 35.4 percent and 31.4 percent respectively of all immigrants to Penang in 1980 (Malaysia, Department of Statistics, 1983a: 300–302).

Another aspect of the new labour force is that nearly half of the workers are in the unskilled labour category although this feature is unequally distributed among industries. For example, the percentage of unskilled labour in the total workforce for rubber-based industries is 54.1 percent while that for the electronics/electrical industries is 20.1 percent, and that for textiles/garments is 15.8 percent.

*Structural changes.* The rapid pace of industrialization in Penang has resulted in a diversified economic base. This is evident in the structural shifts in Penang's economy from 1970 to 1980. Table 3 shows that manufacturing, which accounted for 21 percent of Penang's GDP in 1971, had increased to 37.2 percent by 1980, a share far exceeding the national manufacturing share of 21.2 percent. The growth rate of this sector from 1971 to 1980 was 11.6 percent, representing the highest performance among all the states in Malaysia (with the exception of Trengganu). Manufacturing in Penang from 1980 to 1983, however, has been affected by the overall depressed world economic situation. It the same period. In terms of employment, agriculture, forestry and fishing declined from 31.4 percent in 1970 to 13.3 percent in 1980. However, jobs in manufacturing increased from 10 percent to 13.3 percent in the same period.

*Socio-demographic Impact.* This section highlights in some detail the socio-demographic features which characterize a Penang Free Trade Zone (Bayan Lepas) surveyed in 1981–82.[3] As shown in Table 2, the study of this FTZ showed a predominance of *Bumiputeras* (Malays) in the labour force. 95 percent of the total production-line workforce

TABLE 3

Penang and Malaysia: Penang employment by industry group, gross domestic product by industry of origin, Penang and Malaysia 1970–80

| Industry group | Penang Employment 1970 | 1980 | 1971 Penang | 1971 Malaysia | 1980 Penang | 1980 Malaysia | 1983 Penang | 1983 Malaysia |
|---|---|---|---|---|---|---|---|---|
| Agriculture, fishing, hunting, forestry | 31.4 | 13.3 | 14.6 | 30.5 | 5.9 | 22.9 | 4.2 | 22.8 |
| Mining, quarrying | — | 0.1 | — | 6.6 | 8.0 | 4.8 | 0.1 | 4.4 |
| Manufacturing | 10.0 | 13.3 | 21.0 | 14.7 | 37.2 | 21.2 | 42.1 | 18.3 |
| Construction | 3.8 | 2.8 | 5.2 | 4.3 | 3.8 | 4.7 | 4.1 | 5.7 |
| Utilities | 1.0 | 0.1 | 2.9 | 1.9 | 2.5 | 2.3 | 2.5 | 2.5 |
| Transport, storage, communications | 6.2 | 2.1 | 7.7 | 5.0 | 8.2 | 6.7 | 7.7 | 8.1 |
| Wholesale and retail trade, hotels and restaurants | — | 8.9 | 26.1 | 13.6 | 20.6 | 13.0 | 19.1 | 13.7 |
| Finance, insurance, real estate, business services | 47.6 | 1.2 | 10.8 | 8.9 | 8.2 | 8.5 | 8.7 | 8.2 |
| Government services | — | 11.2 | 7.5 | 11.6 | 10.6 | 13.4 | 8.5 | 13.6 |
| Others | — | — | 4.1 | 2.6 | 2.9 | 2.6 | 3.1 | 2.7 |
| Total % | 100.0 | 100.0 | 100.0 | 100.0 | 100.0 | 100.0 | 100.0 | 100.0 |
| Number (in '000) | 210.0 | 666.3 | 827.0 | 12,618.0 | 2,220.5 | 25,376.0 | 2,581.4 | 30,810.0 |

Source: Penang Development Corporation (1973) Malaysia, Dept. of Statistics (1983b); Malaysia, Government of (1981: 100–101, 1984: 153).

surveyed were females, a reflection of the actual composition of the production-line workforce. Males tended to be in more skilled work, such as technicians and supervisors. The workforce was young, the mean age being 22.6 years, with 83.4 percent clustered in the 16–27 age group. This is due to the rigid enforcement of the legal working age of 16 years in corporate sector jobs, the relative recency of the multinational factories in the FTZs, and the fact that young females constitute most of the workforce. Also, there is a preference in such companies to employ young school-leavers (Lim, 1978). In racial terms more Chinese enter the workforce at a younger age than Malays. Whereas 36 percent of the Chinese were 15–19 years, the proportion for Malays was 21 percent. Over 53 percent of the Malays were aged 20–24 years. This pattern is similar to the national one (Malaysia, Government of, 1984). Jobs in the formal sector demand a certain level of education. As many as 70 percent of the workers had been to secondary school. On average they had 8 years' schooling altogether. Malay workers tended to have more schooling than Chinese: 80 percent compared to 51 percent.

Penang became a net in-migration state during the 1970s owing to the industrialization programme and the development of the FTZs. Thus, 45 percent of the respondents were born outside Penang. While Malays came from a wider catchment area than the Chinese, the significant point was that 82 percent of Malays were from rural areas, drawn from the peasantry, compared with 7 percent of the Chinese. Interestingly, this pattern reflects the national migration patterns of those who moved between 1965 and 1970, which showed Kedah and Perak as major sending states to Penang (Young, 1982). The shorter distances (these states are adjacent to Penang), the growth of FTZs demanding female workers, and the aggressive recruitment drives of the multinational companies all help to explain these patterns.

While this is a case study of one major FTZ in Penang, the socio-demographic characteristics of its workers are a product of the particular nature of industrialization in Penang in the 1970s and are similar to this type of industrialization in other developing countries (Salih et al., 1985).

This part of the chapter has highlighted the development impacts of export-processing industrialization which enabled Penang to grow rapidly in the 1970s. While that industrialization has solved the problems of unemployment in Penang, particularly among the youth, it is clear that we are now entering a phase of uncertainty in the 1980s. Changes in the world economy and the national economic outlook require a reconsideration of the strategy for Penang. The 1970s strategy was based on the relocation of industry to the outlying areas by multinationals to take advantage of new production technology and the availability of cheap labour. A new state industrialization strategy for the 1980s is required for two reasons. First, these industries which form the core of Penang's industrialization are now undergoing a new round of restructuring due to the prolonged downturn in the world economy. Second, the national economic situation in the 1980s will be affected by this downturn as well as other new development policies now being considered by the government.

We should note the following trends for their direct bearing on the future prospects for industrialization in Penang. Rising protectionism in the industrialized countries, and selective imposition of quotas for textiles, for example, will affect the very sectors where Malaysia has a comparative advantage. Trade frictions among the industrialized countries (such as those between the United States and Japan) may result in a solution which proves beneficial to developing countries, especially if the result is a general opening-up of Japan. However, the outcome may be a mutual accommodation between Japan and the USA involving concessions which adversely affect the developing countries. A third trend is industrial restructuring in the United States and Europe, and the impact of deskilling and unemployment which have weakened the bargaining power of labour in the industrialized countries. These have induced governments to begin considering new industrial policies, particularly to assist the recovery of their worst-affected regions, and thus promote the returning-home of their offshore investments. An added feature of this trend is reverse investment (as for example Japanese investment in the United States) in order to overcome the threat of protectionism and to placate union pressure. Another aspect of this industrial restructuring involves, besides the 'sunset industries', the high-technology industries where developments in microprocessor technology and semiconductors have contributed to cost reductions and higher productivity, and led to large-scale rationalization of industrial sectors (for example, the use of robots and computers). The possibility of the developing countries participating actively in this second industrial revolution is rather limited, especially in research and development, though this could have led to some measure of technological independence for them.

All these developments in the world economy have a particular significance in finding the proper niche for Penang's future industrialization, and more specifically, for whether it should continue to push for more investment in electronics and textiles, the two dominant industries in the 1970s, or shift to other activities such as downstream processing and fabrication of Malaysia's primary products. The choice of strategy at the state level will also depend on national policy. Nonetheless, the proper consideration of international forces, together with national-level factors must form the basis of this decision.

*Penang's Problems and Prospects:*
*the Case of the Semiconductor Industry*

These trends and outlook at the national and world level have very important implications for the direction of Penang's future industrialization. Penang's fate has become inextricably tied up with developments in the world economy and its cycles. From a manufacturing base of light small-scale industries based on local raw materials, Penang has become dependent on a narrow industrial base centred on electronics and textiles, and therefore more vulnerable to international business cycles. The manner and effectiveness in which the national economy and government policy respond to these developments will determine Penang's industrial future. This point may be best illustrated by analysing the case of the semiconductor industry in Penang which, besides being dominant in Penang's industrialization during the 1970s, may also enable us to identify possible elements for a new industrial policy for the state.

The reasons for selecting the semiconductor industry for a case study are three-fold. First, the semiconductor industry was the major component in Penang's industrialization programme of the 1970s and foremost in the export-led drive. Second, it is a classic example of capital transfer from developed countries to developing countries which was part of the process underlying the new international division of labour in the 1970s (Henderson, 1986). The search by multinational companies for cheap labour during the late 1960s and 1970s coincided with the entry into the labour market of a large cohort of young and educated youths in developing countries, a product of the post-war baby boom and the health care revolution. Third, the electronics industry, and therefore, the semiconductor component of it, owing to its high technology input and responsiveness to the rapid changes in this technology, is particularly sensitive to demand which in turn is dictated by world economic cycles. These cycles are the underlying causes of many of the problems associated with narrowly-based sectoral development in Penang including the lack of linkages among industries (Chi, 1980), instability of employment, and other aspects of the labour formation process.

Although the electronics industry covers more than semiconductors, the emphasis here is on the latter because most of Penang's electronics factories are involved in the production of semiconductors. In fact, Malaysia produces 40–70 percent of the world's share of 64K chips, Penang alone being the leading exporter of these chips. This is clear from Table 4 which shows the extent of offshore investment by United States, Japan and West European semiconductor firms in developing countries. Note the large increase in electronics firms in Malaysia between 1971 to 1974. By 1979, Malaysia had the largest

TABLE 4

Development of offshore investment in various Third World locations by major US, Japanese and West European semiconductor firms, 1971–79

| Country | Number of firms present | | | |
|---|---|---|---|---|
| | 1971 | 1974 | 1976 | 1979 |
| *Southeast Asia* | | | | |
| Korea | 6 | 8 | 8 | 8 |
| Hong Kong | 1 | 6 | 6 | 7 |
| Indonesia | 0 | 3 | 3 | 3 |
| Malaysia | 0–2 | 11–13 | 13–14 | 14 |
| Philippines | 0 | 3 | 1 | 6 + 1 planned |
| Singapore | 9 | 10 | 12 | 13 |
| Taiwan | 3 | 3 | 6 | 8 |
| Thailand | — | — | 1 | 1 |
| *Latin America* | | | | |
| Brazil | 0–2 | 2 | 5 | 5 + 3 planned |
| Mexico | — | — | 12 | 13 |
| Barbados | 0 | 0 | 0 | 1 |
| Puerto Rico | — | — | 2 | 3 |
| El Salvador | — | 1 | 1 | 2 |
| *Mediterranean Basin* | | | | |
| Morocco | — | — | 1 | 1 |
| Malta | — | — | 1 | 1 |
| Portugal | — | — | 2–3 | 3 |

TABLE 5

Share of United States imports of integrated circuits, 1981

| Country | Linear | Bipolar Digital | MOS Logic | MOS Memory | Total | |
|---|---|---|---|---|---|---|
| Malaysia | 29.1 | 28.7 | 25.7 | 27.2 | 3.4 | 26.4 |
| Singapore | 12.9 | 15.9 | 11.7 | 26.5 | 14.1 | 19.0 |
| Philippines | 13.9 | 10.6 | 20.8 | 15.8 | 8.4 | 15.1 |
| Korea | 12.2 | 11.6 | 4.9 | 3.7 | 5.3 | 6.8 |
| Thailand | 2.3 | 4.6 | 7.0 | 2.1 | 0.2 | 3.6 |
| Taiwan | 8.3 | 4.2 | 2.5 | 1.4 | 13.6 | 3.5 |
| Japan | 4.7 | 8.6 | 4.5 | 13.5 | 16.7 | 9.7 |
| Others | 16.6 | 15.8 | 22.9 | 9.8 | 38.3 | 15.9 |
| Total % | 100.0 | 100.0 | 100.0 | 100.0 | 100.0 | 100.0 |
| Amount ($US million) | 325 | 693 | 592 | 1222 | 121 | 2953 |

*Source:* United States Department of Commerce, cited in *Press Journal* (1984).

number of semiconductor plants in the Third World. This is confirmed by Table 5 which illustrates the source of United States imports of integrated circuits (ICs). Malaysia again ranked highest with a total of

US\$26.4 million in 1981. Malaysia's share in the export of ICs (unassembled) to Japan is fifth in terms of value (Y63 billion), after Singapore, Hong Kong, the United States and the Philippines (*Press Journal*, 1984).

Figure 1 shows the high absorption of ICs by the United States and Japan since 1978. In fact, while the amount (in US\$) for Europe and Japan declined somewhat between 1978 and 1982, that for the United States continued to increase. The United States and Japan are not only the major consumers of ICs but also the major producers of products using semiconductors. They are also the leaders in research and development in semiconductors and the electronics industry as a whole.

FIGURE 1
International demand for integrated circuits

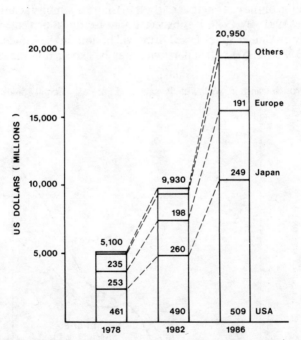

*Source:* Japan Electronic Machine Industry Forum, 'Report of Survey on Present Status and Future of Electronics Industry in Japan, Europe and USA', cited in *Press Journal* (1984).

The international division of labour in the production of semiconductors is made possible by the separation of four functions in its production process: (i) research and development; (ii) wafer fabrication; (iii) assembly of ICs; (iv) testing. Beginning with Fairchild's first offshore establishment in Hong Kong in 1961, the

assembly phase was the earliest facility deployed overseas; later some of
the testing functions followed (Henderson, 1986). The growth of
international sales of ICs and the number of Far East assembly plants is
shown in Figure 2. A slight dip is suggested in the 1974 to 1975 recession
following the first 'oil shock'. An apparent 10-year cycle is suggested in
the semiconductor industry with the current slump in the world market.
A 'shake-out' in the industry appears to be taking place, associated with
the introduction of more capital-intensive technology pushing out old
lines. The life-cycle of the dynamic RAM (random access memory) is
illustrated in Figure 3 showing the replacement of 64K by 256K chips,
which in turn by 1987 to 1988 will be replaced by the 1-Megabyte chip
(see Figure 4). With the expanding capacity of these memory chips and
increasing capital-intensity in production techniques, the labour cost
advantages of offshore facilities are expected to decline; and an
acceleration of the phasing-out of these offshore assembly facilities had
begun by 1981. By 1989, it is expected that nearly 40 percent of chip
assembly by United States-based firms will be done in the United States
(Ernst, 1982/83: 57). A similar trend may be expected in the case of

FIGURE 2
Growth trends in worldwide IC sales and Far East assembly plants

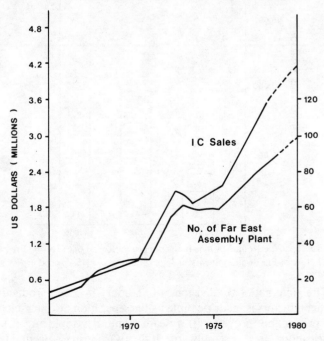

*Source:* Rosen Associates (1980), cited in Ernst (1982/83: 43).

FIGURE 3
Life-cycle of dynamic RAM

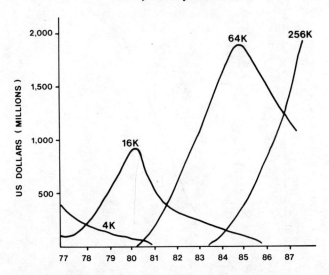

*Source:* as for Figure 1.

FIGURE 4
Development of dynamic RAM

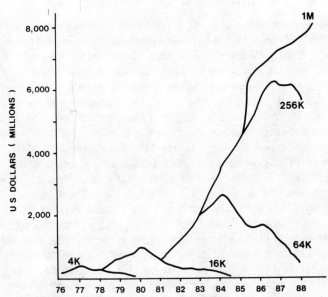

*Source: Press Journal* (1984).

FIGURE 5
World demand of 64K dynamic RAM

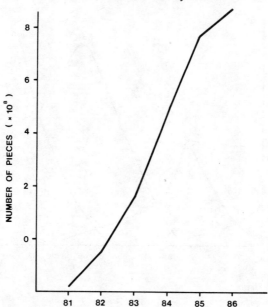

*Source: Press Journal* (1984).

Japanese semiconductor firms. Demand for ICs continues to climb for 64K RAMs (Figure 5), but bloated inventories between 1984 to 1985 are causing layoffs (Wilson, 1985). Part of this 'high-tech crisis' in the United States is associated with the trade deficit with Japan.

Penang's growth in the 1970s was associated with the assembly of 64K RAMs and the state has become a major producer of these chips. Precisely at the time the 64K chip is beginning to be replaced by the 256K chip, some firms in Penang are encountering over-capacity. The current slump in the export market has led to retrenchments and layoffs in many factories in Bayan Lepas FTZ. Retrenchment is perhaps the most controversial issue today and adds to the numbers of growing unemployed.[4] The numbers retrenched, as in the case of the unemployed, are closely linked to the fluctuations of the world economy.[5] Some manufacturing industries, such as electronics, textiles, rubber products and plywood are more prone to these fluctuations owing both to the nature of the industry (as in the case of electronics) and to the extent of its export-orientedness (for example, electronics and textiles). Thus an examination of the pattern of retrenchment shown in the *Economic Reports* (Malaysia, Ministry of Finance, 1973 to 1984) indicates that the first significant batch of retrenchments was in the first half of 1975 when 2,230 persons (over half in electronics) were retrenched.[6] Retrenchment continued into 1976, the numbers falling off until 1983 when the figure rose to 4,303 (again, mainly in electronics and textiles). Judging from reports of the numbers retrenched, the present recession is proving to be very severe. According to Malaysian Trade Union Congress estimates, 30,000 workers from the organized sector were retrenched between September 1984 and September 1985. This does not include the vast numbers who have been retrenched outside the organized sector.

A rough estimate of retrenched workers by type of industry indicates the seriousness of the problem. Within the primary sector it has been estimated that 16,000 workers have been retrenched from plantations, particularly rubber, in the last three years. Between December 1984 and May 1985, 6,000 workers were laid-off. In the mining industry, tin has been badly affected, retrenching about 20,000 workers in the last five years, and thus reducing the workforce from 40,080 in July 1980 to 22,761 in April 1985. Among industries in the manufacturing sector, electronics has retrenched about 30,000 workers. The increasing speed of retrenchment here is demonstrated by the fact that between August 1984 and March 1985, a matter of seven months, over 6,000 workers were laid-off. The pace has continued to increase, for between April and September 1985, 4,200 workers have been retrenched. Retrenchments in electronics continued unabated throughout the last quarter of 1985.[7] It was not until April 1986 that a slight upturn in business was felt in the electronics companies. Table 6 shows the extent of reported layoffs by industry between 1982 and 1984. Manufacturing has been the worst hit especially during the second half of 1982, and the first half of 1983 and 1984. This is followed by the wholesale, retail, restaurants and hotels sector, mining and quarrying, and agriculture.

The implications of layoffs and retrenchment on the welfare of workers are considerable. Unfortunately, there is very little research on retrenched workers. The fragmentary data available are derived from preliminary research on electronics and textile workers (Ariffin, 1985).[8] What emerges from the analysis is that an overwhelmingly large section of those retrenched are women, and indeed Malay women, because they make up the bulk of production workers in the electronics factories. There is evidence that many of the women who have been laid-off are in the 'older' age groups, that is over 25 years, and are, owing to their age, having problems securing another job (Ariffin, 1985: 15–16). Thus the dictum, 'first in, last out' has not been adhered to by the multinational companies who have, in order to cut down production costs, retrenched the older workers whose wages are higher than the more recently recruited workers (Salih et al., 1985). Because these workers are older, many are married, and hence their retrenchment has important

TABLE 6
Retrenched workers by industry, 1982–84 (in percentages)

| | 1982 | | 1983 | | 1984 | % change | |
|---|---|---|---|---|---|---|---|
| | 1st half | 2nd half | 1st half | 2nd half | 1st half | 1st half | |
| *Industry* | % | % | % | % | % | 83/84 | 82/83 |
| Agriculture, forestry, and fishing | 23.4 | 1.3 | 3.8 | 0.3 | — | — | − 15.4 |
| Mining & quarrying | 15.9 | 17.5 | 15.6 | 52.8 | 14.3 | — | 137.7 |
| Manufacturing | 26.3 | 67.5 | 73.9 | 35.5 | 83.0 | — | 87.5 |
| Electricity, gas, water | — | — | — | — | — | — | — |
| Construction | 12.3 | 3.7 | 0.4 | 4.6 | — | — | − 58.7 |
| Wholesale, rental trade, restaurant, hotel | 21.1 | 8.4 | 4.9 | 0.8 | 2.3 | — | − 39.5 |
| Finance, insurance real estate | — | — | 0.2 | — | — | — | — |
| Community, social & personal service | 0.7 | 1.0 | 2.3 | 5.6 | — | — | − 467.4 |
| Transport, storage | — | — | — | 0.5 | 0.3 | — | — |
| Others | — | 0.6 | — | — | — | — | — |
| Total % | 100.0 | 100.0 | 100.0 | 100.0 | 100.0 | — | 70.5 |
| Number | 1026 | 3741 | 6314 | 1813 | 2596 | | |

*Source:* Malaysia, Ministry of Labour and Manpower (1982, 1983, 1984).

implications for family income and future job placement. These workers have been substantial family income earners, and the loss of their job has meant serious cut-backs in expenditure on their family, particularly in food and education. Because these retrenched workers are women, and as the unemployment rates for women are higher than men, especially in the urban areas, many have had to wait up to a year to secure another job. As marriage tends to be associated with restricted geographic mobility, most have not been able to find jobs of equal earning power.

The retrenchment problem becomes more crucial for workers who are sole income earners, with very poor parents in rural areas depending on them, or having dependent children. This situation is aggravated when both husband and wife are retrenched, as in the rubber estates, mines and some of the factories. Recent evidence points to the increasing importance of these Malay women, whether single, married or divorced, as vital contributors to household income. Not only are parents dependent on them for survival but brothers and sisters have their education paid for by these women workers. The situation is similar to that in Hong Kong where working daughters delay marriage to elevate their family's economic situation (Salaff, 1981). The

FIGURE 6  Employment in the electronics industry, Penang, 1977–84

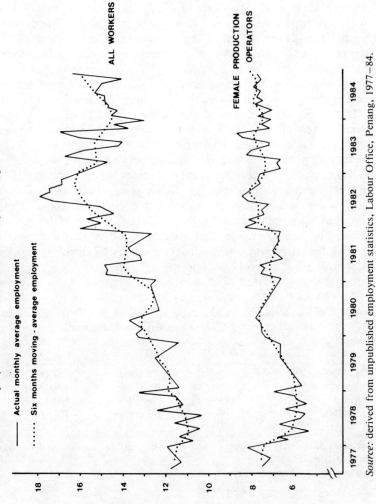

—— Actual monthly average employment

......... Six months moving - average employment

ALL WORKERS

FEMALE PRODUCTION
OPERATORS

NUMBER OF EMPLOYEES ( IN HUNDREDS )

*Source:* derived from unpublished employment statistics, Labour Office, Penang, 1977–84.

seriousness of retrenchment, then, is heightened by the fact that most of those retrenched are women who have become primary income earners.

Although the number of workers employed in Penang's FTZs increased between 1982 and 1983 (Table 2), this masks the true impact of the cycles of expansion and contraction in production and sales. Figure 6 shows more accurately the employment effects in terms of the average monthly total employment in electronics in the FTZs and the total number of female operators. The trend clearly shows the amplitudes, particularly when smoothed out through the six-month moving average, which reflected the cycles in the semiconductor sector.

Those who were retrenched during the downslide of the market situation were absorbed into other industries, have returned to their villages, or have remained in the urban areas seeking employment. Over the long term, some restructuring of the workforce at the factory level has taken place, as in the case of the electronics factories between 1974 and 1975, and again in 1984−85. The current retrenchments affect a much wider field of production than just electronics because of the impact of a general slowdown in the world economy on Malaysia as a whole. The consequence of this situation has been that it has been difficult for retrenched workers from electronics and textiles factories to be reabsorbed into other sectors.

TABLE 7

Average wages for unskilled and semiskilled workers in ASEAN electronics industry (current US$ per month, rounded figures)[1]

| Countries | Around 1970 | Mid-1970s | Around 1980 |
| --- | --- | --- | --- |
| Singapore | 65 (1968) | 90 (1976) | 250 (1982) |
| Malaysia | 30 (1971) | 60 (1976) | 120 (1980) |
| Thailand | 25 (1971) | 35 (1978) | 100 (1979) |
| Philippines | 45 (1971) | 57 (1978) | 100 (1979) |
| Indonesia | 20 (1971) | — | 25 (1982) |

[1] In Indonesia and the Philippines, figures refer to labour costs; in other countries, they refer to wages.

*Source:* Cited in Chaponniere (1984: 139).

Thus, the integration into the world economy of the Penang economy, by means of its FTZs, has exposed the local economy to the conjunctural effects of production and accumulation on a world scale. While the short-term effects are beyond the control of the state, the situation has reflected the policy response to pressure and problems affecting the local situation. However, these short-term fluctuations mask the underlying trends in the position and role of Malaysia, as reflected in the experience of the Penang economy. Capital is constantly seeking new profit centres on the world economic stage, and peripheral countries constantly compete with each other in order to provide a home for this itinerant capital. As shown in Table 7, wages are low in Penang when compared with those for similar work in the United States or Japan (the major reason for relocation of factories off-shore), but are higher than those of her ASEAN neighbours except Singapore. It is these structural changes at the level of the world economy which, together with state mediation of competing capitals and its control of labour, help to promote capital accumulation. It is these processes which continually determine the location and role of Malaysia and its constituent parts, such as Penang, in the international division of labour.

## Conclusion

In this chapter we have described the transformation of the Malaysian economy from the period when it was subject to a colonial division of labour to its present role in the 'new' international division of labour. This historical transformation was the product of the interplay of internal social forces — the various racial groups and class factions and their reflection within the state — with the changing structure of the world economy. Though the transformation has benefited the majority of the population, it has not resulted in a greater degree of autonomy for the Malaysian economy: the basic relations of dependence remain. As Malaysia continues to play a subordinate role in the international division of labour, it remains exposed to the vissicitudes of capital accumulation and decision-making processes at the global level. Thus in the future, as in the past, the realities of economic development in Malaysia will be determined by the articulation of the changing global structures with social and political interests internal to the society itself.

## Notes

1. This section is derived, in part, from an earlier paper (Salih and Young, 1985a).

2. In other words, the large size of these companies means that they have to adhere to the racial quota stipulated by the government. Besides, the formal nature of labour recruitment allows the intake of Malays to be based on achieved features, such as level of education, rather than the informal ascribed factors such as kinship, dialect groups, etc. so typical of small-scale family-run enterprises (see Young, 1982; Salih et al., 1985).

3. Data drawn from the Participatory Urban Services Study in Penang (Salih et al., 1985).

4. Parts of this section are taken from Salih and Young (1985b).

5. This does not account for the hundreds who have voluntarily resigned from textiles and electronics factories, for fear of impending retrenchment.

6. As in the case of the unemployed registrants, not all retrenched workers appear in the government statistics, for it is not mandatory for companies to report the number of retrenchments.

200 Global Restructuring and Territorial Development

7. A survey of English-medium newspapers such as *The Star and New Straits Times* shows that there was a news item on retrenchment practically every day between September and October 1985.

8. Ongoing research on Household Responses to Industrial and Urban Change in Malaysia carried out by the authors and based at the Universiti Sains Malaysia (1984–87) is also studying retrenched electronics workers.

## References

Ariffin, R. (1985) 'Retrenchment: An Exploratory Study of the Retrenchment Experience of the Textile and Electronic Workers in Penang'. Penang: School of Social Sciences, Universiti Sains Malaysia.

Bank Negara Malaysia (1984) *Annual Report, 1983*. Kuala Lumpur: Bank Negara.

Chaponniere, R. (1984) 'The ASEAN Integrated Circuit: the Electronics Industry in ASEAN — Issues and Perspectives'. *ASEAN Economic Bulletin*, 1(2): 136–151.

Chi, S.C. (1980) 'Industrial Estates and Regional Economic Development: A Case Study of the Prai Industrial Area'. Ph.D. thesis. Penang: Universiti Sains Malaysia.

Ernst, D. (1982/1983) 'Review: Restructuring World Industry and New Information Technology', *Asian Exchange*, December–March: 51–59.

Frobel, F. (1982) 'The Current Development of the World-economy: Reproduction of Labor and Accumulation of Capital on a World Scale', *Review*, 5(4): 507–555.

Goh, B.L. (1976) 'Survey of Small-scale Industries in Butterworth Town'. Penang: Centre for Policy Research, Universiti Sains Malaysia.

Henderson, J. (1986) 'The New International Division of Labour and American Semiconductor Production in South-east Asia', in C. Dixon, D. Drakakis-Smith and H. Watts (eds.), *Multinational Corporations and the Third World*, pp. 91–117. London: Croom Helm.

Hoffman, L. and S.E. Tan (1980) *Industrial Growth, Employment, and Foreign Investment in Peninsular Malaysia*. Kuala Lumpur: Oxford University Press.

Jomo, K.S. (1986) *A Question of Class*. Kuala Lumpur: Oxford University Press.

Kreye, O. (1980) *Perspectives for Development through Industrialization in the 1980s: An Independent Viewpoint on Dependency*. Tokyo: UNU Project on Goals, Processes and Indicators of Development, United Nations University.

Li, D.J. (1982) *British Malaya: An Economic Analysis*. Kuala Lumpur: Insan.

Lim, C.Y. (1967) *Economic Development of Modern Malaya*. Kuala Lumpur: Oxford University Press.

Lim, L.Y.C. (1978) 'Women Workers in Multinational Corporations in Developing Countries: The Case of the Electronics Industry in Malaysia and Singapore'. *Women's Studies Program Occasional Paper No. 19*. Ann Arbor: University of Michigan.

Lim, M.H. (1980) 'Ethnic Relations and Class in Malaysia', *Journal of Contemporary Asia*, 10(1–2): 130–154.

Lim, M.H. (1981) *Ownership and Control of the One Hundred Largest Corporations in Malaysia*. Kuala Lumpur: Oxford University Press.

Lim, T.G. (1977) *Peasants and Their Agricultural Economy in Colonial Malaya 1874–1941*. Kuala Lumpur: Oxford University Press.

Malaya, Government of (1956) *First Malaya Plan 1956–1960*. Kuala Lumpur: Government Press.

Malaysia, Department of Statistics (1983a) *State Population Report, Pulau Pinang*. Kuala Lumpur: Department of Statistics.

Malaysia, Department of Statistics (1983b) *General Report of the Population Census*, Vol. 1. Kuala Lumpur: Department of Statistics.

Malaysia, Government of (1961) *Second Malaya Plan 1961 – 1965*. Kuala Lumpur: Government Press.

Malaysia, Government of (1966) *First Malaysia Plan 1966 – 1970*. Kuala Lumpur: Government Press.

Malaysia, Goverment of (1971) *Second Malaysia Plan 1971 – 1975*. Kuala Lumpur: Government Press.

Malaysia, Government of (1981) *Fourth Malaysia Plan 1981 – 1985*. Kuala Lumpur: Government Press.

Malaysia, Government of (1984) *Mid-term Review of the Fourth Malaysia Plan 1981 – 1985*. Kuala Lumpur: Government Press.

Malaysia, Ministry of Finance (1973 to 1984) *Economic Reports 1972/73 to 1984/85*. Kuala Lumpur: Ministry of Finance.

Malaysia, Ministry of Labour and Manpower (1978 to 1984) *Labour and Manpower Reports of 1979/80 to 1985/86*. Kuala Lumpur: Ministry of Labour and Manpower.

Muzaffar, C. (1979) *Protector?*. Penang: Aliran.

Penang Development Corporation (1973, 1974, 1983, 1984) *Annual Reports*. Penang: Penang Development Corporation.

Press Journal (1984) *Nihon Handotai Nenhan 1984* (Japan IC Annual Report). Tokyo.

Rao, V.V.B. (1976) *National Accounts of West Malaysia 1947 – 1971*. Singapore: Heinemann Educational Books.

Roff, W.R. (1976) *The Origins of Malay Nationalism*. Kuala Lumpur: University of Malaya Press.

Saham, J. (1980) *British Industrial Investment in Malaysia 1963 – 1971*. Kuala Lumpur: Oxford University Press.

Salaff, J. (1981) *Working Daughters of Hong Kong*. New York: Cambridge University Press.

Salih, K. (1981) 'Malaysia and the World System: a Perspective Essay on Incorporation, Social Groups and the State'. Paper presented at the Research Workshop for Interdependence and Development. OECD, April.

Salih, K. and J. Tan (1985) 'Impact of Industrial Development Corporations and Industrial Estates on Regional Development: Case of Malaysia'. Paper presented to the International Centre for Public Enterprises in Developing Countries Workshop on the Role of Public Enterprises in Regional Development in Developing Countries. New Delhi, 25 – 30 March.

Salih, K. and M.L. Young (1981) 'Malaysia: Urbanization in a Multiethnic Society — Case of Peninsular Malaysia', in M. Honjo (ed.), *Urbanization and Regional Development*, Vol. 6, PP. 117 – 147. Singapore: Maruzen Asia.

Salih, K. and M.L. Young (1985a) 'Penang's Industrialisation: Where do we Go from Here?'. Paper to the Malaysian Economic Association Convention on the Future of Penang, 6 – 8 May.

Salih, K. and M.L. Young (1985b) 'Employment, Unemployment and Retrenchment in Malaysia: The Outlook and What is to be Done about it?'. Paper to the MTUC Conference on Unemployment and Retrenchment in Malaysia. Penang, 10 October.

Salih, K., M.L. Young, L.H. Chan, K.W. Loh and C.K. Chan (1985) 'Young Workers and Urban Services: A Case Study of Penang, Malaysia'. Final report of the Participatory Urban Services Project. Penang: Universiti Sains Malaysia.

Snodgrass, D.R. (1980) *Inequality and Economic Development in Malaysia*. Kuala Lumpur: Oxford University Press.

Tham, S.C. (1977) *Malays and Modernisation*. Singapore: Singapore University Press.

Wilson, J.W. (1985) 'America's High-tech Crisis: Why Silicon Valley is Losing its Edge', *Business Week*, 11 March: 44 – 50.

Young, K., W.C.F. Bussink and P. Hassan (1980) *Malaysia: Growth and Equity in a Multinational Society*. Baltimore: Johns Hopkins University Press.

Young, M.L. (1982) 'Migrants and Niches: Economic Structure of Migration Streams in Peninsular Malaysia 1965–1970'. *Staff Discussion Paper No. 7*. Penang: School of Social Sciences, Universiti Sains Malaysia.

# IV
# THE URBAN DIMENSION OF GLOBAL RESTRUCTURING

## 9

## The Fixers:
## the Urban Geography of International Commercial Capital

### *Nigel Thrift*

> In the final analysis, a world paper money of obligatory usage presupposes a world state, a world government, that is, the disappearance of inter-imperialist competition, that is, superimperialism. We are further from that than ever. (Mandel, 1975: 14)

In this chapter I shall make a number of points in a preliminary fashion about the present phase of the internationalization of capital. In particular, my concern is with the internationalization of what might be called the 'intermediary economy', not banking or industrial capital but rather commercial capital (in its broadest sense). The function of this international intermediary economy is to organize and adjudicate all manner of international economic exchanges — for a fee. Its territory is the 'international financial centre'. I shall concentrate on the changing geography of one such centre, the City of London, through consideration of the recent activities of a number of its larger denizens.

### International Commercial Capital

*At the Most General Level ...*
Until quite recently most interest has focused on the internationaliz-ation of industrial (or productive) capital and the internationalization of banking (or interest-bearing) capital (Thrift, 1985a). Clearly these are both important tendencies with highly visible effects, whether these be export processing zones or the eurodollar market, 'developed' country deindustrialization or 'developing' country debt. But the role of commercial capital has tended to be forgotten.

The reasons for this state of affairs are difficult to divine, particularly because, as I shall argue below, it has been commercial capital that has been responsible for much of the growth of international financial centres. One reason may be that there has been a general tendency in Marxist and Marxist-related theory, from Marx onwards, to down-grade the importance of commercial capital within capitalism by seeing it as a 'parasitic', or even 'relict' form to be relegated to the sidelines of capitalist production (see Ingham, 1984, for a critique). Another reason may be that banking and commercial capital are often occluded, especially in accounts that draw on the concept of finance capital (see Minns, 1981, for a critique).

What, then, is commercial capital?[1] Briefly, commercial capital mediates in the circulation of commodities for a fee. It does not retain any direct or long-term ownership or control of these commodities. Commercial capital can be subdivided into merchant capital which mediates the circulation of commodity capital of various kinds, and money-dealing capital which mediates the circulation of money capital of various kinds (and especially credit money having 'fictitious value'; see Harvey, 1982: chapter 9).

Certainly, given this description, commercial capital can be seen as 'parasitic' within capitalist production. As Harvey (1982: 71–72) puts it, 'On the one hand, the relationship is parasitic, in the sense that the merchant creates no value but merely appropriates it . . . On the other hand, merchants' capital can expand the surplus value realised by the producer through accelerating the turnover of capital and reducing the necessary costs of circulation'. Commercial capital, in other words, performs a vital enabling function within the capitalist productive system. The costs of circulation can also be benefits.

Just as certainly, commercial capital cannot be described as a relict form, although it is possible to find such a scenario in Marx, a scenario in which commercial capital dies out as the barriers to capitalist production are removed by its internationalization. But in reality, the role of commercial capital has become more, not less, important as capitalism has internationalized. Partly this is the result of the ingenuity which commercial capitalists have brought to bear in inventing new markets for commodities of all kinds, and most especially those which mobilize credit money. Even more importantly, a complex and wayward system of nation-states has grown up round the world with each state in economic competition with the others, necessitating the raising of all kinds of barriers to trade such as laws, and central bank regulations, and with each state founding its own national money with its record of stability and trust (Giddens, 1985). Thus

> International commercial capital is not merely based on the existence of the 'simple circulation of commodities and money'. The political system of nation states creates a set of conditions which renders international trade quite distinct from 'trade in general'. (Ingham, 1984: 94–95)

The four main reasons why commercial capital continues to thrive are as follows. First, it performs a vital function oiling the wheels of capitalist production. This function, in many cases, because of economies of scale, is performed more cheaply than could be achieved by internalizing its functions within industrial or banking capital. Second, it has ceaselessly created new markets for its services, especially in the burgeoning international credit system. Third, it has been able to take advantage of the barriers to trade implicit in the international capitalist economy. And, fourth, it provides much of the wherewithal for speculation. Thus, commercial capital forms a vast intermediary economy between industrial capital, banking capital and the state.

In spite of the above, commercial capital is still continually under threat from banking capital and industrial capital. There is no reason, in principle, why many of its functions — from making markets to accounting to information gathering to underwriting — cannot be performed internally by banking and industrial corporations. Indeed many are, to a point, and the boundary is continually shifting back and forth. There are two reasons why these functions have not been entirely absorbed by industrial and banking capital. The first reason relies upon the fact that considerable economies can be gained from subcontracting specialist services, not just because particular services can be carried out on a larger scale and therefore more cheaply by commercial capital, but also because, as the social and technical division of labour has increased in complexity, so specialist information can be pooled more easily by specialist firms, certain specialists can only be employed full-time within such firms, and so on. Of late, evidence seems to be mounting that modern banking and industrial capital is actually referring a number of previously internalized functions to commercial capital in a 'decentralization of administration' that parallels the 'decentralization of production'.

The second reason why commercial capital has not been absorbed is that it has raised numerous barriers that permit only selective access to participation in markets. Thus a constant element of the structure of commercial capital is the fencing off of markets by means of associations of various kinds. These associations are often backed up by the power of the state and by being linked to various criteria of social acceptability. Thereby, the forces of state and civil society are harnessed to the economic survival of a part of capital as a distinctive entity.

Of course, throughout history, commercial capital has had to deal with the problem of technological change. In the constant bidding to cut the circulation time of money capital, enormous technological strides have been made which have threatened the integrity of commercial capital as a separate entity. Of late, for example, pressure has been put on commercial capital by the converging technologies of computers, communications and information vending. But, so far, the evidence is that commercial capital has been able to capitalize on its extant expertise, mobilize its forms of association in new ways and move into new areas of expertise in such a way that it has been able to keep particular markets more or less to itself.

*More Particularly . . .*

What, then, are the different kinds of organizations and practices that go to make up commercial capital? There are four main clusters. The most ancient of these clusters of organizations are those that are concerned with mediating the exchange of commodities of various kinds, from agricultural produce (e.g. cocoa, coffee, sugar, rubber, wool, soya meal) to metals (copper, lead, tin, zinc, nickel, aluminium) to bullion (gold, silver). Merchant capital still exists, arranging the buying and selling, insurance, shipping and finance of raw materials exchange, usually within a fixed marketplace. However upon the raw materials market has been built an extensive money capital market, especially through the use of fixed-time, fixed-price bills of exchange known as futures which can be used by corporations to insure against commodity price rises and falls, or for speculation. Futures markets expanded considerably in the 1970s, especially as a result of the founding of new exchanges. In the late 1970s and early 1980s futures markets were given a further boost when they finally became fully integrated into the credit system with the establishment of markets in purely financial investments like eurodollars, municipal bonds, stock market indices, even interest rates. In the United States the number of contracts drawn on the futures markets increased from less than 20 million in 1970 to 150 million in 1984.

A special case of the market in commodities is the market in real estate. Clearly not all of this market is of concern to the subject matter of this paper since much of it is to do with the simple shifting of revenues. But certain kinds of real estate, especially office property but also large retail units, large industrial units and the like, are now traded as commodity money (Feagin, 1983). This development has only been bolstered by the appearance of institutions like property trusts and the development of secondary mortgage markets. The chief elements of commercial capital active in this property market are real estate agents (who are essentially brokers) and merchant banks.

A second cluster of commercial capital organizations is concerned with mediating monetary exchange. In the money markets commercial capital acts as a wholesaler. The grandparent of these markets is the discount market (Coakley and Harris, 1983). But, as capitalism expanded from the mid-1950s onwards it ran into a series of national rules and regulations on borrowing and lending which had to be surmounted. The new markets that resulted were co-ordinated by various 'fixers', especially the merchant banks. Of these markets the most important is the eurocurrency market, which is essentially a short-term interbank market. The eurocurrency market has grown dramatically since 1970 (for a dated but still useful account see Mendelsohn, 1980).

The foreign exchange markets have also grown rapidly. They are simply markets that shuffle foreign exchange about the world at the request of customer corporations and for purposes of speculation. In 1984 these markets had a daily turnover of $150 billion (*Economist*, 1985a). Again, the chief organizations that run these money markets are various merchant banks, acting as brokers, as well as other kinds of broker and dealer. These organizations act as processors and organizers of foreign exchange for a fee. Until recently, they have generally had little to do with lending.[2]

The third main cluster of commercial capital organizations deals in securities (stocks and shares) issued to raise capital by companies or governments (the primary market) then bought and sold in a speculative fashion (the secondary market). The organizations act as the mediators of exchange in a series of fixed marketplaces to which there is restricted access (stock and government bond exchanges).

A final important cluster of commercial capital organizations is focused on the selling of corporate services. The most important of these services is non-life insurance and reinsurance (in which insurance is reinsured to spread the risk) with its insurance companies, brokers and underwriters. This market has over time become more centralized around fixed exchange points.

Further important parts of the cluster of service organizations are as crucial to commercial capital as they are to banking and industrial capital. Since they charge a fee and are intimately involved in the process of exchange they are included in this paper as commercial capital. The profession of *accountancy*, which dates from the 1940s in its modern form, is pivotal to the capitalist system (Tinker, 1984). Accountants adjudicate the process of exchange. Through a series of historically evolved rules they define what is profit and what is not. They apply these rules to a sample of the exchanges that a corporation makes and then derive a statement of what the corporation is worth. *Advertising agencies* charge a fee for publicizing the availability of commodities for exchange. They help to create and sustain markets. Advertising agencies date from the 1820s, but it was not until the 1880s that agencies came into their own, spurred on by the growth of mass consumption of goods and the establishment of popular newspapers which gained much of their revenue from advertising (Fraser, 1981). *Legal services* have become increasingly concerned with defining and adjudicating contracts for the exchange of commodities in the presence of legal systems from many nation- states. *Tax consultants* provide the expertise for minimizing different nation-states' tolls on exchange. *Information services* provide all kinds of commercial information from analysis of transactions in markets (e.g. spot prices of currencies and securities) to analysis of competitors in particular markets. Whatever the cause it is becoming increasingly the case that information about money is money. The list of service firms goes on almost endlessly. These firms are the 'fixers' of capitalism.

**International Financial Centres**
The natural habitat of commercial capital is the 'financial' centre. For three interrelated reasons the organizations of commercial capital tend to group together in these centres. The first reason is to be near clients, especially the headquarters offices of banking and industrial corporations, but also major state departments and other commercial capital firms. (Commercial capital is a social as well as an economic network.) The second reason is to be in close proximity to relevant markets, many of which operate from fixed exchanges and all of which operate under quite severe spatial constraints. The third reason is to tap into information on markets and the operations of banking and industrial corporations and the state rapidly and efficiently. It is no surprise, then, to see most concentrations of commercial capital in selected cities.

Until recently most of these concentrations have served domestic national markets. Commercial capital in cities like Chicago and Tokyo is still essentially oriented to exchange within their domestic economies. With a few notable exceptions like the City of London, New York and Paris, these concentrations were not internationally oriented. In the 1970s, this all began to change. Nearly every key activity of commercial capital began to internationalize for three interrelated reasons. Partly this was a response to the internationalization of key customers amongst banking and industrial capital. This imperative required the setting up of office networks mirroring the multinational networks of plants and offices of banking and industrial capital in order to retain custom. Partly it was a consequence of the internationalization of the markets themselves, which was linked to the internationalization of banking and industrial capital and to new market opportunities afforded by developments in a number of countries. And partly it was the result of technological changes which were initially an enabling factor but which have now become a determinant in the markets.

There therefore came into being a worldwide network of *international 'financial' centres*, trading posts serving the international market (Figure 1).[3] The main activities of these international financial

FIGURE 1
The hierarchy of international financial centres in 1980[1]

---

**First order Supranational Centres**
London        New York


**Second order Supranational Centres**
Amsterdam     Frankfurt      Paris
Tokyo         Zurich


**First order International Financial Centres**

| | | | | |
|---|---|---|---|---|
| Basel | Bombay | Brussels | Chicago | Dusseldorf |
| Hamburg | Hong Kong | Madrid | Melbourne | |
| Mexico City | Rio de Janeiro | Rome | San Francisco | |
| Sao Paulo | Singapore | Sydney | | |
| Toronto | Vienna | | | |


**Second order International Financial Centres**

| | | | |
|---|---|---|---|
| Bahrain | Buenos Aires | Kobe | Los Angeles |
| Luxemburg | Milan | Montreal | Osaka |
| Panama City | Seoul | Tapei | |

---

[1]Derived from hierarchical cluster analysis and stepwise multiple discriminant analysis performed on sixteen variables.
*Source:* Reed (1983: 227).

centres are similar, in some ways, to those carried on in domestic financial centres but they are arranged in a hierarchy that spans the globe. These activities are as follows.

*International commodity exchange.* Every significant international financial centre has a whole battery of commodity exchanges. Currently, the important growth area is in futures exchanges. Some of these are now being linked together to enable 24-hour futures trading to take place eventually. For example, since January 1985 the Chicago Mercantile Exchange (CME) has been linked to the Singapore International Monetary Exchange (SIMEX) for trading in a range of futures including eurodollars, eurodeutschmarks and interest rates. Another important element of international commodity exchange is the international property market. It is over the last 15 years that a truly international property market has come into being, one that relies on the activities of a select band of international real estate brokers to form a commodity market (Bateman, 1985; Thrift, 1984a, 1985b). This property market is mainly concerned with office buildings, although selected retail and industrial buildings and some expensive residential buildings can also be included. An irony of this market is that it is to a great extent concentrated on international and domestic financial centres. Thus the activities of commercial capital can form both supply and demand.

*International monetary exchange* (including the arrangement of eurocurrency loans). International currency clearing is one of the very important monetary exchange activities of commercial capital in international financial centres and access to clearing is an equally important determinant of location in international financial centres by offices of banking and industrial corporations. In 1982 New York cleared approximately $160 billion every day, followed by London ($17 billion), Frankfurt and Paris ($12 billion each), Tokyo ($7 billion), Zurich ($4 billion) and Amsterdam ($2 billion) (Reed, 1983).

*International securities dealing.* Until the last two or three years trading in foreign stocks and shares was an unusual activity. But now high-volume trading is taking off. There is considerable interest in the promotion of an international securities market, boosted by the attention of institutional investors like pension funds intent on internationalizing their portfolios. Thus, there are now 16 US globally oriented national funds. In turn, overseas institutions now own about 3.8 percent of US stocks. The New York Stock Exchange is now a major trader of the shares of British companies and there are 200 US companies listed on the London Stock Exchange. The current ambition is to link a series of stock exchanges round the world in such a way as to enable 24-hour trading. The New York Stock Exchange is linked with the Pacific Exchange in San Francisco. The Boston and Montreal Exchanges are linked. There is a task force investigating the linkage of the New York and London Exchanges (Pagano, 1985).

*International services.* International insurance broking used to be confined to the City of London. Now it is spreading round the globe. In North America exchanges in New York, Miami, Toronto and Chicago are taking some of London's international business and there are plans for a further exchange in Atlanta. The New York Exchange has experienced a remarkable growth since its opening in March 1980, from a premium volume of $72.5 million in 1981 to $450 million in 1984. But as yet these exchanges are still struggling to find international business (Manser, 1985). Other international services like accountancy and legal services also form important clusters of commercial capital within international financial centres.

The formation of international financial centres has been boosted by two developments. The first of these is the multinationalization of commercial capital. The result is that the ownership of commercial capital in international financial centres has become more and more cosmopolitan. In the City of London, for example, there are more

TABLE 1
Foreign banks in London and New York[1]

|  | London | New York | Difference |
|---|---|---|---|
| 1970 | 163 | 75 | 88 |
| 1971 | 176 | 81 | 95 |
| 1972 | 215 | 85 | 130 |
| 1973 | 232 | 98 | 134 |
| 1974 | 264 | 114 | 150 |
| 1975 | 263 | 127 | 136 |
| 1976 | 265 | 144 | 121 |
| 1977 | 300 | 177 | 123 |
| 1978 | 313 | 208 | 105 |
| 1979 | 330 | 244 | 86 |
| 1980 | 353 | 253 | 100 |
| 1981 | 353 | 255 | 98 |
| 1982 | 379 | 285 | 94 |
| 1983 | 391 | 294 | 97 |
| 1984 | 403 | 307 | 96 |

[1]Includes only foreign banks directly represented through a representative office, a branch office or a subsidiary.
*Source: The Banker*, 1984.

foreign banks than British banks. The same goes for New York (Table 1). Similarly, there are many foreign insurers in London. For example, the present membership of the Institute of London Underwriters is 40 percent foreign. In New York, there are 70 foreign insurers operating.

The second development has been the role of the converging technologies of communications, computing and information gathering. Reed (1983: 230) sums up the importance of this convergence:

Jet travel has made it possible to move important people and documents from one location to another, anywhere in the world, within 24 hours. This quick and relatively inexpensive means of moving highly skilled people is perhaps the single most important factor in diminishing the need for (all) financial centres to be expert in a number of ancillary activities (i.e. accountancy, advertising, law, printing, etc.). The international financial centres can export much of the needed ancillary services to other centres at substantially lower costs than would be incurred if each centre had to generate these skills internally.

The non-personal form of communication may involve airmail or telephone, telex or sea mail. Important documents such as letters of credit, trade bills, term loan agreements and cheques can now be moved overnight by air courier. This has improved the operating efficiency of centres and their clients in those matters that require the movement of a physical document. Telephone, telex and other types of transmission make it possible to send and receive instructions almost simultaneously.

Indeed the rapid development of completely automated systems of exchange and information on exchange, whether for commodity, share, currency or insurance dealing, further boosts the role of the international financial centres (Langdale, 1985; *Economist*, 1985b). These systems further reduce the turnover time of capital through better co-ordination and distribution of information about exchange, as well as exchange itself:

> Better, more reliable communication links have encouraged round-the-clock, round-the-world trading in what is becoming, as the cliche correctly has it, a global market place. Bonds have been following foreign exchange down that route; now the elite of world class equities are on the move as well. Better, easier-to-use computers have given firms the ability to process millions of transactions a day, investors the intelligence to track dozens of variables in scores of places. Both have made possible higher volumes and greater velocity, and allowed a wider range of more complicated instruments. They have also contributed to the rapid growth and sophistication of electronic and screen-based telephone markets. (*Economist*, 1985b: 10)

The result is that international financial centres are becoming more and more important and their importance is undoubtedly synergic: 'influence of the centres is far greater than the total reach, scope, and influence of their various institutions when measured separately' (Reed, 1983: 234).

**The City of London**
The doyenne of the international financial centres is still the City of London. The City has reigned supreme amongst centres of international commercial capital since the eighteenth century (McRae and Cairncross, 1984). By 1832 the City had already taken on much of its present form with, for example, the discount houses in place and several of the 'classical' fixed markets. Already in that year Nathan Rothschild could observe that

> this country in general is the Bank for the whole world . . . all transactions in India, in China, in Germany, in Russia, and in the whole world, are guided here and settled through this country. (cited in Ingham, 1984: 93)

Already, the City's international role meant that it was becoming divorced from the British domestic economy and indeed it had little to do with the industrial revolution or subsequent developments. By the turn of the century this divorce was almost complete. From 1865 to 1913,

> income from interest and dividends on foreign investments, from shipping credits, insurance, banking and the financing of foreign trade increased from a total of around $80 million to $340 million. (Ingham, 1984: 41)

This moved the UK's balance of payments into surplus. The City's earnings declined relatively before World War II, mainly because of the worldwide depression, then increased again after the war was over. The form of the City's institutions is not immutable but Figure 2 attempts to summarize its present state. Numerous introductions to the City exist which would make a longer summary superfluous (e.g. Wilson Committee, 1980; Coakley and Harris, 1983; McRae and Cairncross, 1984; Harris, 1985).

FIGURE 2
The structure of the City of London: basic commercial practices and institutions

| Commodity | Practices | Institutional structure | Organizations |
|-----------|-----------|------------------------|---------------|
| Money | Arranging loans, clearing | Wholesale money markets; foreign exchange markets | Overseas banks; Discount houses; Merchant banks (including accepting houses); arms of clearing banks; foreign exchange dealers |
| Securities | Issuing, broking, jobbing | Stock Exchange | Issuing houses; stockbrokers and jobbers |
| Commodities | Merchanting, broking | Various commodity markets and exchanges (e.g. LIFFE, LME) and other more diffuse markets | Brokers associates; Merchant banks, etc. |
| Services (a) Insurance | Underwriting, broking | Lloyds and other more diffuse markets | Lloyds, insurance companies |
| (b) Freight | Chartering | Baltic Exchange, Lloyds Shipping Register, etc. | Chartering companies |
| (c) Accountancy, legal services, advertising, public relations, tax consultants and advisers, management consultants, etc. | Adjudicating, publicizing, minimizing costs of exchange, etc. | Diffuse markets | Relevant companies |

*Source:* Ingham (1984: 16).

By 1983 the total overseas earnings of the City stood at $5,378 million, with $2,754 million of this amount coming directly from the fee-earning activities of commercial services. The City-controlled assets double the size of Britain's GDP (Harris, 1985). Arguably, the City is still the world's leading international financial centre, despite a strong challenge from New York in the 1970s and 1980s. Specifically, the City has been able to retain its supremacy as the chief nexus of a number of markets, including:

1. *The insurance market*. London is still the major international insurance centre in the world, despite a strong challenge from New York (which is still mainly concerned with domestic insurance). It has retained its position by actively developing the world reinsurance market and encouraging, to a limited degree, foreign names and insurance companies (Manser, 1985). Already by 1978, the City's annual premium income had overtaken the gross domestic product of New Zealand (McRae and Cairncross, 1984).

TABLE 2

The growth of London as a merchant banking and broking centre, 1970–84

|  | 1970 | 1975 | 1980 | 1984 |
|---|---|---|---|---|
| Number of foreign banks directly represented through a representative office, a branch office or a subsidiary | 163 | 263 | 353 | 403 |
| Number of foreign banks, indirectly represented through a share in a joint venture or a consortium bank | — | 72 | 50 | 67 |
| Total number of foreign banks directly or indirectly represented | 163 | 335 | 403 | 470 |
| Number of foreign securities houses (dealers in bonds and securities) | — | — | — | 96 |
| Numbers employed by foreign banks and foreign securities houses in London | 11,813 | 20,881 | 31,132 | 39,175 |

*Source: The Banker*, various issues.

2. *The money market*. London is one of the largest of the foreign exchange markets. It is also the major node of the eurocurrency markets. Of the $2,000 billion of eurocurrency extant in the world at the end of 1982, one-third was on the books of London merchant banks (McRae and Cairncross, 1984), many of them from overseas (Table 2). Because of the shadow of developing country indebtedness

it seems sensible to assume that the City will not see a boom through the 1980s comparable to that of the second half of the 1970s. It is quite possible too that London may shrink vis-a-vis New York, which at the end of 1981 set up offshore banking legislation to permit US banks to book loans in New York without going over the hurdle of US tax and domestic monetary controls. Within a year these International Banking Facilities, as they are called, accounted for 8 percent of the total euromarket deposits, as against London's share which was held steady at around the 35 percent mark. In bank loans booked through the different centres, London's lead was narrower: 27 percent against 14.5 percent for New York.

It is a useful warning that London can be challenged. For the time being, to be sure, London may not have much to fear. Not only do the Americans and other foreign banks already have an enormous investment in the City which will tend to keep the business here, but New York has not proved as efficient a place to raise euromarket deposits as London, and most of the loans being booked through New York have to be funded by dollars bought in established euromarket dealing centres, of which London is by far the largest. (McRae and Cairncross, 1984: 71–72)

3. *The commodity markets*. London still leads the other international financial centres in a number of commodity markets such as gold bullion. However the largest commodities markets now are futures markets. Of these futures markets, the largest is the Chicago Mercantile Exchange but this is still mainly a domestic market, although its International Monetary Market, dealing in financial futures, has had enormous influence. The largest international futures markets are in New York and London. London has the edge in cocoa, sugar and coffee futures but New York has taken the lead in many other futures. For example, COMEX in New York is easily the largest market in the world for gold futures. In the early 1980s, however, London responded to the challenge of Chicago and New York by setting up a range of new futures exchanges including the London Gold Futures Market and the London International Financial Futures Exchange (LIFFE).

TABLE 3
Employment in the City of London, 1976

| Sector | Employment ('000s) | Percent |
|---|---|---|
| Banking | 76 | 24 |
| Insurance | 40 | 12 |
| Stockmarket and other financial | 20 | 6 |
| Exchange markets | 22 | 7 |
| Accountants and lawyers | 17 | 5 |
| Subtotal | 175 | 54 |
| City total | 321 | 100 |

*Source:* Jones, Lang and Wootton, 1980.

4. *The service centre.* As a centre of services, and especially accountancy and legal services, the City of London is still pre-eminent.

The fortunes of many people in Britain now rely on the continuing success of the commercial activities of the City of London (Table 3) (King, 1985). The judicious use of social exclusion, the constant creation of new credit money markets (such as eurocurrency markets) and allowing the selective entry of foreign institutions have so far enabled the City to retain its position as the leading international financial centre, unbolstered by any significant national market. As Manser (1985: 115) points out with respect to the London insurance markets:

> it is important to distinguish between the 'UK market' and the 'London market'. The UK market is no more than a market of national insurers. . . . The London market is much more than a geographical expression. It is an international insurance centre which, apart from certain advantages of language and communications, is based in London largely by historical accident. . . . The speciality of London is (international) finance, where that of Detroit is motor manufacture and that of Dusseldorf is steel.

But as some of the examples above make clear, London is feeling the chill winds of competition which have, for example, already forced it to review many of its traditional barriers to integration of elements of commercial capital. It can never expect to be again unambiguously the world's major international financial centre. It is no surprise, then, that just as foreign firms based in other international financial centres have moved their operations into the City or bought into City firms in order to capture business, so City-based firms are moving their operations into other international financial centres abroad or buying into them to ensure that they are not left behind in the race for these centres' business. The City firms are trying to make sure that they are represented in every significant international financial centre. The next section examines this process of internationalization.

**The Internationalization of the City of London**
The City's major commercial firms have been internationalizing since the turn of the century. But it has been in the 1970s and 1980s that they have seriously moved overseas. The impact of this movement on other international financial centres has been quite substantial and has actually rebounded on London. New York, for example, owes much of its success as a foreign exchange trading centre to an influx of British-owned broking firms, with their expertise and contacts, into the city in the 1970s. Another example: London's major corporate lawyers (43 in the City, 101 in London as a whole)[4] (Investors Chronicle, 1984) have extensively internationalized in the last 15 years with a resultant concentration of their offices in particular international financial

centres. For example, Stone James Stephen Jaques now has offices in New York, Sydney, Perth and Canberra, while Linklaters and Paines has offices in New York, Paris, Brussels and Hong Kong. Twenty-three foreign law firms now have offices in Singapore. Nine of these firms are based in the City of London. Thus pockets of the City of London can now be found in all the major international financial centres.

Clearly, however, there is a need for more detailed case studies of particular forms of internationalization and the next two subsections of the paper provide a survey of the internationalization of two key sectors of the City — accountants and real estate agents — via case studies of two of the largest firms in each sector.

## *Accountancy*

The accountancy profession adjudicates exchange for which it receives a fee. It informs shareholders of an industrial or banking company what they have received in exchange for their investment. It allows creditors to assess the security of their claims. It helps the state to decide whether the revenues it received from the company are sufficient. And so on. The profession of chartered or public accounting is relatively recent. Originally, it came into being in Great Britain in the 1850s as a result of state action: the introduction of the companies acts and the bankruptcy acts. In the decades following the US Civil War, British chartered accountants crossed the Atlantic to monitor British capital investment in the United States:

> By protecting shareholders and maintaining investor confidence, accountants performed the primary service of stimulating capital accumulation in the United States in the early twentieth century. The (British) firm of Marwick Mitchell helped J.P. Morgan avert a bank collapse and restore investor confidence in the Knickerbocker Trust Co., thereby ending the panic of 1907. The State's ratification of an income tax constitutional amendment in 1913 led to a substantially increased demand for professional accountancy services, as did the call for official accounting standards and guidelines by the Federal Trade Commission and the Federal Reserve Board. But it was the stock market crash of 1929 and the Securities Acts of 1933 and 1934 that produced the largest growth in the demand for accountants. Peat, Marwick, Mitchell's experience provides some indication of the magnitude of this growth. In 1947, the firm's revenues stood at less than $10 million; by 1981 revenues had reached $979 million. British accounting experienced a comparable growth as a result of the 1948 Companies Act; Britain today (with some 100,000 chartered and certified accountants) has more accountants per head than any other advanced capitalist country. (Tinker, 1984: xvi)

The core of the accountancy business is still the audit. An audit is a summary of economic transactions. Typically, a large corporation makes millions of transactions in any year, so audits are concerned with designing a sample frame that captures the significant features of these transactions. This requires a three-phase exercise. The first phase involves the assessment of the quality of the internal controls of corporations to check if the corporation can be audited. The second phase consists of tests for errors in the corporation's recording of transactions (e.g. matching shipping documents to invoices). In the final phase additional testing is carried out (Stevens, 1982).

Recently, three trends have touched the accountant's world. The first trend has been computerization. Now auditing programs are a vital part of any audit. Many of these programs are copyrighted and have become a business in themselves. The second trend is diversification out of auditing into other services. Tax consultancy was an early favourite. Management consultancy and related business services (e.g. insolvency) are the current major areas of expansion. Accountants are also heavily involved in services to central and local government, in development consultancy, in charity consultancy, and so on. The third trend is litigation. Most accountancy firms are run as partnerships but this form of organization is now coming under considerable strain as they become subject to more and more law suits from creditors alleging careless auditing practice after companies go bust. In the United States suits against accountants are running at one a day. But even in less litigious countries accountants are now being sued. The result is that insurance cover is becoming increasingly hard to obtain and increasingly expensive. It is quite possible that, as a result of this pressure, the larger accountants may become limited companies, so protecting the partners from personal bankruptcy.

The accountancy profession is dominated worldwide by the 'big nine' firms (Tables 4 and 5), all of which are sizeable multinationals. In 1981, these nine firms between them audited 493 out of the *Fortune 500*

TABLE 4
The nine largest multinational accountancy firms,
1984, by number of audits

|  | USA Fortune 500 major audits | Rest of world Fortune 500 major audits | Total |
|---|---|---|---|
| Price Waterhouse | 151 | 72 | 223 |
| Peat Marwick Mitchell | 156 | 37 | 193 |
| Arthur Anderson | 159 | 17 | 176 |
| Ernst and Whinney | 136 | 37 | 173 |
| Coopers and Lybrand | 98 | 52 | 150 |
| Deloitte Haskins and Sells | 116 | 31 | 147 |
| Arthur Young | 83 | 48 | 131 |
| Touche Ross | 71 | 25 | 96 |
| Klynveld Main Goerdeler | 12 | 48 | 60 |

*Source:* Price Waterhouse, 1985.

TABLE 5

The nine largest accountancy firms in the UK, 1983, by number of audits

|  | UK Times 500 major audits | UK Times 1000 major audits |
| --- | --- | --- |
| Price Waterhouse | 88 | 145 |
| Peat Marwick Mitchell | 60 | 133 |
| Deloitte Haskins and Sells | 62 | 102 |
| Coopers and Lybrand | 51 | 80 |
| Ernst and Whinney | 38 | 66 |
| Arthur Young | 34 | 58 |
| Arthur Anderson | 28 | 55 |
| Touche Ross | 20 | 45 |
| Thomson McLintock | 19 | 41 |

*Source:* Price Waterhouse, 1985.

firms. (This can be an extensive commitment: Deloitte Haskins and Sells employs 1,400 people full-time just to audit General Motors). In 1981 the big nine employed 170,000 people worldwide in some 2000 offices in more than 100 countries. In the United States alone the big nine had over 15,000 partners and employed 30,000 Certified Public Accountants. The firms employ enough lawyers to be regarded as some of the largest law firms in the world and enough management consultants to be regarded as amongst the world's largest management consultancy firms (Clairmonte and Cavanagh, 1984; Stevens, 1982; Tinker, 1984).

Of the top nine firms six are nominally City headquartered firms. There is, however, some difficulty in judging the nationality of ownership of partnerships. Historically, City accountancy firms have tended to expand overseas in part by linking with other accountancy firms to form a loose alliance of country partners all operating under the same name. Since in each of these firms the United States practices are much larger in terms of number of partners than any other and partners have, nominally at least, equal voting rights, ownership and control of these City firms is problematic. Whatever the case, currently there are 30 major accountants based in the City of London and 63 in London as a whole (Investors Chronicle, 1985).

Of these firms, one which still regards itself as a 'true blue' City firm is Price Waterhouse which, on a range of measures, is the largest of the big nine. The firm was founded in the City of London in 1849 by S.H. Price and Edwin Waterhouse. It was able to attract distinguished partners, including Knights of the Realm, and with this social background was quickly able to find impressive accounts. It has used social networks for economic gain ever since.[5]

The firm went multinational early on in its history. At the turn of the century it joined with the New York firm, Jones, Caesar and Co. By the mid-1930s it already had 57 branch offices around the world and 2,500 employees in all (Stevens, 1982). By 1984 its complement had grown to 26,500 employees (including 1,854 partners) working from 354 offices in 95 countries. In 1984 Price Waterhouse as a whole earned $1,150 million in fees (Price Waterhouse, 1985). Price Waterhouse's main activities continue to be in audit. In both the United States and the UK, for example, about 70 percent of its chargeable hours has come from this course. However taxation services are growing fast (18 percent of chargeable hours in the United States, 16 percent in the UK), as is management consultancy (about 10 percent of chargeable hours in both the United States and the UK). The firm is also involved in businesses like insolvency, business services to small firms and services to central and local government. The movement into new services has come about partly through organic growth and partly through merger. For example in 1983 Price Waterhouse UK merged with Urwick Orr and Partners, one of the City of London's major management consultancy firms. The firm has tried to merge on a larger scale than this with other accountancy firms. For example, in 1983 it tried to merge with another of the big nine, Deloitte Haskins and Sells, but partners in the two firms threw the proposal out (a problem of the partnership form).

Over time, the company has tried to act more and more like a centralized multinational corporation by adding a world tier of administration — the 'world firm' based in the City of London. The world firm co-ordinates the operations of each of the country partnerships (which was organized as 20 member firms responsible for major markets like the United States, Canada, Australia, South Africa, Asia and so on) at the world scale. It is run by a nine-member Policy Committee, a 20-member Council of Firms and a Council of Partners. The world firm is responsible for international marketing, promotion of a world image, the development of computerized auditing and other systems which can be used by each of the member firms. It would certainly be an exaggeration to say that the company is entirely run from the City, but it is subject to centralized control of a sort.

The firm has become international for two main reasons. The first is a constant search for new country markets offering profit opportunities for accountancy. The second is the fact that its clients became international and in order to continue to obtain work it was necessary to be able to display an international office network likely to match their own locational pattern. This is also vital in obtaining new audits.[6] On a worldwide basis 40 percent of all clients audited by the firm have international operations. The result of these factors is that Price Waterhouse has an employment structure which matches closely to the pattern of international financial centres (see Table 6), for that is where

TABLE 6
Price Waterhouse employment structure, 1984

(a) *Employment by chief geographic area*

| Area | Employment ('000s) |
|---|---|
| UK | 3.1 |
| North America | 12.1 |
| Pacific and Far East | 4.1 |
| Europe | 2.7 |
| South America | 2.2 |
| Africa, Middle East and Asia | 2.3 |
| Total | 26.5 |

(b) *Employment in largest offices*

| Office | Employment | No. of partners |
|---|---|---|
| London (less National HQ) | 1,695 | 87 |
| New York (less National HQ) | 1,252 | 73 |
| Hong Kong | 807 | 29 |
| Toronto | 635 | 43 |
| Sydney | 567 | 43 |
| Buenos Aires | 405 | 26 |
| Kuala Lumpur | 404 | 12 |
| Sao Paulo | 402 | 26 |
| Dublin | 400 | 29 |
| Calcutta | 388 | 13 |

*Source:* Price Waterhouse, 1984.

custom is to be found and that is where the existing clients are. 'More and more, bidders with the strongest presence in all the world's commercial centres win the multinational accounts. For this reason there is great pressure ... to expand internationally by passing money and talent into overseas offices or by merging with established firms in Europe, Asia and the Americas' (Stevens, 1982: 70).

Another example of a City-based accountancy firm is Touche Ross. The firm was founded in the City in the 1880s. It reached across the Atlantic to form a United States partnership in 1905 and has linked with many other firms round the world since. By 1984 its employment had grown to 22,000 personnel operating out of 380 offices in 87 countries (Touche Ross, 1984). As with Price Waterhouse, the firm's main activities are in audit. Again, taxation consultancy, management consultancy, insolvency and services to small business are growing fast. In addition, the firm is involved in services to the voluntary sector and computer security. Like Price Waterhouse, the constituent firms of

Touche Ross are co-ordinated worldwide by a central body, Touche Ross International. Touche Ross International

> has adopted the policy of linking in each country with well established professional local firms. These practices are run by nationals of the country who have an in-depth knowledge of local business and conditions. . . . Clients have all the advantages of dealing with a national firm backed by the strength of a coordinated international organisation. (Touche Ross, 1984: 7)

### *Real Estate Agents*

There are 101 major estate agents in the City of London, and 153 in London as a whole (Investors Chronicle, 1984). City of London-based international real estate agents, or international real estate consultancies as they now prefer to be called, head the international real estate consultancies of the world. Their eminence has come about because of the early existence in Britain of chartered surveying as a

TABLE 7

Equivalent net rents and occupation costs for a suite of 10,000 square feet of air-conditioned offices in a central location, May 1985

| City | Equivalent net rent sq.ft. p.a. (£) | Total occupation cost sq.ft. p.a. (£) |
|---|---|---|
| London — City | 33.00 | 56.20 |
| London — West End | 25.00 | 37.70 |
| Manchester | 7.00 | 13.30 |
| Glasgow | 7.50 | 15.70 |
| Brussels | 5.42 | 7.95 |
| Paris | 19.92 | 24.49 |
| Amsterdam | 6.39 | 7.77 |
| Frankfurt | 9.25 | 11.65 |
| Madrid | 9.12 | 11.57 |
| Barcelona | 5.70 | 7.12 |
| New York — Mid Town | 38.75 | 52.84 |
| New York — Down Town | 27.17 | 40.25 |
| Chicago | 17.07 | 27.30 |
| Los Angeles | 20.65 | 27.53 |
| San Francisco | 25.35 | 33.15 |
| Sao Paulo | 6.52 | 9.05 |
| Singapore | 15.10 | 23.55 |
| Hong Kong | 21.68 | 25.59 |
| Tokyo | 37.19 | 44.98 |
| Johannesburg | 5.58 | 6.97 |
| Melbourne | 13.22 | 16.81 |
| Syney | 16.56 | 19.93 |
| Perth | 6.48 | 9.90 |

*Source:* Richard Ellis, 1985.

profession. The Institute of Chartered Surveyors was founded in 1868. Its Royal Charter was granted in 1881. As with accountancy, this body of expertise was then exported, though at a much slower rate.

These consultancies are essentially commodity brokers dealing in four variants of the same commodity — office buildings, retail buildings, industrial buildings and expensive residential real estate. Over the last 15 years the market for commodities of this kind has become truly international under pressure from institutional investors wanting to internationalize their property portfolios and corporations rationalizing extant portfolios and building new ones. The market is divided amongst the international financial centres since it is here that the highest returns are possible (Table 7) and the judicious construction of a portfolio for a client means that, at any one time, buildings can be bought or developed, rented or sold in such a way that the worst vagaries of land price and rental downturns can be avoided. Other developments have also spurred the creation of an international property market. New forms of (mainly) institutional investment like property unit trusts have appeared on the scene. New forms of finance such as property leasing and other forms of forward funding have been made available by banking capital, often with merchant banks acting as fixers. In addition there is now a substantial secondary mortgage market, handled by elements of commercial capital like brokers and merchant banks, which trades mortgages (Daly, 1982; Feagin, 1983). The net result is that the international property market is a market where buildings are increasingly treated as money commodities in a context which can be divorced from the rest of the economy. For example,

> property prices in Central London have risen by an average of just over 15.7% compound since 1974. In 1984 the index rose 16.9%. The prices are no longer dependent on Britain's economic performance as *Central London is now part of the international property map. (Far Eastern Economic Review*, 1985, my emphasis)

International real estate consultancies have grown rapidly under the impetus provided by this market, helped by a number of trends, of which two are particularly significant. The first of these trends is computerization. In particular, the building up of computer data banks of properties allows clients to pick up international property portfolios more easily and, at the extreme, without even sighting them. The second trend is diversification. Over time, the functions of real estate consultancies have been added to. Clearly the firms are still involved in the traditional functions of chartered surveyors — agency, estate management, surveying, valuation, rating consultancy and the like. But increasingly they have also moved into services with which they have not been traditionally associated, including advice on and management of property portfolios, location consultancy and, taking on some of the functions of merchant banks, arrangment of finance, especially forward funding.

   Like accountancy firms, real estate agents are partnerships and this organizational form has influenced the way they have internationalized. A range of options has been taken up including organic growth through branch offices, merger with extant firms in other countries, and alliances with several overseas firms. In many cases a partner from the UK has been seconded to a branch office as the representative of the City firm. The problems of co-ordination of the international network have undoubtedly become greater over time. Some firms have solved these problems by appointing partners from accountancy firms to deal with administrative and financial matters!

TABLE 8
Direct representation of major British real estate agents in international financial centres

**First order Supranational Centres**

| London 27 | New York 7 | | | |
|---|---|---|---|---|

**Second order Supranational Centres**

| Amsterdam 4 | Frankfurt 3 | Paris 5 | | |
|---|---|---|---|---|
| Tokyo 1 | Zurich 1 | | | |

**First order International Centres**

| Basel 0 | Bombay 0 | Brussels 3 | Chicago 3 | Dusseldorf 1 |
|---|---|---|---|---|
| Hamburg 1 | Kong Kong 4 | Madrid 3 | Melbourne 2 | |
| Mexico City 0 | Rio de Janeiro 1 | Rome 0 | San Francisco 2 | |
| Sao Paulo 1 | Singapore 4 | Sydney 3 | | |
| Toronto 0 | Vienna 0 | | | |

**Second order International Centres**

| Bahrain 0 | Buenos Aires 0 | Kobe 0 | Los Angeles 2 |
|---|---|---|---|
| Luxembourg 0 | Milan 0 | Montreal 0 | Osaka 0 |
| Panama City 0 | Seoul 0 | Taipei 0 | |

**Others**

| Antwerp 1 | Barcelona 1 | Dallas 1 | Dover 1 |
|---|---|---|---|
| The Hague 1 | Houston 2 | Miami 1 | Rotterdam 1 |
| Vancouver 1 | | | |

Direct representation refers to a branch, representative or joint office and the offices of a firm in which an estate agent has a shareholding. Associate firm office networks (e.g. Hillier Parker's European Commercial Property Associates) are *not* included. The estate agents are Goddard and Smith; Gooch and Wagstaff; Healey and Baker; Hillier Parker, May and Rowden; Jones Lang Wootton; Knight, Frank and Rutley, Pepper Angliss; Richard Ellis; St. Quintin; Savills; Weatherall, Green and Smith.

   Whatever the case, the net spatial result of all these developments has been a concentration of the offices of British international real estate consultants in international financial centres. Table 8 shows the pattern of office location of some of the major British international real estate consultancies.

Jones Lang Wootton and Richard Ellis are two of the premier British real estate consultancies. Jones Lang Wootton was founded in the City of London as early as 1783, and has developed steadily since. From 1945 onwards it has grown particularly fast and now employs 1,500 people (including 150 partners) round the world working from 40 offices in 17 countries. It is now the largest real estate consultancy in the world, as well as the largest (with 500 employees and 80 partners) in the UK. Its international commitment is bolstered by modern communications and information systems linked up worldwide, including the COMPUTON system, a worldwide property data base system, and PPAS (Property Performance Analysis System), a suite of computer programs aimed at carrying out automatic analysis of the performance of property portfolios. In addition, in 1985 an international research department was set up in Brussels which will augment the sizeable research departments in other cities (for example, the London research department employs 20). These research departments can earn considerable income by providing information on the international property market, carrying out consultancy and issuing publications.

Richard Ellis was founded in the City of London in 1773. The firm grew steadily until 1960, when it had 80 staff worldwide. By 1972 there were 200 staff, including 35 partners. The firm's present complement of just over 1,000 employees worldwide (including 100 partners), works from 32 offices in 14 different countries, illustrating how rapidly it has grown in the 1970s and 1980s. It is the second largest real estate company in the world and one of the largest agencies in the UK (with 375 staff and 78 partners). Like Jones Lang Wootton, the firm has well established research departments.

The pattern of internationalization of Jones Lang Wootton and Richard Ellis is shown in Table 9 and Table 10. From these tables it is possible to see how in the 1970s and 1980s the two firms have moved out from the old Commonwealth countries like Australia, in which their international activities had been concentrated (and in which considerable activity still takes place; Jones Lang Wootton has a staff of 230 in Australia) to other areas of the world. Jones Lang Wootton now has offices in Europe, the Far East, and the United States. Richard Ellis has offices in Europe, the Far East, Africa, South America and the United States. Quite clearly the opening of these new offices has corresponded with the activities of particular clients in the manufacturing and financial spheres coupled with the attractions of serving particular real estate markets. For example, in Europe:

The nature of the firm's business dealings in the various European countries has tended to vary from market to market. In some the emphasis was more on

TABLE 9
The office network of Jones Lang and Wootton, 1984[1]

| *Number of offices in:* | | *Opening of first office in:* | *Number of partners, associates and directors in:* |
|---|---|---|---|
| London | 4 | 1939 | 97 |
| Glasgow | 1 | 1962 | 6 |
| Edinburgh | 1 | 1970 | 4 |
| Jersey | 1 | 1970 | 1 |
| UK total | 7 | | 108 |
| Dublin | 1 | 1965 | 6 |
| Paris | 1 | 1971 | 7 |
| Amsterdam | 1 | 1972 ⎫ | 5 |
| Rotterdam | 1 | 1970 ⎬ | |
| The Hague | 1 | — | |
| Frankfurt | 1 | 1973 ⎫ | |
| Hamburg | 1 | 1974 ⎪ | |
| Dusseldorf | 1 | 1974 ⎬ | 4 |
| Brussels | 1 | 1965 ⎪ | |
| Antwerp | 1 | 1973 ⎭ | — |
| Europe total | 10 | | |
| Sydney | 3 | 1958 | 18 |
| Melbourne | 1 | 1958 | 6 |
| Perth | 1 | 1958 | 6 |
| Brisbane | 1 | 1958 | 7 |
| Adelaide | 1 | 1958 | 4 |
| Canberra | 1 | 1958 | 1 |
| Auckland[2] | 1 | — | 0 |
| Christchurch[2] | 1 | — | 0 |
| Australia and New Zealand total | 10 | | 42 |
| Hong Kong | 2 | 1973 | 14 |
| Singapore | 1 | 1973 | 10 |
| Kuala Lumpur | 1 | 1973 ⎫ | 4 |
| Penang | 1 | 1973 ⎬ | |
| Jakarta | 1 | 1980 | 2 |
| Tokyo[2] | 1 | 1984 | 1 |
| Far East total | 7 | | 31 |
| New York | 2 | 1975 | 11 |
| Los Angeles | 1 | 1978 | 1 |
| Houston | 1 | 1980 | 2 |
| San Francisco | 1 | 1982 | 1 |
| Washington DC | 1 | 1982 | — |
| USA total | 6 | | 15 |
| Overall total | 40 | | 224 |

[1]Date of opening of first office only is given; offices have subsequently been moved within city.
[2]Representative or associate office only.

TABLE 10
The office network of Richard Ellis, 1984[1]

| Number of offices in: | | Opening of first office in: |
|---|---|---|
| London | 2 | 1973/1960 |
| Manchester | 1 | 1978 |
| Glasgow | 1 | 1965 |
| UK total | 4 | |
| Paris | 1 | 1969 |
| Amsterdam | 1 | 1973 |
| Brussels | 1 | 1973 |
| Geneva | 1 | |
| Madrid | 1 | 1974 |
| Barcelona | 1 | |
| Europe total | 6 | |
| Sydney | 1 | 1965/1981 |
| Melbourne | 1 | |
| Perth | 1 | 1966/82 |
| Brisbane | 1 | |
| Adelaide | 1 | 1969 |
| Australia total | 5 | |
| Hong Kong | 1 | 1978 |
| Singapore | 1 | 1976 |
| Jakarta[2] | 1 | 1982 |
| Far East total | 3 | |
| Johannesburg | 1 | 1969 |
| Cape Town | 1 | 1969 |
| Durban | 1 | 1969 |
| Pretoria | 1 | 1969 |
| Harare | 1 | 1978 |
| Africa total | 5 | |
| Rio de Janeiro[2] | 1 | 1979 |
| Sao Paulo | 1 | 1980 |
| South America total | 2 | |
| New York | 1 | 1982 |
| Chicago | 1 | 1976 |
| Atlanta | 1 | 1978 |
| Houston | 1 | 1981 |
| Dallas[2] | 1 | 1982 |
| San Francisco[2] | 1 | 1980 |
| Los Angeles | 1 | 1982 |
| United States total | 7 | |
| Overall total | 32 | |

[1] Date of opening of first office only is given; offices have subsequently been moved within city.
[2] Representative or associate office only.

> providing a service to British companies — perhaps associated with one of the
> major pension funds — that had overseas interests and were seeking suitable
> property for investment purposes in a country where they were operating,
> although the firm has always aimed to build up a local clientele as quickly as
> possible. In others the firm has found itself more consistently involved with
> local clients engaged in property investment or development, or who simply
> required in a local context the agency, appraisal or management services that
> Richard Ellis specialises in. (Richard Ellis, 1982: 27)

Sometimes the movement into Europe has had effects on the UK
market. Thus, 'occasionally, the firm has been able to assist EEC clients
with an eye on expanding in Britain to acquire either property or
property investments in the UK' (Richard Ellis, 1982: 27).

In South America, by contrast, the emphasis has been very much on
serving British corporate interests, like Unilever:

> Here, the firm has moved in mainly as advisers to the many long-established
> British trading houses that have built up strong business connections in the
> South American markets, and in the process have acquired substantial
> property holdings throughout the subcontinent. Now many of the firms, in
> line with current practice in the UK, feel the time is ripe to ensure that these
> holdings represent a positive asset to their organisation or, if they do not, to
> obtain professional advice on the steps that need to be taken to make the most
> of their value. (Richard Ellis, 1982: 28)

The very recent expansion of both firms into the United States is
particularly interesting because it is so clearly a long-term strategic
move, planned in advance. The expansion clearly coincides with the
increased activity by British multinational corporations like Dixons in
the United States in the 1970s and 1980s but, more importantly, stems
from the lifting of exchange controls in 1979 and the consequent
internationalization of the investment portfolios of British pension
funds, insurance companies and marketing companies (current practice
being that 33 percent of such portfolios should be in property). Take,
for example, the case of Richard Ellis:

> It was in January 1975 that the firm, attracted by the potential of the vast
> American real estate market, but as yet quite unversed in the intricacies of
> operating within it, undertook an extensive study of the possibilities. The
> results of the research operation were sufficiently encouraging to justify the
> opening of the first Richard Ellis office in the United States — in Chicago,
> Illinois in October 1976. The firm decided from the start on judiciously
> combining the traditional expertise of the British chartered surveyor with
> local real estate know-how, and the staff were consequently drawn partly
> from the firm's London investment department and partly from Americans
> knowledgeable in real estate operations. (Richard Ellis, 1982: 28)

Richard Ellis now manages the powerful American Property Trust.

> The American Property Trust was set up in 1974 with eleven unitholders, amongst whom were the British Steel Pension Fund, South Yorkshire County Council Staff Superannuation Fund, South of Scotland Electricity Board Fund, British Rail Fund, and the Electricity Supply Nominees.... Between 1974 and 1979, the American Property Trust raised $11.5 million for direct property investment in the USA. By 1984, the trust had assets of $250 million and its participants had grown in number to forty-nine, including major concerns such as Imperial Chemical Industries, Rank Xerox and Reed International. Its geographical distribution of ownership had shifted from a concentration in the south-east of the USA to include properties in Atlanta, Dallas, Houston, Washington, Chicago, Denver, Los Angeles and Kansas City.... [Its activities] are sufficiently powerful to compete directly with domestic US investors. (Bateman, 1985: 117)

The other major area of expansion of offices by Jones Lang Wootton and Richard Ellis has been in the Far East, coincident with the Pacific Basin's rapid economic growth and the elevation of a number of cities, like Hong Kong, Singapore and Tokyo, to international financial centre status, and therefore to inclusion in the international property market. Most recently, both firms have tried to engage with the elusive Japanese property market, a market that is difficult because of its state restrictions, its ownership by a few large Japanese land companies and the tendency of Japanese corporations to internalize property buying. But it is also a market which promises long-term dividends both because of the possibility of investment in Japanese real estate and, more importantly, because of potential to direct Japanese investment into real estate around the world. Most real estate agents continue to operate in this market via, at best, a Japanese national based in London acting as link-person. On 1 May, 1984, however, Jones Lang Wootton opened the first British real estate agent's office in Tokyo:

> According to [the] Chairman of JLW's London partnership, 'the opening underlines our continued evolution as a truly worldwide integrated operation'. Japan has been seen as perhaps the last of the international property markets for UK surveyors to try to enter and JLW are first in. Initially the Tokyo office will be a representative one, setting out to help JLW provide an improved service to JLW clients who require property advice and service in the UK and Europe, USA, Australia, Hong Kong, Singapore, Indonesia, Malaysia and New Zealand. They will also be giving on-the-spot professional advice on the domestic property market to both existing clients and to non-local Japanese firms. (*Estates Gazette*, 1984)

## Conclusions

This brief foray into the urban geography of commercial capital leads to at least three conclusions. First, and most obviously, commercial capital is still thriving. It still plays a role in national economies, insofar as it is still possible to talk about a national economy (Radice, 1984; Thrift, 1985a). More importantly, commercial capital has played a vital part in the most recent internationalization of capital (the so-called 'new international division of labour'). The new international system of credit money that has come about, with its multiple, piggybacked financial markets intended to spread risk and maximize short-term investment profit, would never have succeeded without the ability of commercial capital both to create new markets and, in large part, manage the system. It remains to be seen, of course, whether the improvisatory powers of commercial capital can finally surmount the current crisis (Harvey, 1982; Brett, 1983).

Second, it has become clear that the tendency *within* the organizational structure of commercial capital is towards large multinational service corporations offering a veritable supermarket of commercial services. Thus, management of the international credit money system is being centralized into the hands of fewer and fewer decision-makers.

Third, international commercial capital has had an important impact on selected cities like London and is now in the process of exporting the social relations involved to a number of other cities around the world. In the new system of international financial enclaves, commercial capital intervenes in quite forcible ways. Thus, it provides an important and growing component of demand for office accommodation, specialized labour, particular services (like telecommunications), particular types of housing and so on (see Thrift, 1985b on Hong Kong). And, it has the social power — especially through its extended social- political networks — to enforce what it demands. In turn, the results of the demands it makes change the social make-up of these cities, making parts of them the preserve of a professional middle class, of gentrified housing (Hamnett, 1984), and a whole host of other effects, quite out of proportion to the numbers of people involved. Thus, the internationalization of commercial capital poses a considerable economic, social and political challenge to a number of cities which shows no signs of abating (Coakley and Harris, 1983; GLC, 1985).

## Notes

1. I have followed Ingham's usage here, rather than that of Marx. Marx refers to merchant capital in general and then distinguishes commercial and money-dealing capital. Ingham (1984: 256, fn. 9) uses 'commercial capital as the general form of profit-making through the repeated and continuous buying and selling of commodities (including money)... rather that the archaic merchant capital of Marx's work'.

2. Merchant banks are now obtaining their own capital base, usually coincident with their takeover by banking capital interested in retailing a whole series of financial services

to corporations. This is a classic case of how the integrity of commercial capital is constantly threatened and must be constantly fought for.

3. Clearly, international financial centres link to the 'world city' literature, but this paper is an attempt to unpack the world city literature by pointing to commercial capital functions only (see Cohen, 1981; Friedmann and Wolff, 1982; Noyelle, 1983; Thrift, 1985a).

4. Numbers noted here and for accountants relate only to firms that serve one or more of the *Times 500* companies.

5. Members of the firm are expected to cultivate contacts at all opportunities. These may well be functional to the business. Thus accountants in general, and all members of commercial capital, tend to have an above-average representation in any community.

6. Thus Stevens (1982: 72) discusses a Peat Marwick Mitchell bid for the Caltex audit:

> The proposal was designed in fourteen sections. Key segments covered the greater glory of Peat, Marwick International, the firm's oil industry experience, an overlay map of Peat and Caltex locations worldwide, a review of the audit scope, and a description of PMM's consulting and tax services.

## References

*Annual Investment File* (1985) 'Chartered Surveyors Survey', *Annual Investment File*: 51–68.

Bateman, M. (1985) *Office Development: A Geographical Analysis*. London: Croom Helm.

Brett, E.A. (1983) *International Money & Capitalist Crisis: The Anatomy of Global Disintegration*. London: Heinemann.

Central Statistical Office (1984) *UK Balance of Payments 1983*. London: Her Majesty's Stationery Office.

Clairmonte, F. and J. Cavanagh (1984) 'Transnational Corporations and Services: The Final Frontier', *Trade and Development*, 5: 215–273.

Coakley, J. (1984) 'The Internationalisation of Bank Capital', *Capital and Class*, 23: 107–120.

Coakley, J. and L. Harris (1983) *The City of Capital*. Oxford: Blackwell.

Cohen, R.B. (1981) 'The New International Division of Labour, Multinational Corporations and Urban Hierarchy', in M.J. Dear and A.J. Scott (eds.), *Urbanisation and Urban Planning in Capitalist Society*, pp. 287–318. London: Methuen.

Cowell, C.K. (1983) 'The International Marketing of Services', *The Service Industries Journal*, 3: 308–328.

Crawfords (1984) *Crawfords Directory of City Connections*. London: Economist Publications.

Daly, M.T. (1982) *Sydney Boom, Sydney Bust*. Sydney: Allen and Unwin.

Darling, J. (1984) 'The Role of Financial Intermediaries in Australian Urban Investment', in C. Adrian (ed.), *Urban Impacts and Local Investment in Australia*. Canberra: Australian Institute of Urban Studies.

*Economist*, The (1985a) 'Round the World on $150 Billion a Day', *The Economist*, 30 November.

*Economist*, The (1985b) 'The Other Dimension. Technology and the City of London', *The Economist*, 6 July.

*Estates Gazette* (1984) 'JLW Open in Tokyo', *Estates Gazette*, 28 April: 260.

*Far Eastern Economic Review* (1985a) 'Property '85', *Far Eastern Economic Review*, 28 February: 45–74.

*Far Eastern Economic Review* (1985b) 'Banking '85', *Far Eastern Economic Review*, 25 April: 53–110.

Feagin J.R. (1983) *Playing Monopoly in Real Money*. Englewood Cliffs: Prentice-Hall.

Fraser, W.H. (1981) *The Coming of the Mass Market 1850–1914*. London: Macmillan.

Friedmann, J. and G. Wolff (1982) 'World City Formation: An Agenda for Research and Action', *International Journal of Urban and Regional Research*, 6(3): 309–394.

Gaedeke, R.M. (1973) 'Selected US Multinational Service Firms in Comparative Perspective', *Journal of International Business Studies*, Spring: 61–66.

Giddens, A. (1985) *The Nation State and Violence*. Cambridge: Polity Press.

GLC (1985) *GLC Financial Strategy*. London: Greater London Council.

Hamnett, C. (1984) 'Gentrification and Residential Location Theory: A Review and Assessment', in D.T. Herbert and R.J. Johnston (eds.), *Geography and the Urban Environment*, Vol. 6, pp. 283–329. Chichester: Wiley.

Harris, L. (1985) 'British Capital: Manufacturing, Finance and Multinational Corporations', in D. Coates, G. Johnston and R. Bush (eds.), *A Socialist Anatomy of Britain*, pp. 7–28. Cambridge: Polity Press.

Harvey, D. (1982) *The Limits to Capital*. Oxford: Blackwell.

Ingham, G. (1984) *Capitalism Divided? The City and Industry in British Social Development*. London: Macmillan.

Investors Chronicle (1984) *The City Directory 1984–85*. Cambridge: Woodhead Faulkner.

Jones Lang Wootton (1980) *Offices in the City of London*. London: Jones Lang Wootton.

Jones Lang Wootton (1982, 1983, 1984) *International Property Review*. London: Jones Lang Wootton.

Kindleberger, C.P. (1979) *The Formation of Financial Centres*. Princeton: Princeton University Press.

King, A.D. (1985) 'Capital City: Physical and Social Aspects of London's Role in the World Economy', *Development and Change*, 16.

Langdale, J. (1985) 'Electronic Funds Transfer and the Internationalisation of the Banking and Finance Industry', *Geoforum*, 16: 1–13.

Longstreth, F. (1979) 'The City, Industry and the State', in C. Crouch (ed.), *State and Economy in Contemporary Capitalism*. London: Croom Helm.

McRae, H. and F. Cairncross (1984) *Capital City. London as a Financial Centre*. London: Methuen.

Mandel, E. (1975) *The Generalised Recession of the International Capitalist Economy*. Brussels: Imprecor.

Manser, W.A.P. (1985) *The International Insurance Market. A View from London*. Economist Intelligence Unit Special Report 193 London: Economist Publications.

Mendelsohn, M.S. (1980) *Money on the Move*. London: McGraw Hill.

Minns, R. (1980) *Pension Funds and British Capitalism*. London: Heinemann.

Minns, R. (1981) 'A Comment on Finance Capital and the Crisis in Britain', *Capital and Class*, 14: 98–110.

Noyelle, T.J. (1983) 'The Implications of Industry Restructuring for Spatial Organisation in the United States', in F. Moulaert and P.M. Salinas, (eds.), *Regional Analysis in the New International Division of Labour*, pp. 113–133. Boston: Kluwer Nijhoff.

Noyelle, T.J. and T.M. Stanback (1985) *The Economic Transformation of American Cities*. Totowa: Rowman and Allanheld.

Pagano, M. (1985) 'Does 24-hour Trading Mean More Business or the Same Amount Spread Thinly?' *The Guardian*, 1 July: 19.

Price Waterhouse (1984) *An Introduction to the UK Firm of Price Waterhouse*. London: Price Waterhouse.

Price Waterhouse (1985) *Annual Review 1983 – 4*. London: Price Waterhouse.

Radice, H. (1984) 'The National Economy — a Keynesian Myth?', *Capital and Class*, 22: 111 – 190.

Reed, H.C. (1981) *The Pre-eminence of International Finance Centres*. New York: Praeger.

Reed, H.C. (1983) 'Appraising Corporate Investment Policy: A Financial Centre Theory of Foreign Direct Investment', in C.P. Kindleberger and D.B. Audretsch (eds.), *The Multinational Corporation in the 1980s*, pp. 219 – 244. Cambridge, Mass.: MIT Press.

Richard Ellis (1982) *Two Centuries of Service*. London: Richard Ellis.

Richard Ellis (1982, 1983, 1984) *International Property*. London: Richard Ellis.

Richard Ellis (1985) *World Rental Levels*. London: Richard Ellis.

Sargent, J.R. (1979) 'UK Performance in Services', in F. Blackaby (ed.), *Deindustrialisation*, pp.102 – 123. London: Heinemann.

Spence, M. (1985) 'Imperialism and Decline: Britain in the 1980s', *Capital and Class*, 25: 117 – 139.

Stevens, M. (1982) *The Big Eight*. New York: Macmillan.

Taylor, M.J. and N.J. Thrift (eds.) (1982) *The Geography of Multinationals*. London: Croom Helm.

Thrift, N.J. (1984a) 'The Internationalisation of Producer Services and the Genesis of the World City Property Market', *UNIDO CRP*, 36.

Thrift, N.J. (1984b) 'Taking the Rest of the World Seriously? The State of British Urban and Regional Research in a Time of Crisis', *Environment and Planning A*, 17: 7 – 24.

Thrift, N.J. (1985a) 'All Change: The Geography of International Economic Disorder', in R.J. Johnston and P.J. Taylor (eds.), *World in Crisis*. Oxford: Blackwell.

Thrift, N.J. (1985b) 'The Internationalisation of Producer Services and the Integration of the Pacific Basin Property Market', in M.J. Taylor and N.J. Thrift (eds.), *Multinationals and the Restructing of the World Economy*. London: Croom Helm.

Tinker, T. (1984) *Paper Prophets. A Social Critique of Accounting*. Eastbourne: Holt Rinehart and Winston.

Touche Ross (1984) *Touche Ross and Co.* London: Touche Ross.

Wilson Committee (Committee to Review the Functioning of Financial Institutions) (1980) *Report and Appendices*, Command 7939. London: Her Majesty's Stationery Office.

# 10
# Global Capital Restructuring and Local Political Crises in US Cities
## *Michael Peter Smith*

Capital flight, foreign investment, multinational corporate competition, and global interdependence of production activities are all dimensions of what has been termed the 'new international division of labour'. This globalization of economic relations has influenced migration from periphery to core and channeled interurban migration within the United States (Portes and Walton, 1981). Leading cities in the emerging international network of production and exchange often are described as 'world cities' (Friedmann and Wolff, 1982). The logic of the development of such cities often is assumed to be driven entirely by the imperatives of transnational capital accumulation. The tendency has been to view world city development from the perspective of the unfolding logic of the world system. Yet political life in world cities (and in other localities importantly affected by the new international division of labour) has been characterized by socio-spatial conflicts between multinational corporate growth strategies and national, regional and local forces demanding a stable economic base.

James O'Connor (1981) has succinctly defined the current economic crisis of world capitalism as an 'interruption in the accumulation of capital' brought about by changed environmental conditions. To cope with this crisis while still reproducing capitalist social relations in the legal, cultural and ideological spheres, a central strategy of big capital sectors within the advanced societies has been capital restructuring. According to O'Connor, capital restructuring may prevent, postpone, or displace the current economic crisis. He does not entertain the possibility, discussed herein, that capital restructuring may also compound and thus prolong the structural crisis of accumulation. It is the premise of this essay that the very unfolding of capital restructuring creates profoundly destabilizing conditions of everyday life in the localities most immediately affected. If this is the case, then we must turn to the realm of local politics, as it intersects with the changing global economy, to comprehend the real consequences of capital restructuring.

Support for this research was provided by the Murphy Institute of Political Economy, Tulane University and by the University of California, Davis.

O'Connor defines a *structural* crisis as an historical period in the development of capitalism during which 'one accumulation model is substituted for another, i.e., where some structures deteriorate and others are built'. A structural crisis may be distinguished from a *sectoral* crisis, which is engendered by processes producing an uneven rate of development among economic sectors or among geographic regions which are based upon unevenly developing sectors (O'Connor, 1981). A central economic process contributing to sectoral crisis is the appropriation of large shares of the economic surplus by sectors of multi-locational capital (global industry, finance and business services) at the expense of localized sectors of the economy. In the current period, multi-locational capital has concentrated investment in some regions of the advanced capitalist societies and has shifted investment to peripheral locations globally to combine relatively advanced technologies with cheap labour (Portes and Walton, 1981; Frobel et al., 1980). This sectoral shift underlies the decline of older industrial areas in developed societies, which suffer rapid disinvestment. Thus, the ongoing sectoral crisis is likewise a *spatial* crisis in places experiencing under-investment, disinvestment, or excessively rapid growth.

In the United States, during the past decade, these three forms of crisis — structural, sectoral and spatial — have been combined and focused in particular regions and cities. The attempt by agents of US multi-locational capital and by political elites to overcome the structural crisis has taken the form of sectoral and spatial shifts of investment patterns both within the United States and globally. The current efforts to restructure capital in the face of new global conditions for profitable accumulation have addressed the structural crisis by technological modernization and spatial reorganization of production. The main result has been the avoidance of a deeper structural crisis at the global level by provoking a new round of sectoral crises at the local level. In the US, local crises are especially pronounced in the Snowbelt, the declining older manufacturing centres of the northeastern and midwestern regions. The other developed capitalist societies, facing similar global conditions, have experienced a similar series of localized sectoral crises (Urry, 1981; Morgan, 1982; Body-Gendrot, 1984).

Local crises, however, are not limited to older manufacturing cities. The rapid growth and presumed prosperity of the Sunbelt also have engendered local crisis conditions. Sunbelt growth attracts both people from the declining Snowbelt and immigrants from the Third World, most of whom have fled economic and political conditions likewise related to the global reorganization of capitalism (Portes and Walton, 1981; Sassen-Koob, 1983, 1984). The resulting population boom in the Sunbelt has intensified pressures on municipal budgets (Firestine, 1977; Lupsha and Siembieda, 1977; Fainstein et al., 1983). This has occurred at precisely the time that the region's own older manufacturing sector, a major potential source of employment for the new migrants, has undergone rapid decline. For example, in California, 979 manufacturing plants were closed down between 1980 and 1982. Over 100,000 jobs were permanently lost in the industrial sector (*New York Times*, 1982: 12). The internationalization of capital brought foreign competition for markets; post-war plants became obsolete as US manufacturers channeled capital into consolidations and mergers, diversification, real estate ventures, and financial markets rather than investing in the modernization of domestic plants.

What have been the local political responses to the global economic restructuring? The forms of resistance and accommodation to local crises of disinvestment or unregulated rapid growth have varied from nation to nation and place to place. Where popular resistance has occurred, its form, development, and effectiveness have depended upon the channels available for expressing discontent; the character of existing or emergent forms of local political organization connecting affected individuals, households, and social networks to the political process; the prevailing structure and culture of local politics; and class and political alignments at the local and national scales in the affected societies.

This essay addresses these issues by examining both governmental and popular responses in US cities to the restructuring of the global economy. Its aim is to assess the political implications of four interrelated political and economic responses to the globalization of capital: the call by state and local government officials for 'enterprise zones' to restore the employment base of declining cities and regions; the spread of new immigration and 'new' sweatshops in US cities; the expansion of the 'informal' economy; and the changing character of urban political mobilization in Sunbelt cities.

**The Uses of Enterprise Zones**
In their quest to reverse local and regional economic decline, both the Reagan administration and state and local government officials from distressed regions have proposed the establishment of enterprise zones to attract new capital investment. Because Democrats in Congress have not wished to allow Ronald Reagan to have a policy symbolizing his concern for urban problems, national enterprise zone legislation has not been passed by the Democratic controlled House Ways and Means Committee. Despite the absence of national legislation, nine state governments, caught in the competitive struggle for business investment with other regions within the global economy, have activated such zones. Ten other states have passed zone legislation, but have not yet designated any zones. Over 60 related bills are pending at

the state legislative level. Specific proposals on the agenda of state and local governments include measures to suspend zoning and building regulations, to lower or remove property taxes, to deregulate environmental and health and safety regulations, to allow sub-minimum wages for all workers or for youth employed in designated zones, and to pass additional 'right to work' laws to weaken union power.

John Walton (1982: 12–13) points out that the model underlying the designation of enterprise zones in declining cities in the US is the practice of multi-locational capital investment in such export-processing and free-trade zones as Hong Kong, Puerto Rico, and the Mexican border. These places are characterized by low wages, widespread poverty, sweatshop working conditions, and, in many instances, renewed capital flight to still cheaper points of production. These characteristics raise the question of what kind of working and living conditions in declining American cities would be needed to render firms that locate in enterprise zones competitive in the global marketplace.

Critics of enterprise zones question the ability of such a policy to create new jobs, at stable wage levels, in depressed urban areas (Walton, 1982; Massey, 1982; Goldsmith, 1982a, 1982b; Aronowitz, 1981; Aronowitz and Goodman, 1981; Malone, 1982). Places like the South Bronx, ravaged by disinvestment, abandonment, arson and high levels of welfare dependency, have become prototypes of the sort of older inner city area the policy nominally is intended to revitalize. Critics point out that the policy does nothing about key features of the urban ghetto context, like low skill levels and high insurance rates, due to actual or perceived high crime rates, which currently are impediments to inner city investment. More importantly, the very logic of the enterprise zone heightens the destructive competition for industry among local governments that already is eroding state and local tax bases and may further undermine workers' already beleaguered protections by encouraging intensified intergovernmental competition leading to the elimination of health and safety protections and organizing rights.

In the context of the new international division of labour, the creation of tax havens to lure 'footloose firms', 'runaway plants', and multi-locational producers of products and services by offering the sort of concessions envisaged in enterprise zone policies, is unlikely to generate net gains in employment in the overall national economy. The world capitalist economy already has been sufficiently restructured to enable large multinational corporations to plan and control global networks of economic activity with production facilities spanning the globe in the quest for cheaper and more controllable labour pools. To the extent that enterprise zones might prove an effective lure (and it is by no means clear that they could offset labour cost and control factors in countries like Korea, Taiwan and parts of Latin America) they are simply likely to encourage the moving around of existing jobs within and among metropolitan areas, states, and even nation-states, playing one set of workers off against another, to the overall political benefit of the big capital sectors of the advanced economies. This sort of 'substitution effect' is especially likely during periods of limited economic growth. Some evidence from Britain (Massey, 1982) suggests, for instance, that many firms within metropolitan areas have simply moved short distances to designated zones at minimal cost to themselves and no net gain in employment in depressed older metropolitan areas. This is not an accidental outcome; it is an inherent feature of the logic of the policy within the evolving global economy. As long as there are cheaper points of production, and in the absence of politically effective constraints on capital flows, the intensified competition among cities, states and national economies will continue to bode ill for the living standards of working people in both the core and the periphery. Enterprise zone policies actually legitimate the process of capital flight from localities where production costs, including labour costs entailing decent living standards, render the areas 'uncompetitive' in the global economy. Goldsmith (1982: 23) and Aronowitz (1981) have shown that the decline in living standards has been precisely the fate of the once booming and now declining economy of Puerto Rico, whose once highly touted enterprise zone policy 'Operation Bootstrap' has now been discredited. The policy's inner contradiction, reflecting the inner contradiction of global competition in late capitalism, has been nicely stated by Goldsmith (1982: 23): 'To the extent that "Operation Bootstrap" succeeded, thereby raising wages, it reduced the attraction for investors, and (eventually) failed'.

Given their dubious worth as a job creation strategy, why are enterprise zones so prominently placed on the political agenda of US cities? What factors underlie their treatment as a serious policy tool? Walton (1982: 14–16) has interpreted them as a strategy of urban political elites to deflect criticism for their inaction on the 'urban crisis' front, while simultaneously serving the interests of those 'who would align themselves with a continued redistribution of income [to capital] and tax burdens [to households and wage earners] for other political purposes.' Walton does not specify what these other purposes might be. Yet if we ask the question 'Who benefits?' several winners are clearly discernable. These include:

1. Republican party elites and their supporters in the world of corporate and finance capital, who currently are seeking to establish a

new ideological hegemony to replace New Deal liberalism with a more limited 'social wage' and a new social contract more favourable to business interests;

2. State and local politicians in both major political parties, whose campaign coffers remain full and whose political support among business interests widens as they define the 'urban crisis' increasingly in terms of the 'problems' of 'inadequate capital formation' and 'population migration' rather than in terms of capital flight, structurally segmented housing and labour markets, or past public policies which have contributed to urban deterioration, deconcentration, disinvestment, and decline;

3. Industrial capitalists who underinvested in the upgrading of domestic plant and equipment for decades, diversified into real estate speculation, built new production and assembly facilities in the Third World, and now seek various public subsidies for 'reindustrialization' within a new context of weakened labour unions, chastened workers and supportive politicians;

4. Suburban, southern, and western Congressional representatives of both major political parties, who view their growing influence in the recently reapportioned Congress as an opportunity to turn yet another economic development policy to their own regional advantage. As Herbers (1980: 4E) has said of past practice:

> The tendency has almost always been to bring in so many areas for help that the plan was rendered ineffective. Just as rural areas received Model Cities money, with political power shifting to the South and West, anyone who has watched Congress in action can envision enterprise zones in the vast suburban expanses where economic growth has been underway, drawing jobs away from the most distressed central cities ...

Given this political current, it is hardly surprising that at the state and local governmental levels, prominent suburban elected officials in all regions already have formed alliances with urban politicians within their regions in support of state level enterprise zone legislation (Merdinger, 1981).

### The New Immigration and the New Sweatshops
Critics of enterprise zone proposals (Glickman, 1981; Goldsmith, 1982a) have aptly characterized them as a method which, if they did 'work' in core cities, would accelerate the spread of new immigrant sweatshops there. The spectre of 'bringing the Third World home' and reproducing the periphery in the core (Sassen-Koob, 1984) already is haunting some core cities in the United States, as the new international division of labour in such sectors as textiles and electronics assembly fosters the employment of cheap and politically quiescent illegal

immigrant labour. Meanwhile, the threat of further capital flight in primary sector manufacturing reduces the bargaining power of remaining middle-income workers, keeps wage structures lower than they otherwise would be, and contributes to income polarization in core cities. Thus, even without national enterprise zone legislation, key conditions anticipated by their critics are already emerging (see Sassen-Koob, 1984; Smith and Judd, 1984).

In contrast to the affluence of technical and scientific professionals, the vast majority of the new 'service' jobs in US cities are very poorly paid. Indeed, 'more than 60 per cent of the service jobs in New York City pay salaries below the Bureau of Labour Statistics' living standard for a low income family of four, while 25 per cent of full-time service workers earn less than the poverty level' (McGahey, 1983: 23). When these trends in the shifting job market are combined with the continuing decline in well-paying manufacturing employment, it becomes apparent that dire predictions of growing polarization of incomes, increased poverty, and possibly heightened class tensions are not far-fetched.

Intraclass conflict among segments of the secondary labour market is one strong possibility as already marginalized occupational groups such as women and minorities face intensified competition from newly displaced manufacturing workers. Another is the prospect of heightened conflict between primary and secondary workers in new employment growth sectors like high technology and services where new jobs are characterized by extreme disparities in pay (Sassen-Koob, 1984; Smith and Judd, 1984; McGahey, 1983).

Organizing the new clerical and service workforce through traditional trade unionism is a limited strategy for driving up wages to maintain middle-class living standards. The supply of surplus workers is being swelled by both the displacement of unionized industrial workers and the inflow of migrant labour at precisely the time the new technologies are giving high-tech companies the option of moving jobs overseas (Serrin, 1983). For instance, in 1983 Atari announced its intention to move 1,700 assembly jobs from California to Asia to assemble home computers and video games for the world market. It joined other high-technology corporations like Intel, Apple and Wang which had already begun to locate assembly plants in Asian countries. The quest for wages as low as $4.00 a day prompted this investment shift to the Pacific Basin and Mexico. The shift was an early sign that not only attempts to restructure the Snowbelt economy but even the process of Sunbelt development were vulnerable to foreign competition.

Finally, assembly of high-tech products like computers still remains largely within the US. Nevertheless, 'as the price of more sophisticated personal computers declines, as profit margins erode, these manufacturers may also move overseas' (*New York Times*, 1983: 1, 21). In such circumstances, those firms that remain in the United States increasingly begin to resemble the new sweatshops that have sprung up in many US cities in textile manufacturing, another highly competitive global industry.

For example, decline of stable markets due to intensified international competition in the textile sector has re-created the classical conditions of over-exploitation portrayed by early twentieth-century social reformers like Jacob Riis and Lewis Hine. Production in the 'new' sweatshops is organized within new immigrant enclaves to make the firms more competitive in the global market. Thousands of small garment factories have been established in many major urban centres in the past decade. Chicago, Boston, New York, Los Angeles and other Sunbelt cities with large Hispanic labour pools have hundreds of sweatshops. New York is estimated to house over 3,000 (Malone, 1982: 28; see also Portes, 1983). Violating labour laws, minimum wage requirements, and health and safety regulations, the owners of these sweatshops are able to survive by over-exploiting a highly vulnerable labour force. Those of the new urban immigrants who have entered the United States illegally lack even the right of citizenship as a political resource.

The spread of new sweatshops as a local response to global economic crisis can be traced to two key dimensions of the new international division of labour. First, as certain manufacturing sectors like textiles become globalized, foreign-produced clothing, relying on inexpensive Third World labour, accounts for an increasing share of the US market. For example, reliable estimates indicate that in 1983 nearly 50 percent of women's clothing was produced abroad. This intensified global competition has forced American clothing manufacturers, operating in an already competitive environment of thousands of small, under-capitalized firms, to cut costs further by relying on sweatshops whenever possible. Second, the dramatic rise in illegal immigration to the United States has made such over-exploitative conditions increasingly possible, for it provides a steady supply of cheap labour.

Just how exploitative these conditions are was recently revealed in a series of articles by Serrin (1983) dealing with 'new' labour conditions in the garment industry in New York City. Beyond describing working conditions as 'hot, bleak, unsanitary, and unsafe', Serrin documents the depressed pay and virtual absence of benefits.

> In many cases, the minimum wage, $3.35 an hour, is ignored. Employers, particularly in nonunion shops, pay few benefits, and often no overtime. Holiday pay is often late or is not given to workers. Sweatshops can be union or nonunion shops. The union label, while it generally means that garments

that carry it have been sewn in shops with better working conditions than have clothes that do not, is no guarantee that government or contractual wage, hour, and workplace standards have been met.

Workers can make $5 an hour, particularly in union shops, although wages can run as low as $1 an hour or, for a time, as high as $9 an hour, because of the complicated piecework wage system that has almost always existed in the industry. The industry and the union consider this system efficient, and there is little effort to change it, although some critics and some workers say it makes the workers both slave driver and slave. (1983: 12–13)

Thus we see that far from transforming the politics of production, US trade unions, weakened by the new international division of labour, have actually colluded in preserving some of the most exploitative features of the 'new' productive relations. Furthermore, it is important to realize that neither sweatshop-like organization of production nor trade union vulnerability is limited to the most competitive sectors. In less competitive industrial sectors, unionized manufacturers frequently contract out to small assembly shops that employ non-union workers. This practice enables large corporations to take advantage of the latter's cheaper wages, limited regulations, and dependent labour force. The response of trade unions has been defensive and ineffectual (Portes and Walton, 1981).

Given the vulnerability of trade unions, what other channels are currently available for people experiencing declining living conditions stemming from the new international division of labour? Historically, two basic modes of response by popular classes to worsening economic conditions have been the pooling of resources by households through informal support networks, and the collective mobilization of demands by adversely affected communities directed at agencies of the state. What have been the responses of households and communities in the US to the new conditions ushered in by the internationalization of production and the attendant fiscal crisis of the welfare state? What are the major political consequences of the growing reliance by households on the 'informal economy' to survive in the face of declining opportunities for making a living through formal wage labour? How are the prospects for grassroots political mobilization affected by the globalization of production relations, the rise of new sweatshops, the spread of the informal economy, and the movement of the fourth great wave of immigrants to the service-based economies of the growing cities of the US Sunbelt?

**The Informal Economy**
Integral to the analysis of local responses in the US to the global restructuring of capital is the spread of the 'informal economy'. Portes (1983: 159) defines the informal economy as 'the sum total of income-

producing activites in which members of a household engage, *excluding* income from contractual and legally regulated employment.' This includes a broad range of activities such as direct subsistence, the production and exchange of goods or services by the self-employed, and the employment of unprotected wage labour (Portes, 1983: 159–161; see also Mingione, 1983). In the US, the provision of personal services, labour exchange, and industrial subcontracting are examples of such 'informal' activity.

The growth of informal production of this sort as a household 'survival strategy' (Mingione, 1983), in the face of global economic crisis, has several important political implications. It reduces the ability of the welfare state to deliver services by weakening its capacity to tax 'in respect to the real volume of goods and services . . . produced' (Mingione, 1983: 320). Because the entire burden of state expenditures falls upon the formal sector, firms in this sector, in turn, seek to avoid the increasing tax burden by informalizing parts of their activities through subcontracting, capital flight and the like. The growing informal sector also puts pressure on the national and local state in the form of deepening fiscal crises. These intertwined processes, by reducing public revenues and formal job opportunities, intensify the need for more and more workers to enter the informal economy as a survival strategy in the face of state revenue and service cutbacks and deindustrialization. Yet, as household barter, labour exchange and self-production come to substitute for public services and purchased goods and services, more and more time is subtracted from the available supply of wage labour. Ironically, this situation complicates the possibilities for labour exploitation and capital accumulation by reducing the scope of the basic form of worker exploitation under capitalism — wage labour. (See Mingione, 1983: 323, for a discussion of other dimensions of reduced availability of labour time as a result of growing informalization).

Consider the following example from California's Silicon Valley. Employment restructuring in Silicon Valley has placed the blue-collar workforce, particularly immigrants and women, in a structurally disadvantaged position. Nevertheless, Katz and Kemnitzer have identified the many ways by which individuals and households knowingly take advantage of the contradictions of their situation. For example, they extract free time and obviate the need for paid day-care services by working at nominally lower paid industrial homework; they increase their income beyond wages available inside factories by subcontracting, job-hopping, and moon-lighting; and they supplement their income derived from wage labour by such informal activities. In these ways, individuals and households 'make choices for themselves that allow not only survival, but assertion of self and flexibility in the arrangement of their work, compatible with their life situation and with their definition and understanding of it' (Katz and Kemnitzer, 1983: 334).

These practices, particularly participation in the informal sector, are double-edged phenomena. In addition to enabling particular individuals and households to survive outside the regulative controls of wage labour, the growing informal sector undermines the fiscal basis of the social wage paid by the welfare state. It also reduces the need for capitalist employers in the mainstream economy to pay direct and indirect wages sufficient to reproduce labour power. Indeed, as Wolpe (1975: 247) has pointed out: 'The most important condition enabling capitalism to pay for labour power below its cost of reproduction . . . is the availability of a supply of labour power which is produced and reproduced outside the capitalist mode of production.'

The growing prevalence of informal household labour outside the formal wage-labour arrangements of advanced capitalism also has implications for how working people are likely to interact with political institutions. Wage labour in the formal sector remains connected to political life through trade unionism, whereas labour in the informal sector is more likely to be connected to the political system through community organization. Several conditions underlie the connection of informal workers to political life through residential community. To begin with, informal workers often engage in petty commodity production and piecework within places of residence (Mingione, 1983; Portes, 1983). Furthermore, they often are concentrated in immigrant communities which lack services, amenities and access to institutions of the wider city and society. In addition, many informal sector workers are women, whose traditional responsibility for social reproduction makes them especially concerned about issues relating to the quality of everyday life in their residential communities (Castells, 1983). Finally, trade unions have made little effort to organize these workers, who are not concentrated in large workplaces. Thus we see that the residential community has become the shopfloor of workers in the informal sector.

### Community Mobilization and the Local State

During earlier periods of mass immigration to US cities, white ethnic groups from Europe and black migrants from the rural south caused problems of social control for local political elites. Political mobilization of these popular classes over issues of employment, public services and the quality of community life led to the development of political relations, first between white ethnics and urban political machines, and later between blacks and public bureaucracies. The purpose of these relations was to co-opt opposition and to confer legitimacy on the political system.

The past decade's migration to US cities has created different problems for local political elites. Consisting largely of illegal workers from Latin America and Asia, the new migrants have not been directly connected to either the mainstream economy or the political system. For the most part, they are part of the 'informal economy'; and lacking rights of citizenship, they are subject to deportation and cannot directly engage in political activities.

Nevertheless, the very presence of large numbers of illegal migrants has compounded the political management problems of local public officials. It has done so by contributing to the growth of the informal economy, thereby reducing the capacity of local governments to tax and provide public services through revenue sharing. The growth of the informal economy thus has contributed to the deepening of the urban fiscal crisis. In this context, alliances between local officials and mainstream constituencies have been threatened by the erosion of the fiscal base for cementing such relations.

It follows that the growing numbers of illegal migrants in US cities may eventually provoke political discontent among *other* social groups. One possibility is that as migrants compete with other lower income US citizens for 'off-the-books' jobs, the latter workers will rebel, as apparently occurred in the 1980 revolt in Miami's black ghetto. For these reasons, what at first glance appears to be a minor matter for local authorities may prove to be a very problematic situation, fraught with considerable potential for mass mobilization and political instability.

The class structure of US cities reflects the sectoral and spatial crises of the national and world economies. In the Snowbelt, 'growth coalitions' of business and government leadership have co-opted some segments of organized labour (Friedland, 1983) but still face the institutionalized political leverage of mobilized neighbourhood organizations (Mollenkopf, 1983); in the Sunbelt, where a growing segment of the workforce lacks the basic right of citizenship, investors and government officials appear at first glance to face much weaker pressures from below (Mollenkopf, 1983; Davis, 1984; Sassen-Koob, 1984).

In addition to lack of political rights, other dimensions of the social, cultural and political structures of Sunbelt cities have been identified as barriers to grassroots political mobilization of the new immigrants. These include: the widespread poverty and low level of education among Mexican-American immigrants, and their past history of alienation from the political arena, which inhibit political participation (Bloomberg and Martinez-Sandoval, 1982: 122); the privatistic ethos of southerners and new southern white migrants which favours good basic local government services but opposes local public expenditures for social and human services (Lupsha and Siembieda, 1977); the scale and forms of 'return migration' as a survival strategy among Hispanic migrants, which might retard the creation of channels for local political influence within Sunbelt cities, as it once did for Italian immigrants to the US in the early twentieth century (Erie, 1985: 16); the prevalence of 'reformed' local political institutions such as at-large and non-partisan elections, which impede neighbourhood-based political mobilization; the lack of the traditional mechanisms — urban patronage and social policy bureaucracies — which integrated older waves of ethnic migrants to the political system (Erie, 1985: 34); and finally, the more limited functions assumed by Sunbelt city governments which limit the use of public sector jobs as both a target of political mobilization and a mechanism of political integration (Lupsha and Siembieda, 1977; Erie, 1985). Despite these structurally unfavourable conditions, grassroots mobilization at the neighbourhood level has become an instrumental force in local Sunbelt politics. The emergent style of neighbourhood politics in Sunbelt cities has included: the rise of neighbourhood associations as interest groups; the use of spatial concentration by both young urban professionals and racial and ethnic minorities as a political resource; the creation of smaller city council districts to reflect and express emergent interests; and the proliferation of community organizations as mechanisms to connect individuals and households to the apparatus of the local state (Abbott, 1981: 212).

The defection of young urban professionals from the pro-growth coalitions which initially created their jobs is due in large measure to the mounting social costs of unregulated growth. The call for an improved 'quality of life' has become the rallying cry of the new neighbourhood movement in Sunbelt cities. The middle-class segment of the new neighbourhood movement has resisted highway expansion and commercial encroachment into residential neighbourhoods and has raised the issue of who should pay for the mounting environmental costs of publicly subsidized rapid growth. According to a major study of the new movement: 'Their concerns also support efforts to preserve and rehabilitate old housing and old neighbourhoods, to slow the rapid turnover in population, and to promote stable racial integration' (Abbott, 1981: 213).

What can be said of the black and Hispanic segments of the new neighbourhood movement? In several Sunbelt cities (as in older American cities in other regions) there has been a shift in political alliances by racial and ethnic groups away from growth-oriented towards neighbourhood-oriented whites (Abbott, 1981: 214). Abandoning the older pattern of making deals with pro-growth forces in exchange for city jobs, favours and marginal increases in public housing, black and Hispanic neighbourhood leaders have discovered that a political restructuring in the direction of ward-based local government electoral forms and neighbourhood targeting of community improvement funds can be used to improve conditions in the ghettos and barrios as well as in gentrified urban neighbourhoods. As a result of this political shift, ward-based voting has been adopted in Atlanta, San Antonio, Richmond, Fort Worth, Albuquerque, and, for a time, in San Francisco; Hispanic mayors have been elected in Denver and San Antonio; and an anti-growth woman now heads Houston's local government. Black mayors have been elected in New Orleans, Los Angeles and Atlanta, though in these instances by maintaining a delicate balance between pro-growth and 'managed growth' forces (Smith and Keller, 1983).

Hispanics in particular are likely to become a more powerful element in Sunbelt politics. In some Sunbelt cities — San Antonio, El Paso and Los Angeles — Hispanics already approach 50 percent of the population. While many of them are not yet citizens, 'the sons and daughters of undocumented aliens born in the United States are citizens and thus ultimately will be eligible voters' (Erie, 1985: 35). Most undocumented aliens are Mexican; and since the average age of Mexican-Americans is 18 — compared to age 30 for Anglos — they will undoubtedly become a crucial electoral force. This is especially true in the leading cities of California and Texas, where 85 percent of Mexican-Americans and undocumented Mexicans live. Their growing electoral influence in these two states is all the more important given that California and Texas now command nearly one-quarter of the votes in the presidential electoral college (Erie, 1985: 36).

It is nonetheless true that the connection between this demographic trend and political mobilization and influence has not yet crystallized into predictable patterns. Although the concentrated numbers of Mexican-Americans in specific cities and neighbourhoods has been a political resource in some Sunbelt cities, such residential segregation may enable local government officials to structure benefits so as to reinforce the political isolation of Mexican-Americans. This possibility may impede the formation of wider political alliances, just as the anti-poverty programme of the 1960s isolated blacks politically (Cloward and Piven, 1974).

## Conclusion
In the contemporary United States, three forms of crisis — structural, sectoral and spatial — have been combined and focused upon particular localities. These forms of crisis, and the local responses to them, are closely connected to the ongoing transformation of the global economy. As US manufacturers relocate to underdeveloped countries,

they become linked to a large pool of cheap labour whose costs of reproduction are subsidized by extensive networks of informal economic activity. The geographic scope of the informal sector is underlined by the fact that US manufacturers need not always locate abroad to take advantage of lower wages and controllable labour pools. Beyond regional differences in conditions conducive to capital accumulation, manufacturers often take advantage of the reduced costs and increased control of 'domestic' labour associated with the influx of Third World migrants to major US population centres. Additionally, the creation of enterprise zones and related proposals to stem the outflow of capital is a sign of a shifting balance of power in favour of accumulation even in regions of previous labour strength. Thus, such proposals cannot be expected to slow the continued growth of the domestic informal sector, which has drawn capital abroad and now attracts it to new peripheries within the core (Sassen-Koob, 1983). The political consequences of the growing informal economy within the US, therefore, should not be taken lightly.

Such consequences start with the reduced capacity of government to tax the actual volume of economic transactions. This, in turn, makes the delivery of adequate public services increasingly difficult to achieve. The inadequacy of public services, in turn, has political ramifications for local politics. While the reorganization of production globally has weakened the political leverage of trade unions, neighbourhood movements for improved services and living conditions have emerged as an increasingly important channel of popular pressure on local governments. In the Snowbelt, local political elites have responded with calls for enterprise zones. In the Sunbelt, local officials are responding with proposals to regulate rapid economic growth and its environmental effects. In both instances, the policies are indicators of shifting balances of political power.

The growth of grassroots political mobilizations in Sunbelt cities is an important development because the former quiescence of the region originally attracted investors there (Mollenkopf, 1983). Thus, ironically, the spread of neighbourhood political mobilization in Sunbelt cities may contribute to the erosion of the quiescent and privatistic style of local politics that was one of the key dimensions of Sunbelt growth.

In the short run, the reliance by households on self-production in the informal economy has conservative political implications — reduced costs to capital of reproducing labour power, the individualism of 'household' rather than 'community' responses to crisis, and the willingness of marginalized people to engage in additional personal labour rather than working to transform the relations of production and politics through collective action. Ironically, in the long run, the cumulative weight of even these 'individual' responses to crisis may serve to undermine the twin pillars of social control under advanced capitalism — wage labour in production relations and the bureaucratic state in the political sphere.

## References

Abbott, C. (1981) *The New Urban America: Growth and Politics in Sunbelt Cities.* Chapel Hill: University of North Carolina Press.

Aronowitz, S. (1981) *South Bronx Revitalization Program and Development Guide: A Critique.* New York: Urban Research and Strategy Center.

Aronowitz, S. and C. Goodman (1981) 'Ghetto Enterprise Zones: A Walk on the Supply Side', *The Nation*, 21 February: 207–208.

Bloomberg, W. and R. Martinez-Sandoval (1982) 'The Hispanic- American Urban Order: A Border Perspective', in G. Gappert and R. Knight (eds.), *Cities in the 21st Century.* Beverly Hills: Sage Publications.

Body-Gendrot, S. (1984) 'Plant Closings in Socialist France'. Paper presented at the Annual Meeting of the American Political Science Association, Washington, DC August–September.

. Castells, M. (1983) *The City and the Grassroots.* Berkeley: University of California Press.

Cloward, R.A. and F.F. Piven (1974) *The Politics of Turmoil.* New York: Pantheon.

Davis, M. (1984) 'The Political Economy of Late Imperial America', *New Left Review*, 143: 6–38.

Erie, S.P. (1985) 'Rainbow's End: From the Old to the New Urban Ethnic Politics', in J.W. Moore and L.A. Maldonado (eds.), *Urban Ethnicity: A New Era.* Beverly Hills: Sage Publications.

Fainstein, S.S., N.I. Fainstein, R.C. Hill, D. Judd and M.P. Smith (1983) *Restructuring the City: The Political Economy of Urban Redevelopment.* New York: Longman.

Firestine, R. (1977) 'Economic Growth and Inequality: Demographic Change and the Public Sector Response', in D. Perry and A. Watkins (eds.), *The Rise of the Sunbelt Cities*, pp. 191-210. Beverly Hills: Sage Publications.

Friedland, R. (1983) *Power and Crisis in the City.* London: Macmillan.

Friedmann, J. and G. Wolff (1982) 'World City Formation', *International Journal of Urban and Regional Research*, 6(2): 309–343.

Frobel, F., J. Heinrichs and O. Kreye (1980) *The New International Division of Labour.* Cambridge: Cambridge University Press.

Glickman, N.J. (1981) 'Emerging Urban Policies in a Slow Growth Economy: Conservative Initiatives and Progressive Responses in the United States', *International Journal of Urban and Regional Research*, 5(4): 492–527.

Goldsmith, W. (1982a) 'Enterprise Zones: If They Work We're in Trouble', *International Journal of Urban and Regional Research*, 6(3): 345–442.

Goldsmith, W. (1982b) 'Enterprise Zones', *New York Times*, 8 February: 23.

Herbers, J. (1980) 'Private Incentives: A New Tonic for Tired Old Cities?', *New York Times*, 28 December: 4E.

Katz, N. and D.S. Kemnitzer (1983) 'Fast Forward: The Internationalization of Silicon Valley', in J. Nash and M.P. Fernandez-Kelly (eds.), *Women, Men, and the International Division of Labor*, pp. 332–345. Albany: State University of New York Press.

Lupsha, P.A. and W.J. Siembieda (1977) 'The Poverty of Public Services in the Land of

Plenty', in D. Perry and A. Watkins (eds.), *The Rise of the Sunbelt Cities*, pp. 169–190. Beverly Hills: Sage Publications.

McGahey, R. (1983) 'High Tech, Low Hopes', *New York Times*, 15 May: 23.

Malone, J.H. (1982) 'The Questionable Promise of Enterprise Zones: Lessons from England and Italy', *Urban Affairs Quarterly*, 18(1): 19–30.

Massey, D. (1982) 'Enterprise Zones: A Political Issue', *International Journal of Urban and Regional Research*, 6(3): 429–434.

Merdinger, W. (1981) 'The Potholed Road to Enterprise Zones', *New York Times*, 7 March: 2.

Mingione, E. (1983) 'Informalization, Restructuring, and the Survival Strategies of the Working Class', *International Journal of Urban and Regional Research*, 7(3): 311–339.

Mollenkopf, J. (1983) *The Contested City*. Princeton: Princeton University Press.

Morgan, K. (1982) 'Restructuring Steel: The Crisis of Labour and Locality in Britain', *Working Paper 30*. Brighton: Urban and Regional Studies, University of Sussex.

*New York Times* (1982), 27 October: 1, 12.

*New York Times* (1983), 19 March: 1, 12.

O'Connor, J. (1981) 'The Meaning of Crisis', *International Journal of Urban and Regional Research*, 5(3): 301–329.

Portes, A. (1983) 'The Informal Sector: Definition, Controversy, and Relation to National Development', *Review*, Vll(1): 151–174.

Portes, A. and J. Walton (1981) *Labor, Class, and the International System*. New York: Academic Press.

Sassen-Koob, S. (1983) 'Recomposition and Peripheralization at the Core', in M. Dixon and S. Jonas (eds.), *From Immigrant Labour to Transnational Working Class*. San Francisco: Synthesis Publications.

Sassen-Koob, S. (1984) 'The New Labour Demand in Global Cities', in M.P. Smith (ed.), *Cities in Transformation: Class, Capital, and the State*, pp. 139–171. Beverly Hills: Sage Publications.

Serrin, W. (1983) 'The New Sweatshop', *New York Times*, 12–13 October: 1, 16.

Smith, M.P. and D.R. Judd (1984) 'American Cities: The Production of Ideology', in M.P. Smith (ed.), *Cities in Transformation: Class, Capital, and the State*, pp. 173–196. Beverly Hills: Sage Publications.

Smith, M.P. and M. Keller (1983) 'Managed Growth and the Politics of Uneven Development in New Orleans', in S.S. Fainstein, N.I. Fainstein, R.C. Hill, D. Judd and M.P. Smith, *Restructuring the City: The Political Economy of Urban Redevelopment* New York: Longman.

Soja, E.W. (1984) 'LA's the Place: Economic Restructuring and the Internationalization of the Los Angeles Region'. Presented at the Annual Meeting of the American Sociological Association, San Antonio, August.

Urry, J. (1981) 'Localities, Regions, and Social Class', *International Journal of Urban and Regional Research*, 5(4): 455–474.

Walton, J. (1982) 'Cities and Jobs and Politics', *Urban Affairs Quarterly*, 18(1): 5–17.

Wolpe, H. (1975) *Urban Politics in Nigeria*. Berkeley: University of California Press.

# Index

*Index compiled by Peva Keane*